For Rachel and Ray,
With appreciation of our years
together in Telluride!

Sue M. Cobb

THE LADY OF
SILK AND STEEL

ADST MEMOIRS SERIES
Series Editors
LISA TERRY & MARGERY THOMPSON

In 2003, the Association for Diplomatic Studies and Training (ADST), a nonprofit organization founded in 1986, created the Memoirs and Occasional Papers Series to preserve first-hand accounts and other informed observations on foreign affairs for scholars, journalists, and the general public. Through its book series, its Foreign Affairs Oral History program, and its support for training at the State Department's Foreign Service Institute, ADST seeks to promote understanding of American diplomacy and those who conduct it. Former Ambassador Sue Cobb's story – of rags to riches, of hard work and undreamt-of success, of an adventurous life well lived – reveals an amazing woman and along the way cuts to the heart of what an ambassador does on the job: lead, manage, and serve the nation's interests.

THE LADY OF
SILK AND STEEL
FROM EVEREST TO EMBASSIES

SUE M. COBB

With
Laura Tanna

A Book in the ADST Memoirs Series

IAN RANDLE PUBLISHERS
Kingston • Miami

First published in Jamaica, 2020 by
Ian Randle Publishers
16 Herb McKenley Drive
Box 686
Kingston 6
www.ianrandlepublishers.com

The opinions in this book are solely those of the author and do not necessarily reflect those of the Association of Diplomatic Studies and Training (ADST), or the Government of the United States.

ADST-Moments in Diplomatic History, State Magazine, and the Council of American Ambassadors have previously published short versions of some material in this book.

National Library of Jamaica Cataloguing-In-Publication Data

Names: Cobb, Sue M., author. | Tanna, Laura, editor.
Title: The lady of silk and steel : from Everest to embassies / Sue M. Cobb
     with contributions from Laura Tanna.
Description: Kingston : Ian Randle Publishers, 2020. | Includes index. |
     ADST memoirs series ; 38.
Identifiers: ISBN 9789768286192 (cloth) | ISBN 9789768286208 (epub) |
     ISBN 9789768286215 (mobi).
Subjects: LCSH: Cobb, Sue M., 1937- – Biography. | Cobb, Sue M., 1937- – Travel.
     Diplomats – United States – Biography. | United States – Foreign relations –
     Jamaica. | Jamaica – Foreign relations – United States. | Diplomacy – Foreign
     relations – United States. | Diplomacy – Foreign relations – Jamaica. |
     Diplomacy – Foreign relations – Iceland. | Florida – Politics and government. |
California – Social life and customs | Mountaineering. | Women philanthropists –
United States.
Classification: DDC 327.730092 -- dc23.

All photographs and images are from Ambassador Cobb's personal collection unless otherwise specified.

Front Cover Image: *A windy day on Kingston's harbor played havoc with Ambassador Cobb and the American flag at the dedication of US fast boats to the Jamaica Defence Force.* Courtesy of the Jamaica Observer Limited©2004.

Back Cover Image: Oil painting by Dave McNally, "Mt. Everest." davemcnallyart.com

Cover and Book Design by Ian Randle Publishers

Printed and Bound in the United States of America

Dedication

All Glory to God

To Chuck, Chris and Toby

To my wonderful daughters-in-law
Kolleen Olivia Pasternack Cobb and Luisa Maria Salazar Cobb

To my beloved grandchildren

Luis Eduardo Salazar Cobb	1994
Frederick Tod McCourt Cobb	1995
Charles Edward Salazar Cobb	1996
Nicholas Ruschmeyer Cobb	1997
Sebastian Griffin Salazar Cobb	1999
Cassidy Elizabeth Cobb	2000
Benjamin Pasternack Cobb	2002

A toast to the virtuous pioneers who settled the Old West.

**And a belated thank you to my taciturn father Ben and
to Ruth, the lost and lonely soul who was my mother.**

Contents

Foreword

The Lady of Silk and Steel: From Everest to Embassies is a remarkable story about a humble girl from the Old West who evolved into a role model for every modern woman. From shooting rattlesnakes with her brother in California to climbing Mt. Everest with the Wyoming Cowboys, from becoming an accomplished attorney who assisted in the resettlement of *Marielitos* in Florida, to living three years in Iceland, from being a wife, mother and becoming a United States ambassador, Sue Cobb is someone you'll want to know.

I first met Ambassador Cobb in 2001 at a diplomatic dinner. Typical of her innovative style and inquisitive mind, a month later she invited me to her office at the US Embassy in Kingston for lunch, saying she found it interesting that an American was writing for *The Gleaner,* a Jamaican newspaper. Ambassador Cobb and I have both lived in California, Jamaica, and Florida, and though ten years apart in age, are kindred in spirit as my grandparents were the last of the original homesteaders in Montana. Learning about her life was a joy and an adventure which she now is willing to share because the events she lived through and those she influenced have impacted the world in which she and those I interviewed have helped to guide.

The many facets of her life include marvelous trips around the world with her husband, two sons, their wives, and now their grandchildren. From being atop a rearing elephant as suddenly, a rhino emerges from an Indian river, to almost dying not only on Mt. Everest but also when open ocean diving in the Galápagos. She was a highly ranked Alpine ski racer who once co-owned a tennis club on Key Biscayne. At thirty-eight she entered law school and remembers that in her first court case her senior partner didn't show up because he had fallen prey to Miami's Cocaine Cowboys, in that era from the 1970s to the mid-'80s when Colombian gangs brought cocaine and violence to the streets of Miami. She still won the case all alone and went on over the years to build an entire public finance department that led the legal firm for which she worked to become one of the biggest and most prestigious in Florida, if not the country. All the while she took care of her family and escaped on side trips skiing and climbing in the Rocky Mountains. This was before she became an ambassador's wife, an ambassador herself, secretary of state in Florida, president of the Cobb Family Foundation and a philanthropist.

As the chapters of her life unfolded, I wouldn't have believed it all if I hadn't interviewed a dozen individuals from her different walks of life, including General Colin Powell, Florida Governor Jeb Bush, Prime Minister P. J. Patterson, Prime Minister Bruce Golding, former Jamaican Minister of National Security, Dr. Peter Phillips, and Everest Exhibition Leader, Courtney Skinner, who not only confirmed things I learned in the nine interviews I had done with Ambassador Cobb, but most actually elaborated on her achievements, something which she found disconcerting, since she is by nature humble, though calmly self-confident.

You'll learn how she climbed Mt. Everest and was just a short distance from becoming the first American woman to reach the summit. If only the Chinese hadn't delayed the expedition along the route, at one point lining the team up against a pockmarked wall where fresh blood was still visible while Chinese military officers decided whether to let them proceed – and then when they did get there…well you'll just have to read on.

Because she is modest by nature, despite her remarkable athletic as well as business and diplomatic accomplishments, she has felt some self-consciousness when reading comments by those who participated in the history of her life, people whose observations have added an unusual dimension to this memoir, but I am here to assure you that all the comments interwoven into her text, which you will read, are absolutely genuine, with nothing untoward omitted.

Enjoy the ride.

Laura Tanna, August 31, 2020

Prologue

LIFE UNFOLDS IN CHAPTERS

A plane hit the World Trade Center. I watched in disbelief, in shock, as a second passenger plane hit the World Trade Center. I knew immediately that it was an act of terrorism. I also knew immediately that there would not be one single person in Washington during the next four years who would care one single bit about what happened in Jamaica. And I was the new ambassador of the United States of America to Jamaica. Yes, on September 11, 2001, I arrived for my first day of work at Embassy Kingston as the US Ambassador to Jamaica. I had prepared for my first day in the embassy to introduce myself to my Country Team, all seasoned career Foreign Service officers. I would seek to gain their confidence in me, which we discuss a lot at Ambassador Seminars, and I knew that was critical. But on 9/11 the whole world changed. Now on duty in Jamaica, I could expect no help from the president or the Department of State.

Seventeen years later in May of 2018, I was seated at dinner in the large and beautiful conference room of the Center for Strategic and International Studies (CSIS) in Washington, DC, celebrating Henry Kissinger's 95th birthday and his remarkable life. An auspicious event and a coveted ticket in our nation's capital.

Henry Kissinger, a fellow trustee of the CSIS, is one of the most distinguished diplomats in recent world history. Thankfully, he expends his efforts on behalf of the United States. CSIS is one of the top policy analytic shops in the world, routinely ranking number one in security and defense studies and in the top three worldwide in the overall broad range of think tank subject matter.

The room was packed with members of the president's cabinet, Justices of the Supreme Court, well-known senators, members of Congress, university presidents, the CEOs of this country's most important corporations, influential people all... and me.

I couldn't help but think: how did a little girl from a small farming community in Chino, California come to be here at this moment? It was the same question I asked myself thirty years earlier on October 12, 1988, when I stood alone at 25,000 feet on the North Ridge of Mt. Everest as a horrific storm approached. That day I wondered if I was going to get off the mountain alive.

The Lady of Silk and Steel: From Everest to Embassies is the story of a life shaped by customs of the Old West that became a series of almost unimaginable adventures. From the public schools of Chino, California, to famed Stanford University; from shooting rattlesnakes with my brother in the dry brown hills of Southern California to living in Elizabeth Taylor's former penthouse on the Potomac; from being a wife, mother, and lawyer to climbing Mt. Everest and becoming a United States ambassador. I am not a genius. I am not beautiful. I've never been in a movie, can't sing, dance, or play a musical instrument. I haven't invented anything, nor done anything heroic...yet I am one of the most fortunate women in the world. At every turn I wondered: how did this happen to me?

Though not an active feminist in the sense that word is commonly used today, I do believe in setting high standards, leading by example and mentoring those with whom I worked in the different chapters of my life – as student, wife, mother, athlete, lawyer, civil servant, diplomat, philanthropist.

I believe that everyone has an Everest inside. For me, Mt. Everest remains the perfect metaphor for life. The route up a mountain is not straight. There are many obstacles. You must often retreat and reorganize to try another day or to try a different route. Frequently, your goal – the peak – will elude you. To face such rigors, it is best to have trusted companions along, for you will find need for solace and encounter joys to share. You will learn many lessons. The biggest lesson I learned on the biggest mountain in the world is that it is not, after all, about the peak – it is about the journey and the people with whom you are traveling.

I hope this book will be of value to men and women divining how far they can move out of their comfort zones, confront new challenges, and fulfill their potential.

SUE McCOURT COBB – FAMILY TREE

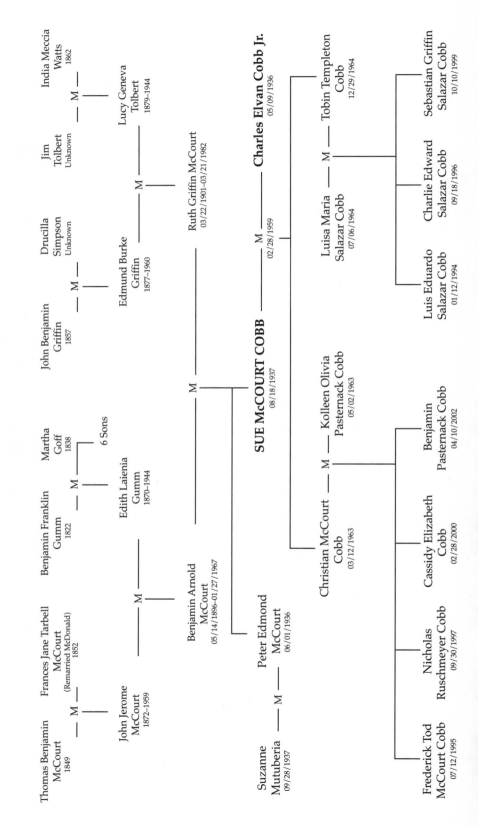

Chapter One

Life shrinks and expands in proportion to one's courage.
Anaïs Nin

RAISED IN THE OLD WEST

How to begin the story of a life? What would interest you most in the trajectory of one woman's life from a small California ranch to ambassador in a country with one of the world's most caring people yet having one of the world's highest murder rates? Maybe I should tell you what it's like to be on Mt. Everest, trying to get back to a camp fifteen miles away, all alone in the darkness, crossing crevasses, which if I make a misstep will lead to certain death? Should I start with describing the two most influential men in my life – one a nuclear engineer and the other an incredibly successful corporate executive and fellow ambassador? Of course, there's also the part about becoming a lawyer at age forty-one and later indirectly influencing the outcome of a presidential election. So maybe I should just start with the whales.

Grandfather Edmund Burke Griffin grew up on a ranch near Houston and was in the first graduating law school class of the University of Texas. In 1898 he fought with Teddy Roosevelt in the Spanish-American War and later practiced law but didn't enjoy it, so he decided to be a sea captain. He started in Portland, Oregon, and went to sea as a whaling captain, capturing what were then known as "monsters of the deep." He was quite successful at whaling and invented a method of preserving whales before there was even a successful means of embalming people. Grandfather Griffin became a partner in the Pacific Whaling Company (PWC) in Oregon, and after moving to California he chartered his two-masted schooner and ran a small museum at the end of the lone pier in Long Beach. He then decided that since people in the Midwest had never seen these giant monsters from the deep, he could probably make money at that. So he used whatever his formula was to preserve whales in Long Beach near his ship, rented a railroad flat car, and took whales across the United States all the way to Miami, Florida. PWC eventually had up to ten shows traveling the country. It was basically a traveling carnival. Tickets to enter the whale's tent and hear the captain's lecture during the 1930s were ten cents per person.

Imagine, in 1927 Henry Ford produced his fifteen millionth Model T, and the population of the United States was 119 million. Fewer than ten percent of the people had cars. They didn't cross the United States in cars or airplanes, so people in the Midwest and the rest of the United States certainly had never seen something like a whale. My mother and father were the "advance team" ahead of the train to put up posters and sell tickets to see the "Monster of the Deep." That's how my parents supported themselves in the Depression of 1929–41.

Actually, Edmund Griffin's daughter, my mother Ruth, was one tough lady. Her mother abandoned her at age three. I do not know the facts, but she had a very difficult childhood that hardened her and left her with a deep residual fear. Later in life she protected herself (and us) with a chain-link fence and trained Doberman Pinchers. She herself kept a WWII attack-trained guard dog on a leash by her side at all times, even while seated in our home at the dining table. "Duke" would not let anyone, my brother Peter and me included, within three or four feet of our mother. If that space were violated, Duke attacked, one time going straight for my face and neck, resulting in serious wounds and serious stitches. Were we scared of Duke? You bet we were. With the chain-link fence and Duke at her side, Mother made sure no one got close to her or to her family without her express permission.

My mother, Ruth Griffin McCourt, was born in 1901 in Van Alstyne, Texas, and lived her first years with her father's sister on a farm near Houston, Texas; but times were tough and at some point, the sister could not keep her. Ruth's mother was nowhere to be found. My mother was forced to leave the farm and was moved to Portland, Oregon in an attempt to have her father nearby, but it was not to be. He immediately left to California. Ruth met her mother for the first time when she was sixteen, but never lived with either her mother or father. She graduated from high school in 1917 and by college age had worked to support herself in fourteen different homes. Mother became a Christian Scientist, which I believe provided a measure of stability and guidance. She entered the University of Oregon in Eugene, living with several different families while doing housework for her room and board. After graduation she moved to Los Angeles, still wanting to be near her father, the whaling captain. She attended a business college, and from about 1922 to 1926, Ruth worked for the Los Angeles County Welfare Department and the Los Angeles Department of Health Auditor's Office.

My father, Benjamin Arnold McCourt, was from a family of Irish-Catholic Democrats, among the fourth generation of Armagh County Irish in the US who had escaped persecution by the Protestants in Northern Ireland. Ben was born in the small mountain mining town of White Oaks, New Mexico, in 1896. A US census showed he was living there in 1904. Later he moved to Redondo Beach, California, finished high school, and entered the University of California at Berkeley. World War I was under way and Ben dropped out of university early in 1917 to join the US Army and was shipped off to France as an enlisted man. He told my brother Peter and me that it was the worst experience of his life to cross the Atlantic in the hold of a transport ship with hundreds of other "grunts." He didn't talk about the war much, but told my brother that if he served in the military, he must be an officer. Thereafter, my brother Peter went to Stanford, joined the Air Force ROTC (Reserve Officer Training Corps,) and became a distinguished US Air Force officer. Peter graduated from Stanford with a master's in mechanical/nuclear engineering after receiving a five-year scholarship from the US Atomic Energy Commission. This brilliant, kind, well-balanced man – fifteen months older than me – remained a major influence throughout my life. He was my first playmate and, if life went wrong, I always felt he was my last hope.

When our father Benjamin was born, my great-grandfather, Thomas Benjamin McCourt, owned and operated a grocery store in the thriving White Oaks mining community. Our grandfather, John McCourt, started working in the White Oaks store in 1890 and remained in the grocery business for the next sixty-five years. He married Edith Levinia Gumm, my paternal great-grandmother, affectionately called Vena, the only daughter of Benjamin Franklin Gumm who also lived in White Oaks. Vena's six brothers were quite notorious in New Mexico Territory. One story had it that two of the brothers worked in a restaurant catering to new arrivals from the East. The boys, wearing roller skates and six-shooters, would skate up to a table, slap down a six-gun, and say, "Now you S.O.B., what do you want to eat?"

My great-grandmother, Dad's grandmother, Francis Jane Tarbell McCourt, and her first husband, Thomas McCourt, divorced. Francis's second husband, William C. McDonald, a mining engineer and a member of the House of Representatives in Santa Fe, New Mexico Territory, went on to become the first governor of the State of New Mexico (1912–18). As a young child my father lived in the "Governor's Mansion" (really just a large ranch house) on a sprawling cattle ranch between White Oaks and Carrizozo where he sat on the lap and listened to the stories of Pat Garrett, the sheriff who famously shot and killed the notorious outlaw, Billy the Kid. Later, around our campfires on fishing trips in the High Sierras, my father would tell spellbinding stories of the "Wild West" to Pete and me.

I had vivid memories of White Oaks, but only from the stories told by my father. Much later in life, I decided to go see White Oaks for myself – which led to one of the most embarrassing events in my life.

In later years, my husband Chuck and I frequently used a small nine-seat Cessna airplane when we were traveling. Our pilot, Mike Lee, worked with us during my Jamaica years. One summer day in 2010 (I think), I was by myself in Telluride, Colorado, where we've long had a home. Chuck was in meetings in California. Mike and the Cessna were nearby. I decided it was a good time to go see White Oaks. I called my office in Miami to make arrangements. They determined that the closest place for me to fly into was Carrizozo, New Mexico, about fifteen miles from White Oaks. They told me, however, that Carrizozo had no rental car agencies. I decided I could solve that when I got there. Mike said the landing strip was run-down, but it was long enough for us to land. Off Mike and I went to White Oaks.

On approach to the runway, Mike had second thoughts. He said he could see grass growing in the cracks of the pavement. I looked – the grass didn't look very tall. I convinced him we should land. He was very tense, but we landed without trouble. No one was in sight. However, out of a small wooden shack (the "control tower"), dressed in cowboy hat and boots came a survivor of New Mexico's Wild West days. He greeted us and I asked him about cars. Politely he said there were no cars available that he knew of. There were definitely no rental cars.

I said, "But I see one next to your building." (It was the only car in sight.)

"Oh, that's my car."

And of course, I said, "I'd like to rent it."

He looked shocked and replied, "Oh no ma'am, the brakes don't work real well, the driver side window doesn't go up... and, she ain't got no air conditioner. You know, she's really old." (I could see that.)

I was wearing Levi's and a plain white man's T-shirt, so I thought I could get away with: "You know, I'm a farm girl. I've driven lots worse. I'll only be gone a couple of hours and I'll pay you $20 an hour."

To that, he agreed, while telling me the other critical potential malfunctions of the old Ford. Mike was horrified as I got into the driver's seat and headed for the hills, literally. White Oaks is up a gorge in the Jicarilla Mountains of Lincoln County. The car was fine. Upon entering White Oaks, I was delighted to see a wooden five-foot-by-five-foot "Welcome to White Oaks" sign with an old but good map of the town. The sign was right in front of the cemetery. So obviously this was going to be my first stop. The Cedarvale Cemetery was, let's say, rustic, with an abundance of healthy weeds. The head stones, however, were clearly marked and I easily found my father's family and relatives of whom he had spoken, including Governor William Calhoun McDonald with whom my father grew up. I also found the headstone of my dad's grandmother, Francis McCourt, who married McDonald in 1881. He had come west from New York in 1880 when the town was in the midst of a mini-gold rush. Dad told me that before becoming New Mexico's first governor,

McDonald was a stout Democrat who had won several local elections first.

The cemetery proved to be a great start as I thoroughly examined a number of tombs and headstones. The big cemetery map provided an easy guide for finding the few short and dusty streets to the family homes that I'd heard about. Leaving the cemetery, I drove through White Oaks – one block of storefronts – that looked just like the towns in every old western movie. It was Sunday; nothing was open and there were no people around. I did notice that the door of the "No Scum Allowed Saloon" was slightly ajar. It did not take long to see the few family houses and the surviving brick schoolhouse, which now acts as the town museum. I found some references to my family, but did not learn much more than I already knew, so I decided I should return the serviceable Ford to its owner at the airport in Carrizozo. Starting back through town, I noticed that the saloon door was still slightly open, so I stopped to check it out and hopefully buy a bottle of water. When I entered the saloon, a middle-aged woman was cleaning the bar and I could see she had already mopped the floor.

I said, "Hello, sorry to bother you, I was hoping to get a bottle of water."

She greeted me pleasantly and said, "Did you come to see the parade?"

"No, I was just passing through…what's going on?"

Now she was quite bubbly, "Oh everyone will be here soon to clean up the sidewalk and the street, best we can."

I said "Oh" and waited.

"Yes, it's a very exciting day for us. I can't remember the last time something like this happened." The words rushed forth from her mouth. "A US ambassador is coming to town… and you know how they have a long line of black cars and the ambassador's car has flags on the front fenders."

Oh My! I was stunned, momentarily speechless, sad, and completely embarrassed! Here I was in my Levi's and T-shirt with my ancient vehicle parked outside for all to see. What would you do? After a few moments, I knew I had to tell her. I stumbled with the words, but soon got the truth out…and quickly started telling her about my father and the McCourt family and the Parker family and the McDonalds…and I was so sorry – I had to run now. Oh, it was sooo embarrassing. I felt sorry for the people in White Oaks. No parade today! Her last words to me as I left the "No Scum Allowed Saloon" were, "Ambassador, please don't go into the cemetery – it's full of rattlesnakes."

In the early 1900s Grandmother Vena went looking for a place where the family could vacation away from the heat of New Mexico. Sometime between 1908 and 1910 she decided to check out Long Beach, California, but upon arriving in Los Angeles by train, she took the wrong streetcar, ended up in Hermosa Beach, and liked it so much that she rented a place for the summer. The family later purchased a modest wooden house on Manhattan Avenue and 25th Street. The McCourt's association with Hermosa continues to this day. My brother Pete and I would spend our summers at the house and Pete eventually purchased it. His daughter Christine lives there now.

After leaving White Oaks, my grandfather John worked first for Armour & Co. in the meat packing industry, then left in 1913 to form the Security Trust and Savings Bank with his friend L. L. Gaines. John didn't like banking and went back to traveling for a wholesale food company in 1917. I met Grandfather John, but never really knew him. The best I can say about my father's family is that they had a varied and colorful history before I ever came on the scene!

After WWI, my father returned to Southern California and became a real estate broker in Palos Verdes, a peninsula south of Redondo Beach. Within a short period of time he met my mother. They married in 1926 on the cusp of the Depression and to earn a living joined Ed Griffin's whale show. They left the whale show in New England in 1932 when the show left for England. My mother Ruth went back to the Health Department in Inglewood and my father became an automobile salesman in Los Angeles. Ruth also went to the Otis Art Institute at night where she learned to sculpt, draw, and paint. They were essentially destitute, except for Ruth's low-paying job. Because Ben had more flexible hours, he got home from his day job earlier than Ruth did, so he always prepared dinner. That remained the case for the rest of their life together. In the absence of having a mother, Ruth simply never learned to cook. In the absence of a mother who cooked, I never learned to cook. That remains true. Ben and Ruth were married for ten years before my brother Peter Edmond McCourt was born on June 1, 1936, in a Los Angeles Christian Science rest home where I was also born the following year on August 18, 1937.

When grandfather Ed Griffin moved to Pomona, our family moved to Pomona not far from Grandfather Ed's ranch. It was 1939 and my father got a job in a gas station. Then in 1941 we moved a few miles away to Chino to a five-acre ranch property, which had an old ranch house and a barn. The property was purchased by my grandfather Ed and subsequently deeded to my mother on February 20, 1945. The first thing Mother did was to build a six-foot-high chain-link fence around the entire five acres. Father, whom Pete and I called "Daddy," was now working as an ice deliveryman. We had iceboxes in those days, not refrigerators. He would pick up a 300-pound block of ice at the Ontario Ice and Cold Storage Plant, in Ontario, California, and then drive to Pomona. If people along his route wanted ice for their iceboxes, they put a card in their front window indicating if they wanted 25, 50, 75, or 100 pounds and he would cut that amount and carry it to their iceboxes.

Edmund Burke Griffin, my dour grandfather,
lawyer and sea captain.

Pfc Benjamin Arnold McCourt, my father, better suited
to being a cowboy than a soldier in France WWI, 1917.

*Ruth Griffin McCourt, my mother, the stoic
Christian Scientist, 1962.*

*Mother and Duke, the US Army WWII attack-
trained Doberman Pincher that guarded mother
day and night.*

Anniversary of Ruth and Benjamin McCourt, May 1966.

Sue, almost four after moving from Pomona, California to a nearby ranch in Chino, 1941.

Sue and brother Peter Edmond McCourt, fifteen months older.

In the mid-1940s, Daddy had a serious ulcer problem, requiring part of his stomach to be removed. We suspect that there had been quite a bit of partying and drinking in the carnival days and alcohol might well have been a contributing factor. This was a very traumatic event for my brother and me because though our father was obviously sick and delirious for days, Mother, as a Christian Scientist, would not call a doctor. Our crying and wailing convinced her to do so and a scary ambulance took my father away for a long time. To the best of our knowledge, he never touched another drop of alcohol in his life, but he and Mother continued to smoke heavily. At first it was the original Lucky Strikes, but in later years Daddy switched to Bull Durham. Squatting on his heels, in Levi's, a flannel shirt and Stetson hat, rolling a Bull Durham, he looked and sounded every bit like the cowboy from New Mexico.

Daddy Ben continued the ice delivery job throughout WWII while Mother made different attempts to get the ranch to pay. They raised and bartered various farm animals and grew vegetables in our yard. We had a World War II "Victory Garden," which was part of our survival. We also gathered walnuts from our orchard to sell. Pete and I helped. They tried raising chickens and selling eggs, but someone stole all the chickens leaving only the mean old rooster that used to chase Pete around the yard. (That was fun to watch.) In 1944 they also had a registered Berkshire pig named Kita de Corte, which Pete and I tried to ride, even though she had lice. This was not a happy sight for my mother when her kids came up to the house from Kita's mud pool. Kita later was slaughtered. I felt really badly about that for a long time because I thought she was killed for playing with Pete and me in the mud pool.

During all of World War II, Daddy served as a block warden for the three or four houses in our area, and was responsible for seeing that we and our neighbors had all the blinds closed when word of a potential air raid sounded and a "black-out" was declared. When we went to Ontario during the war to collect the family's ration stamps so we could buy sugar, gasoline, and other rationed products we passed the Japanese internment camp. I was afraid of the Japanese, but later I learned that immigrants from Japan living in the United States, who had not caused any trouble whatsoever, had most likely done nothing to support the Japanese war efforts or to cause being incarcerated, were picked up and put in this internment camp, essentially jailed. I will never forget that injustice. While I was afraid of the Japanese, I was even more afraid of the Germans during those years. I knew how they took people away in railroad cars.

After we moved to the Chino farm, Mother raised Doberman Pinchers, which she trained and showed (but not Duke) at Southern California dog shows. She became a nationally recognized show judge, including at the Westminster Kennel Club's prestigious New York show and other major shows. This was in addition to maintaining the Victory Garden and helping with the chickens, cows, and pigs raised for butchering. At one point, we even had goats. She did the milking, made butter, and sometimes put up preserves of peaches and plums grown on this fertile property along with oranges, grapefruit, tangerines, avocados, black figs, artichokes, and walnuts. We had a large grape arbor with Thompson seedless and Concord grapes as well as Grandfather Ed Griffin's beehives under the grape arbor. While I didn't know it at the time, what we didn't have was money.

I have fond memories of the ranch in Chino. It was a good place for two kids to grow up in the '40s and '50s. Best of all was mid-summer when I never had to wear shoes, just a pair of Levi's and one of Peter's T-shirts. I remember walking barefoot in the summer on the hot, dusty driveway to pick the sweet tangerines off the tree near the front gate. Sometimes I would walk into the orchard to pluck off a warm juicy peach, but then I would almost always get stickers in my feet, a lot of stickers over the years. I could find shade under a walnut tree and savor ripe black figs right off the fig tree. On the other side of the house, where the walnut grove was, I remember the feeling of the cool mud oozing between my toes as I walked in the irrigation ditches following the paths that Daddy had dug to water the trees. It was a very big deal when the irrigation water was released to an individual farm, on a prearranged date, by the Ontario Water District that controlled water distribution in our valley.

We had our own homemade baseball diamond in the middle of the walnut grove. I desperately wanted to play with the boys and not do my piano lessons, which of course I later regretted. I think one of my last baseball games in that field was when I was the pitcher and Phil Van Pelt, a big strapping neighbor boy, hit a line drive into my forehead right between the eyes. I was knocked to the ground, nearly unconscious. I didn't like baseball much anyway – too much standing around for me. I liked the circus-type swing that hung from a walnut branch outside the kitchen window that Daddy, Pete, and I had made out of rope and a sanded wooden crossbar. We were pretty good acrobats. Mother said it scared her and we would see her at the kitchen window. I figured out later that she was actually in the kitchen to keep an eye on us, because she sure wasn't there to cook! Sometimes she was in the enclosed porch off the kitchen that also had a view of the swing. It had an agitator washing machine and a deep concrete sink where Mother washed my hair. I hated that.

Later Pete and I had a basketball hoop on a tamarisk tree in our yard and spent many hours shooting baskets and playing

"Horse." That served me well. Years later in Miami, I could still beat the members of my sons' high school basketball teams at "Horse." It was very embarrassing to them, and I knew that, but I did it anyway – and I gloated. At the ranch, Pete and I also played cops and robbers, or cowboys and Indians, hiding in and around various ranch buildings, using crude wooden guns we'd carved ourselves. One day Pete convinced me that to prove my courage to be either a cop or a robber, I forget which, I had to jump off the steeply pitched roof of the tool shed, which was almost two stories high, but I did it – injuring my ankle in the process. We were frequently bitten by the red ants with which we shared the yard, so it's no wonder that we sometimes poured gasoline into their mounds, then lit a match to kill them. I was afraid, rightfully, of the black widow spider potential. Mother constantly warned us, so we were pretty cautious around the woodpiles and down in the basement, an eerie place made more so by the stories Daddy's nephew John Porter made up. I was afraid to be down there by myself, even though I liked to delve into the trunk that held Daddy's WWI uniform. John was my father's sister Dorothy's son and was eight years older than me. I have no substantive proof, but I became convinced that John was a US spy during the Korean War. He took lengthy trips, always sat on his haunches, and spoke a strange language.

John also tricked me into admitting that I was the one who took a piece of chocolate out of the Whitman chocolate box Daddy kept on the fireplace mantle, taking a bite of it, and putting it back. John claimed he recognized the marks my two front teeth made in the chocolate (maybe that's why I believed he was in the CIA). I had lied about the candy, was caught, and was mortified. And properly punished. Then there was the time I got caught for stealing a bar of soap from a house down on Vernon, now Yorba Street. I don't remember the details. Pete may have been involved in this caper too, but I got caught and hid from Mother behind the couch in the living room. She found me and I got whipped with a belt for that one. It was not an auspicious sign of my intellectual capacity. Why on earth would any kid want to steal soap?

At some point in our attempts to make money on the farm, we got into the turkey business; that eventually sent Pete and me to college. Turkeys are truly stupid fowl that could be mean. Sometimes a big tom turkey would chase me and try to peck me. I was secretly glad when they panicked as a group, ran into a corner of the fence and suffocated each other. Sometimes we got to watch a pig or cow be slaughtered and butchered (attended by both fascination and revulsion) for freezing for our family provisions or for sale to neighbors. I remember exactly when Kita went to pig heaven. I particularly liked to watch the traveling blacksmith at work when he came to do the horses' hooves. Whatever was going on, on a multi-purpose ranch in the '40s, Pete and I were watching…and we were learning.

If I had to go on my own summary of how Sue became the person that she is, the same things that shaped her are the ones that shaped me. The primary things were being raised on a ranch instead of in a city, which does a lot for your self-confidence and understanding that things have to get done or they don't get done. And it probably is very important that both of our parents were absolutely – I don't know the right word – neither one of them would tell a lie or do something dishonest. It was made very clear to both of us that that was how things [were] to be when we were being raised as children. We were disciplined children. There was no play until all work was done. We worked on the farm and we worked on our studies. Sue developed a tremendous ability to concentrate when she needs to or wants to.

Peter Edmond McCourt, October 9, 2017

Over time, Pete and I learned some pretty good values: that it could be hard to make a living, but that money wasn't the most important thing; that a good education was worth sacrificing for; and that family mattered more than anything. We learned not to lie, cheat, or steal. We learned to ride, fish, and hunt; to work hard; to take care of our animals; and to take care of ourselves. We learned that work and homework both came before play and that if we mopped all the linoleum floors and the cement floor in the living room on Saturday morning, we would each get a quarter to go to the afternoon movies at the Fox Theatre in Pomona. (My favorite was anything with the masked but virtuous Lone Ranger.) Finally, in high school we could ride our bicycles to the Saturday movies, but we still had to earn the twenty-five cents each for our tickets.

We learned that male and female Dobermans like to be together and make babies. And that horses, cows, and other animals did too. We learned to love reading and to be respectful to our elders, particularly Grandfather Griffin whom we were to call "Sir" and to whom we were not permitted to speak until spoken to. We learned to listen to our parents, to recite the Lord's Prayer, and to say a one sentence prayer at bedtime: "Father, Mother, God loving me, guide my little feet up to Thee."

Sometimes it was lonely on the ranch, particularly during WWII when I thought the Germans were coming to our house. There was, in fact, a railroad line about three blocks away. When I heard the mournful whistle of the train, it just scared me to death. I feared the German trains would come along, pick us all up, and we'd be jammed into a boxcar and I wouldn't be able to find my family. If they came into our driveway, they would reach my room first. So I would sneak into Pete's room, but either Mother or Daddy would hear us and make me go back to my room. I remember that really distinctly. It made a big impression on a young child and took decades to digest.

I have a very strong recollection of President Franklin Delano Roosevelt dying and as an eight-year-old in 1945 recall discussions of his policies in my home. I also recall my great admiration for the military, all our armed forces, and for leaders like General Eisenhower and General MacArthur. They were my heroes, the admirals and the generals, except for my even bigger heroes, the Western cowboy stars at the Saturday movies. MacArthur became controversial, but at the time that didn't matter to me. He was a leader. He looked like my Grandfather Ed, he waded through the Pacific Ocean, and he wore a lot of stars on his shoulders. That was the extent of my in-depth thinking. (This is embarrassing.)

After the war ended in 1945, I would curl up under a pile of blankets and listen to the train whistle with its forever haunting refrain as it roared by several blocks away…going somewhere. After the war I wasn't so afraid anymore. Just curious where those people were going.

During the winter there were times that it was terribly cold, because the only heater in the house was in the dining room, which later caused me to set the house on fire – but that's another story. Occasionally during very cold winter nights, we would have to go in our heaviest clothes to help our neighbors keep their smudge pots filled with oil and fired up to try to keep their orange groves warm so that the year's crop of oranges wouldn't freeze. We had some miserable nights, but on our small ranch in Southern California we knew that the warm days would always outnumber the cold ones.

When Pete and I started school in the Chino public school system, we would get picked up by a bus that stopped nearby at the corner of Phillips (our street) and Monte Vista (a half block away). Later the bus stop was moved, and we had two very long country blocks to walk. Mother (we were not allowed to call her mom or mommy) was a voracious reader. She always stayed awake very late every night reading and often didn't get up until late morning, but on school mornings after I was dressed and had breakfast, I would awaken her, she would sit up in bed and fix my pigtail braids before I left to walk to the bus with Pete. Maybe that's why she had my hair cut shorter when I was twelve – no more waking up to braid Sue's hair.

Actually, cutting off my pigtails was a transformative event. Up to age twelve, I was aware that most young girls were wearing pink tutus and playing with dolls, but I was wearing Levi's, hand-me down T-shirts, and toting a Winchester 22 rifle, a gift from my father. When the pigtails went, Mother took me to Pasadena to the Bullock's Department Store and bought me a navy blue knee length wool skirt, a beautiful red cashmere sweater, and brand new shiny black shoes. I was to start junior high school in the fall, take dance classes, and learn to be a proper young lady. Mother made Peter and me go to Cotillion. We hated it. She tried to talk me into going to Scripps College School for Girls in Claremont. I would have none of that and got away with considerable defiance. But thereafter whenever I really displeased Mother, I was immediately threatened with Scripps School for Girls. Geez I didn't want to go there. To this day, I do not know how she paid for the few luxuries that Pete and I had, like piano and dance lessons. We still only got twenty-five cents a week, and only if we did our chores.

Mother's reading selection I remember to be very eclectic, from the Bible and her copy of Mary Baker Eddy's *Key to the Scriptures* (the authoritative Christian Science interpretation of the Bible), always by her bed, placed next to current best-sellers and some really trashy mystery novels and everything in between. Of course, since there was no television allowed in the house until after Pete and I had gone to college, reading was the norm. Daddy sat in his big armchair in the living room near the fireplace with the mantle that held the Whitman chocolates. He read a lot too, mostly history. He went to bed quite early, particularly after his hospital stay. Mother was not a relentless

Christian Scientist, but she was a strong Christian Scientist. Peter and I both attended Christian Science Sunday school until we were about fourteen. While I remember little specifically about the teachings, Mother's beliefs and the strength they generated in her were a strong and a largely positive influence in my life.

Christian Science is frequently misinterpreted as some kind of cult. The inclusion of the word "science" is also rather misleading. This is my understanding: the beliefs of Christian Scientists include the major beliefs of all Christians – belief in God the Father, Jesus Christ, the son of God, and the Holy Spirit; the holiness of Church and the Communion of Saints; the resurrection; salvation of the faithful; and other Christian tenets. The difference in my experience related to the concept of "divine mind healing" for both spiritual and physical health. In totally inadequate, truly layman's terms – the mind is so powerful that it can overcome pain and even cure illness and physical disabilities. Of course, you have to believe in the mind's power and you also have to be a good Christian through prayer. To be frank, many people do not believe Christian Scientists correctly interpret the Bible and would likely not agree with my simplification. But it is what I learned as a child.

In those early years, I had as playmates only Pete and Phil Van Pelt who was the same age as Pete. Phil lived a block away, played football, the trumpet, and had a cute older brother named Frank. When I was eight or nine Phil explained that he and I would be getting married, because there just weren't any other girls and boys around. That sounded pretty grim to me, though Phil turned out to be a brilliant and distinguished surgeon. Pete and Phil were partially responsible for me becoming a competitor and an athlete. Of course, I had my horses which, I frankly admit, were at that time far more important to me than a brother or any friend. My first horse was a small Pinto that Pete and I shared, but Pete wasn't too interested in horses.

Sue and Cindy, 1950, the half Arabian/half standard bred mare, my closest companion until I left for Stanford University in 1955.

Then we got two or three other horses, one of which was an old, but beautiful Standard-bred mare named Pearl. When I was ten, Cindy was born to old Pearl following an arranged marriage to a dashing young registered Arabian. Cindy (short for Cinnamon, her color) became my best friend and my ride to freedom.

Mother used to worry about me riding by myself so much, particularly down near the Chino prison, but I loved it – just my horse and me. I guess she thought someone was going to escape and harm me, but I thought that was pretty silly. I also loved the small-town rodeos. I was very good at barrel racing. Wooden barrels are lined up along a distance of about 100 yards and you guide your steed around the barrels as fast as possible to get back to the start before the next rider. (In retrospect the concept is exactly like a slalom race in skiing.) I was also very good at calf roping (excuse the bragging), because I was a fearless rider and had excellent eye-hand coordination. Cindy and I had many great adventures and it nearly broke my heart to leave her when I went to college. I wanted to take her to Stanford, as some of my new friends were able to do with their horses, but we couldn't afford it. Gradually I rode less and less, only visiting Cindy when returning occasionally to Chino. Even though Daddy had many offers to buy Cindy and year after year Mother said it cost too much to feed Cindy, I was deeply pleased that Daddy would not let Mother sell her. Cindy died peacefully on the ranch at age twenty, shortly after Daddy died in 1967 at age seventy-one.

In 1945 after the war, Daddy acquired a used US Army three-quarter-ton 1941 International Harvester pick-up truck in which both Pete and I learned to drive, mastering the compound gearshift system. California law allowed children living on farms to get their licenses early to help with farm work, so we both got our driving licenses when we were fourteen. By that time the McCourt Turkey Ranch had built up to about ten thousand turkeys a year, which was a large operation at the time. It was year-round, starting with hatching in January and extending through the Thanksgiving and Christmas operation of the dressing plant that Daddy built on the ranch. He had one hired hand during most of the year but ten to fifteen more people when the dressing plant was operating for the holidays. Mother did the financial work and selling to markets all over Southern California. But her work did not include cooking our meals. The family always had dinner together after dark – when Daddy's ranch work was done he cooked our dinner. Almost always the menu included fried meat, fried sliced potato, whatever vegetables were available (often canned) and a canned fruit dessert.

During those early years on the ranch we didn't travel anywhere because we didn't have the money. We would occasionally take a hunting trip to shoot rabbits or a fishing trip, always by car, usually to Deep Creek in San Bernardino County, where I caught my first trout. Although Daddy loved the mountains, my mother's father loved the desert. Grandfather Ed had some property near Palm Springs, so sometimes we drove out to the desert for a change of pace. The real desert is as different from ordinary life in Southern California as are mountains with snow. Palm Springs was a small dusty hamlet. There was nothing on my grandfather's property but rocks, cacti, and Gila monster lizards. Having grown up in New Mexico Territory when it was still the Wild West, my father knew how to fish, hunt, and carve up what was killed for food. He wanted to teach us those skills, including shooting, so we'd practice out in the desert starting when I was seven or eight. Peter and I took a course in gun safety that I will never forget, in the basement of some dusty old city building in Pomona. My father was very big on safety. So my brother and I really learned how to care for, clean, and manage guns.

Sue with 22-gauge single shot Winchester rifle, a gift from father for my tenth birthday, 1947.

Daddy had given me my own Winchester 22 single shot rifle for my tenth birthday and Pete got a bigger 22. Later I also got a 410 shotgun, but I loved my 22. Pete and I would "cover" each other when we got into rattlesnake territory. Once, holding my one-shot rifle at my hip, I shot a coiled rattler right through the neck, believing a gun-to-shoulder movement would spook the rattler, while Pete stood cover with his shotgun. I was super excited and couldn't wait to tell Daddy.

Shortly after the war ended, I believe it was in 1947, we began our yearly summer trips to the Eastern flank of the High Sierras. (The Mammoth Mountain Ski Resort had just opened as a commercial venture, featuring one very short rope tow.) It was from those trips that I gained my deep and abiding love of the mountains, which would lead to adventures and events that I could not possibly have imagined at the time. To my father I credit those trips – along with growing up on a ranch under his guidance and somehow being able to go to Stanford University – with having had the most profound and lasting effect on my life.

We camped first in Agnew Meadows with our old International panel truck parked at our side. Mother never came on those trips. Daddy slept in the truck; Pete and I slept outside on the ground. We'd hike to the San Joaquin River every day to fish, where I got to be a pretty decent fly fisherman. In the evenings, Pete and I would sit at the meadow edge and shoot prairie dogs with our 22s. When the Boy Scout troops started coming to the meadow, we couldn't shoot anymore. Then we moved our camp to the juncture of the San Joaquin River and Shadow Creek. We had to pack in with mules and horses. From there we'd climb to Shadow Lake and Thousand Island Lake for long days of fishing. Sometimes we'd go all the way up to the Ice lakes for Golden Trout. Because we couldn't afford air mattresses, Pete and I slept for years under a canvas lean-to on fresh pine bough tips we'd harvested from nearby trees. Once in a while we'd have to go to Agnew Meadows for supplies. I remember on at least one occasion, we ran the narrow trail almost all the way in both directions, a roundtrip of eight or ten miles. One year when one of the pack station guides got injured, I found myself collared by the manager to be a wrangler taking other folks into the mountains with their pack train. I was very young and very proud of being given that responsibility.

As more crowds began to arrive in the Agnew Meadows area, we began packing out of Reds Meadows and going far back into Fish Creek. There we were safe from most visitors, except for one regular who camped not far away curing his year's supply of venison by hanging the carcass on a branch of a nearby pine tree during his summer stay. Daddy rode a horse in and out in those years. Pete and I and whoever was with us (often my best friend since second grade, Suzanne Mutuberria) would always hike in and out. Suzie's parents were first generation French Basque. They had a sheep farm not far from where we lived. Suzanne got a full scholarship to Stanford so Pete, Suzie, and I were in college together. In 1958 Suzie and Peter got married. They still live in Southern California. From our different camps I hiked and scrambled all over the Sierras…the prelude to skiing and climbing adventures yet to come.

Daddy and Mother were one generation removed from the settlement of the Old West. Mother maintained a strong interest in the culture of the Southwest and collected Indian baskets and Indian rugs, many of which I have now in our Telluride, Colorado home. Although she didn't dress up often, I do remember that when Mother dressed up, she looked absolutely elegant. She had a terrific sense of style. I especially remember a brilliant sapphire blue dress and a chocolate brown one, both with modest beading and gorgeous matching hats. Mother's upbringing had made her strong, quiet, and extremely independent. In a way, Mother seemed just like the masked and righteous Lone Ranger. She hid her emotions and her vulnerability and always insisted on doing what was right. She protected her family fiercely. It could well be that it was my mother, her Christian Science beliefs, her independent nature, and her stoic approach to life, which had the most profound and lasting effect on my life.

Strangely, I cannot remember what Mother wore on a daily basis, but I remember each and every piece of Daddy's clothing and exactly what he wore. It was almost always brown wellington boots, Levi's, a long-sleeved flannel or cotton shirt, either denim or red plaid, with two pockets on the front, a Levi jacket or occasionally his deerskin jacket, and a Stetson brand hat, but not a cowboy one. In the winter he wore wool plaid Pendleton shirts and washed them in tubs of white gasoline on top of the farm's old cistern.

Daddy's campfire stories and mannerisms reflected his upbringing. Ever hear of the stories of Pat Garrett and Billy the Kid? Or the tip of the hat and the expression "much obliged?" As Pete says, Daddy was a kind and a gentle man. You know, I eventually had the barrel of the Winchester rifle he gave me engraved with his name, Benjamin Arnold McCourt, and mine, with the date of my tenth birthday. Then all the gun issues came up and my husband and I moved to an urban area and one simply didn't use rifles or even talk about them. Nonetheless, it was meaningful to me and on my grandson Benjamin's tenth birthday in 2012, I had the rifle barrel engraved with his name as well, to give him as a gift. It's a relic now. That entire approach to life was over when my dad died in 1967. It was just over. The Old West died with my daddy.

Phil Van Pelt, Sue, Suzanne Mutubarria, my closest friend, and my brother Peter (on right) in the High Sierras, 1954.

Peter and Suzanne in front of our Chino ranch house, 1958.

Chapter Two

The function of education is to teach one to think critically.
Intelligence plus character — that is the goal of true education.
Martin Luther King Jr.

MEETING THE LOVE OF MY LIFE

In 1954 my brother graduated as valedictorian from Chino High School, the modest public high school we attended. I graduated in 1955. Peter had all A grades and received a full scholarship to Stanford. Providentially, his scholarship allowed me to follow him there as we could not have afforded the $750 tuition (without room, board, and books). Also, Pete's high school record benefited me enormously because my teachers assumed that I too had a brain and were extra supportive of me. I'm sure I was bumped up one grade in every class because of Peter's superb performances. Given his experience in the US aerospace industry working on rocket engines and then becoming an executive in space-oriented companies, we of course called him a "rocket scientist."

My best friend Suzanne Mutuberria and I wanted to go to college together, but we didn't think either of us would get into Stanford. However, my parents thought I would and made me apply. So I simply got it into my mind that I was going to go there too and I didn't apply anywhere else. Talk about naiveté. Luckily, I was accepted to Stanford. With Grandfather Edmund Griffin's help, my parents had been able to save enough money for me to attend that expensive school. Peter and I each received $65 a month as our personal allowance to cover the cost of books and our very modest social lives.

Suzanne's family had no savings at all, but as salutatorian in our high school class, she received a scholarship from Stanford. So Pete, Suzie, and I stayed together as we started our college years. We naturally drifted into our own circles. Pete and Suzie continued to date, and it was in our junior year that they married. As our lives pursued different paths, we saw less of each other and gently drifted apart. Nonetheless, deep in our hearts we have remained very close over the years.

Arriving at Stanford University in the fall of 1955 was a shock for me. Although Stanford is casually called "The Farm," it was nothing like my farm or any I'd ever seen. I stood on the corner of Stanford's quad, listening to all the different languages being spoken in animated conversation. It was, in fact, a world for which (except for my unreasonable innate self-confidence) I was quite ill prepared. It did occur to me that academics just might be a problem at this school.

When I started going to classes and meeting people who all appeared to be totally brilliant, I got scared. I remember one of my first-quarter incidents – a double date with a girlfriend of mine and two guys we had met at a freshman mixer. Both young men had gone to the prestigious Phillips Academy, often cited as the best high school in the country. We had just had our first important college exam in a year-long course called "The History of Western Civilization." To me the test was very, very hard. I was petrified as to what kind of grade I would receive. That night on our double date, both guys were joking and laughing. One said, "Boy, if Stanford is this easy it's going to be a real snap. We learned all that when we were juniors in high school." I did not say a word but thought, "I'm in trouble." I recognized then that my high school background was very different from many people at my college, but, it turned out, not from everyone. I met others like me and realized that some of us had led similarly sheltered lives through age eighteen. Stanford opened my eyes as to how much more there was to do, see, and learn about the world, and I was eager to experience it all.

I was not struggling for my identity as some college freshmen do, because growing up on a ranch with the guidance of my parents and Grandfather Ed, I knew my values and I knew who I was. I demonstrated, abundantly, in college that I was fun loving, but also fundamentally a serious, disciplined, analytical person. I was determined to have a good time in college, while swallowing whole all the new material being thrown at us. Internally I was stoically, and completely unreasonably, confident.

One of the factors that helped me become quickly integrated at Stanford was my high school athletics record. Suzanne and I dominated our high school sports teams. Of course girls' sports in those days were completely, thoroughly, and absolutely unimportant. It was probably in the late '50s that girls were first allowed to even wear shorts to play sports, rather than skirts. Tennis was an acceptable individual sport and girls played soccer, softball, field hockey, volleyball, and basketball at many schools. My unusually well-developed eye-hand coordination was a gift from birth, so all the team sports and tennis suited me well. I became captain of every single sports team in my high school and was a four-year player in all. As a high school freshman, I turned down the opportunity offered by the boys' football coach, only half facetiously, to be the quarterback of the boys' high school team.

Sports were fun for me. I liked to win. Sports for girls are actually important for the same reasons they are important for boys. We learn teamwork and discipline, how to win and how to lose, how to support and how to console our friends, and how to be resilient and keep on trying. Additionally, while it was not my best sport, tennis was socially acceptable for girls, so I took it up on the side and did well in Southern California tennis tournaments. Later I played on the Stanford tennis team and remain to this day a member of Stanford's varsity athletes Block S Society.

Traveling my first day to Stanford, I flew (the second flight of my life) from Los Angeles International Airport to the San Francisco airport, got into a cab, and went to a campus I had never seen before. When I walked into my freshman dorm, everybody else had already checked in. Girls were putting their things into their assigned rooms and chatting in the hallways. As I came up the stairway, I heard somebody yell, "Sue McCourt's here, Sue McCourt's here!" That was a surprise. Everybody stopped what they were doing and came to meet me. As it turned out, another girl from Southern California who knew of me had been "bragging" about my high school athletic feats. So there I was, I didn't know anyone, but they all knew me. You can imagine that gave me a huge (and unwarranted) boost in confidence.

One of the wonderful reasons for a woman to go to Stanford in the mid-1950s was the ratio of males to females: five to one. I never saw that as an obstacle for women, I always saw it as a big advantage for us. The more men around, the better! I think that may have been because growing up, I had no others in the area to play with except my brother's male friends. Or it might have been because of sports. Or maybe it was just because I was an eighteen-year-old girl at the time. In any event I was extremely comfortable around boys, young men, all men and have been all my life. Was I conscious of the feminine anger and of inequalities? No, not until years later. After settling in that first quarter and figuring out how I was going to manage studying and the workload, I concluded that Stanford was just a wonderful place to be, especially with all these brilliant guys around. I could see we would be learning and growing together.

I was invited to join the Rally Committee, which was at the time an exclusive, invitation-only small group, which supported our major male-only sports teams. We got to lead cheers at Stanford Stadium! Important stuff! And I discovered parties. We had no parties in my high school. I had never had a sip of any alcoholic beverage. But at Stanford I discovered parties and I liked those. I made sure to get my work done so I could go to any good party that came along. I remained my phlegmatic self, as I had been described by classmates, and became consciously socially active my first two years at Stanford. It was not only fun, having many male friends was a good defense against those young gentlemen who wanted some kind of closer relationship that I wanted to avoid.

These were the Eisenhower years. I was not interested in any political movements at all. I was interested in my friends and me at that time, which was every bit as immature as it sounds. The only political movement that I paid attention to was in my junior year, my brother Pete's senior year, when he managed the campaign for the young man, Jim Messinger, who became Stanford's 1957–58 student body president. I just wasn't interested in politics or matters of governance. I'm not sure why, because I chose Political Science as a major, and I really liked all the classes.

It's true. I partied a little too much at Stanford and I studied just enough to end up with a respectable GPA. Frankly, some kids – at least farm kids like me – are too young to go to college. We just did not understand the importance and the value of those to whom we were exposed, or the knowledge being laid at our feet. On the other hand, students like my future husband and my brother, were very focused at early ages. It could have been the difference of how men and women were raised in those years. Women were not expected to be breadwinners, so focusing on career objectives was not a priority. Without such pressure, I played tennis, went to a lot of parties, enjoyed my friends, and studied only on a need to know basis when a test was imminent. My parents were satisfied. I finished college in three years only because I was interested in everything and took as many courses as I could handle, accumulating enough credits to graduate in December 1958. Stanford was a superb experience. The extraordinary exposure across many fields gave me a foundation for life. However, the most important event of my years at Stanford was undoubtedly meeting the man who has been my husband since 1959, Charles Elvan Cobb Jr., Stanford Class of 1958, from Fresno, California.

Our partnership for life began in a most inauspicious manner. Chuck was a big track star – later an Olympian – and a big man on campus. His friends were telling him that he would really like me, and my friends were telling me that I would really like him; and you know when friends try to fix you up, you always say, "No." But enough of that went on that, even though he didn't know me, he called to invite me to the biggest party of the year. Three fraternities from Stanford and three fraternities from the University of California at Berkeley met together annually for one big black tie dance at the St. Francis Hotel in San Francisco. Everybody wanted to go to that party, including me.

I was living on $65 a month but managed to save a little bit (well, truth is, Pete always loaned me money) to buy a new dress for the St. Francis formal event. Then I got sick. I thought I was getting a little temperature, but the doctor put me into the Stanford nursing home – a large house on campus segregated from the active student body and monitored by house staff. But the doctor wasn't really attuned to his patient, because he put me on the second floor with a window. Of course, I got out. There was an overhang that covered the ground floor front door of this building, and my room window happened to be right over the front door. I easily got onto that overhang roof and then I just went down a pipe on the side of the building. I knew where my dress was, and I knew that Stanford and Cal insisted that all transportation be by bus. So I dressed, met my date in front of the Phi Delta Theta house, and together we got on the bus. On the bus ride, Chuck was drinking some kind of fruity beverage in which he overindulged (significantly overindulged).

We got to the St. Francis and the ballroom was just gorgeous. I was wearing my first strapless evening gown and felt very sophisticated. I thought I looked lovely in my dress – a little white organza number with a red rose in the center of my breasts. Everybody, all the women looked so pretty, the men so handsome, and the music was wonderful (the Dave Brubeck Quartet), but I could see that my date wasn't going to pay any attention to me at all. He had been in charge of putting this whole six-fraternity gala together, working with the hotel, with the guys at Berkeley, with the fraternities at Stanford, with the transportation personnel – all in great detail. Now that it had all come together, he was happily celebrating, and he forgot about our first date. I looked for friends and sat with one of my closest girlfriends, Nancy Page Ostrom, and her date, Paul Violich, a really cute Beta on whom I had a secret crush. It was not the evening I had anticipated, so I decided that I would just get on the first bus returning to Stanford, which I did.

The next day Chuck was extremely embarrassed. He was just apoplectic. He called me immediately the next morning to apologize and tried to explain that he had been so busy and had worked so hard on helping put the event together that maybe he had "relaxed" too much. I'm fairly direct, so I said to him, and I truly felt this way, "It's really not a problem. Things happen with people. Yeah, sometimes people don't hit it off. Don't worry about it, it was one date, it's over. I don't see any reason to see you again at all, but I don't hold it against you. Things happen, we're done. Don't bother calling again."

Well, he did call again, and being a competitor, he called every single night for nine months (he says six months, I say nine). I would hang up on him in the beginning or just tell him I was busy. But he was persistent. He kept calling. I knew, from his friends and mine, that he really was a very decent person. I just felt it was a waste of time to go out with him. I also felt that it would look bad if I continued to see this guy who had basically dumped me. But during all those phone calls, I really got to know who he was, how he thought, what he was like, what his parents were like, what his major aspirations were, what his goals in life were, how he responded to the good things and the bad things that routinely happen, to the important things and the unimportant things, why he was training so hard, and why he was going to Stanford Memorial Church most every Sunday. I really got to know him. He had been so persistent that after I began talking to him, I began to expect his calls and looked forward to them (but of course I didn't ever tell him that). Every night, sometime between six and nine, he would call. I would put time aside, and we would frequently talk for close to an hour. I wasn't devoted to him. I was going out with other men. But one night near the end of my sophomore year while we were both studying for finals, he called and said, "Let's go get a cup of coffee." I said, "Yes, let's do." And that was it.

Chuck was always an extremely focused individual who does not tolerate frivolity and focuses on using time constructively. He is a "doer" – extremely impatient about getting things done. We really had not been dating very long and one night we were talking about what we each were going to do in the future. Talking not as a couple, but individually, about what we were going to do in our lives. After about ten dates, he said, "Well, I know what I'm going to do next year when I'm a senior. Just so you know, I will be president of my fraternity, I will have at least a B+ average for my undergraduate years at Stanford, I will be captain of the Stanford track team, I will be commissioned in the United States Navy, and I will marry you." I, of course, was stunned. I was offended. "How can you say that? What are you talking about?" But he had already figured out what his life was going to be for his senior year and stated it very forthrightly. The only response I could muster was: "I just don't appreciate being fifth on your list." He succeeded in every single goal.

We both left school for the summer break but kept in touch. In my junior year, 1957–58, after he came back from his summer ROTC (Reserve Officers Training Corps) midshipman cruise, we were inseparable and soon thereafter became "pinned" (the equivalent of "going steady"), and later engaged. I finished Stanford in December 1958; and in February of 1959, we were married in Stanford Memorial Church. I was twenty-one and he was twenty-two.

I was told that only five or six women in our Class of 1959 went immediately on to pursue a higher degree. I believe most of us were still unsure of what would become of us. In the era in which I grew up, an educated girl's goal was to finish college having met a reputable guy who could get a job, get married, have children, and live happily ever after. That is what society (and the movies) told us to do.

Chuck was a good man and a leader. He was a commissioned officer in the Navy and was doing his required two years of active service. Meanwhile I was still at Stanford and then by the end of December 1958, back home with my parents. Just prior to our wedding, Chuck was stationed on an aircraft carrier based in San Diego. He was soon deployed for three months on that carrier to the Taiwan straits where Taiwan and China were fighting over the islands of Quemoy and Matsu. They lobbed bombs at each other every other day. On the days they were not at war, international shipping could continue in the straits. It was quite dramatic.

Lt. j.g. Charles Elvan Cobb Jr.
Naval Officer, 1958.

Chuck, the fifth best high hurdler
in the world, training for the
Olympics, 1959.

Sue and Chuck, Stanford University, first date, 1957.

Because Chuck was a world-class athlete and the 1960 Olympics were coming up in Rome, Italy, the Navy plucked him from the carrier and reassigned him to the Naval Special Services Branch for Olympic training. He was then attached to the ROTC unit at Stanford to train under Stanford's famous track coach, Payton Jordan. Chuck spent a few months at sea and then was stationed back at Stanford, where we lived on campus. For the track indoor season, he was transferred to the Naval Academy in Annapolis, and we lived in a charming cottage on the Chesapeake Bay. Chuck and I traveled together with the US Olympic track team around the United States and then on to Europe in the summer of 1960.

Chuck won the Armed Forces Championship in the 110-meter high hurdles in what was then world record time. Prior to the Olympics, Chuck was ranked as the fifth best high hurdler in the world. Unfortunately, three of the top five were Americans, so while he was on the Olympic Team for the games, he was destined to be the alternate. The three Americans who actually got to race in Rome won gold, silver, and bronze medals. During the games, some of the top alternate team members were invited to tour the Scandinavian countries to run at several track meets. Chuck said he would go if he could bring his wife. We toured the Scandinavian countries and the invited Americans competed in track meets every four or five days in different cities. That was an exciting time and a broadening educational experience. Because Chuck is such a disciplined person, he has stayed in top athletic shape his entire life.

As soon as Chuck finished his Navy service, he entered the Stanford Graduate School of Business, so we returned to Stanford. In total we lived on or in the shadows of the Stanford campus for eight years. Starting at age eighteen, for our formative young adult years, Stanford University was our home and our culture. This is one of the reasons that both of us are so pleased that our one and only granddaughter, Cassidy Elizabeth Cobb, is part of Stanford's Class of 2022. Chuck and I moved to Miami in the early '70s, and we have been closely involved with and love the University of Miami, but deep in our hearts our blood runs cardinal red.

In a fitting conclusion some years later, for his athletic career, for his leadership, for his devotion to and support of Stanford, the magnificent track at Stanford University was named Cobb Track.

Wedding of Sue McCourt and Charles Elvan Cobb Jr. at Stanford Memorial Chapel, February 28, 1959.

Chapter Three

Whether you think you can or you can't, you're right.
Mark Twain

BECOMING A WIFE, MOTHER, AND CHAMPION SKIER

After our European excursion for the Olympics, we came back to Palo Alto in the fall of 1960. I got a job teaching at Crystal Springs School for Girls, a prestigious private school on the old Crocker Estate in Hillsborough just south of San Francisco. It was at that time purely a girls' school, grades seven through twelve, later to become co-ed. Without the requisite degree in education, I was not eligible to be a teacher in California public schools, but the private schools liked to hire what they called well-rounded or well-educated young men and women. I taught physical education and a senior seminar on world affairs, which required me to continually study in order to understand the historical context and current events of the time. Being totally immodest, I was good at both.

Prior to teaching at Crystal Springs, I had a couple of other part-time jobs while at Stanford. When I walked into a shoe store in the Stanford Shopping Center one day in 1957 to buy shoes, I noticed that a clerk at that very moment was quitting. As he walked out the door, I said to the manager, "I can do that job." He hired me on the spot and I worked as a part-time shoe salesperson the rest of that year. I was just being practical.

Engagement announcement at Cobb residence, Fresno, California, July 1958.
I am wearing the discounted shoes from my first job at Stanford Shopping Center.

I wanted the twenty percent discount on shoes. Right after we were married, I got a job as a clerk in a men's store in Menlo Park. Anything to keep busy and to earn a little bit of money, so I did whatever opened up before my eyes. It was easy for me to get jobs, but it was hard for me to stay with them, because they were about as menial as one could find. When I got the teaching job, thanks to the recommendation of my Stanford friend Nancy Page Ostrom, I was really happy. I was a full-time teacher the two years that Chuck was at Stanford Business School and continued for about two more years on a part-time basis.

The families of the girls in the private school were financially secure. Several of them had homes at the Sugar Bowl ski resort, near Donner Summit in the Sierras. I had skied only one time before I started skiing regularly with my students in 1961. My first ski excursion was memorable. It was in February of 1959 just before Chuck and I got married. I was home in Southern California when a Stanford friend who lived in Los Angeles called and said, "Why don't you come to Aspen with me next week? My uncle and I are going skiing."

I said, "That sounds like fun, but I don't have any skis, I really don't have the money for a flight, and I don't know anything about skiing."

She replied, "Don't worry, we're going in my uncle's plane and I have extra skis and clothes at my house in Aspen." I couldn't resist.

My Stanford friend was Pat Gregson and her uncle was Bill Janss, one of the founders and builders of the Aspen Ski Resort. When we went into their home in Aspen, we went to Pat's bedroom and I remember so clearly, I saw along the wall three pairs of skis. One was red, one was white, and one was blue. Then Pat started looking for clothes for me to wear. In her closet she had beautiful ski suits. One was red, one was white, and one was blue. My eyes opened wide. I mean, this was just out of my league. I didn't know what to do. I had bought an army surplus jacket from the Army-Navy store in Pomona, because that was all I could afford. I'm sure I embarrassed Bill Janss, but he never let on. They found some skis for me, a jacket that was presentable (in fact, it was beautiful), and Uncle Bill personally gave me my first ski lesson. Obviously, I wasn't very good, but I instantly loved skiing.

We had landed in Aspen in his plane at what was then a very small airport. A storm came during the week, so he had the plane moved to Glenwood Springs about seventy miles away. As we were leaving Aspen by car to drive to that airport about twelve miles after we had left the town of Aspen, Bill pointed out a whole mountain range on our left, and said, "I own those mountains and I'm going to build a fabulous new ski resort there." He did. Those mountains became Snowmass. In later years I skied Snowmass, always thinking about Bill. When he finished Snowmass, he bought and built out the remainder of the Sun Valley Ski Resort. This was the man who got me started skiing! After Aspen I wasn't able to afford skiing again until I started teaching at Crystal Springs, where parents of my students hired me to chaperon their daughters to Sugar Bowl with full expenses paid.

Crystal Springs was just a wonderful transition for me. We had some income, Chuck was studying day and night, my hours and my commute from Stanford to Hillsborough were short, plus I met a lot of wonderful people. The girls always wanted to go skiing, and the parents couldn't always go due to other obligations. I was chaperoning high school juniors and seniors, seventeen and eighteen years old. I was twenty-two. They were good skiers, so I wanted to be better. Since their families paid for us to take ski lessons, I probably took over one hundred lessons in two years and got better very quickly. I totally fell in love with the sport.

When Chuck graduated with his MBA, he accepted a job with a wealth management firm in San Francisco called Dodge & Cox, subject to a six-month training period at Brown Brothers Harriman in New York. We spent the summer of 1962 living in a tiny apartment at 355 East 55th Street. It was exciting. The prior summer, in 1961, we were also in New York where Chuck had gained experience at Citibank. That summer we had lived on West 103rd Street on the Upper West Side in a rental apartment in quite a different environment than East 55th Street. I had no job and no children, so I played tennis in Central Park and "went shopping" in Fifth Avenue's elegant stores. I tried on a lot of clothes but never made purchases because I couldn't afford anything. It was just entertainment.

Back in San Francisco with his job at Dodge & Cox, we moved to a lovely two-bedroom apartment on Lyon Street at the end of Union Street just below Pacific Heights and right on the Presidio Wall. Chuck's career was important to both of us. My main job was to be sure that I was put together properly for various occasions in the fabulous city in which we lived. In those days, men and women still wore hats and gloves in San Francisco. I did my best to dress properly, be polite, and keep quiet. I had learned that everyone likes to talk and my best means of an ongoing education was to just keep my mouth closed and listen. Chuck is inquisitive and can be provocative. He asks lots and lots of questions. And people eagerly answer. There's no need for me to say a word. I just watch, listen, and absorb everyone's thoughts and positions. I put their words into my mental filing cabinet under the correct subtitle.

I remained fairly removed from the 1960's "revolution" in full swing in San Francisco. I just wasn't a "Flower Child." Some big lessons came from the faculty members with whom I worked at Crystal Springs. Two or three of them were members of the "hippie" movement. One colleague, quite enraptured with the movement, took me to her apartment in Haight Ashbury, a district named after a normal street intersection – but a district inhabited by a new group of young (mostly) American non-conformists. There were maybe ten to twelve people living in my friend's three-room apartment. In the middle of the day when I visited, several of her roommates were lying on the floor, others on old over-stuffed couches, all puffing away, reeking of what we then called "m-j" or marijuana. I couldn't believe it. In the middle of the day they were sleeping or dyeing T-shirts or just lying around puffing their own types of pleasure. In my young mind it was un-American not to be working for your livelihood. I truly believed they should all clean up, find jobs, and pay attention to their lives. It was a shocker to me. Haight Ashbury was real, and my friend – a respected teacher at an elite school – was deep into that vogue. I don't know whatever happened to her. What had caused the type of rebelliousness we were seeing in the early sixties? I started paying attention to politics, governance policies, the state of our state, and the state of our country.

In 1964 I became engaged in the organization of the Republican National Convention being held in San Francisco's Cow Palace, at which Barry Goldwater was the eventual Republican nominee. For the convention I was in charge of arranging hotel rooms in the Bay Area for all Young Republicans coming from around the country. I was reasonably successful in that chore and attended several exciting days at the convention. But US voters were not keen on Barry Goldwater. In fact, they totally rejected him in favor of Lyndon B. Johnson, the savvy Senate majority leader from Texas.

That was the beginning of a long process of being engaged with the mechanics of politics. Although my father was originally an Irish Catholic Democrat, from my mother and grandfather Edmund Griffin we all had absorbed a kind of conservative approach to life, which emerged as Chuck and I began to be civically and politically active. I remember as a college student that Chuck followed politics and paid close attention to elections and to government policies. After he started working with the investment managers, he was exposed to many political and economic discussions.

Chuck has always had a big influence on my thinking, whatever the subject matter; so while I didn't exactly mean to, I was getting a political and policy education over dinner. To the extent that one of us was not off traveling somewhere, the two of us have talked over dinner together every night for over sixty years. We each have our own personal associations, then we come together, always talking about the nation's problems and the interesting ideas of the times. We had and still have serious dinner discussions and often challenge each other's thought processes and conclusions. It has been an enriching component of our long relationship, which I think actually started with our long phone conversations from a dorm room in 1957.

In the early '60s we were both considered well educated. Chuck had a good job; we had a reasonable income for our age group, and in 1963 and in 1964, I had successive baby boys, fifteen months apart. I reduced my part-time teaching at Crystal Springs and then became a full-time mom. Christian McCourt Cobb was born on March 12, 1963 and Tobin Templeton Cobb on July 6, 1964 – both at Children's Hospital in San Francisco. I don't remember either of my sons having serious illnesses or terrible two's tantrums, or other serious childhood problems. I never thought that being a mother and taking care of children was a problem or impinged on my life as some women do. When the boys were very young, I just took them with me wherever I was going. We frequently went up to the Sierras – about a three-hour drive from our apartment in San Francisco – or down to Santa Cruz where Chuck's father and mother had a small house on the beach. As they got old enough to understand, I expressed my approach clearly to my boys: "These are the rules we'll abide by, and they're A, B, C, D, E, and just understand that's the way it's gonna be, and if it doesn't happen that way, you're gonna have a lot of trouble on your hands." They learned at an early age that I was serious about rules. I didn't have many, but those that related to safety and to my peace of mind, which I explained carefully to them, were enforced.

When they were very young, I used to take a playpen and some toys to the marina and put them into it next to the park tennis courts. I met a "regular" at the tennis courts who managed "deadhead" vehicles for Hertz Rental cars. One day he said, "Look, I can get you a car free anytime you want, between Los Angeles and San Francisco because there's always an imbalance in our fleet and we need drivers to adjust the fleet. Just let me know." I had been driving our own car back and forth visiting my parents in Southern California, and Chuck's parents in Fresno, so a free car was great for me. But kids and long car rides are not a good combination, so I started driving mostly at night. When they were with me and started acting up – crying and hitting each other as kids are prone to do – I would say to them, "I'm going to count to three and if this hasn't stopped, I'm going to pull over and stop this car for a serious discussion."

My voice could be so stern that they would abide. They knew they could count to two and often did, but before three whatever they were doing would cease. I just set the rules firmly and they lived by them (mostly). As boring as it was, driving back and forth was a good way for their grandparents in Fresno and Chino to see the boys and vice versa. From those drives and the beach house in Santa Cruz, I got to know Chuck's parents Elvan and Mildred Cobb very well, as did their grandsons Chris and Toby. Charles "Elvan" Cobb, Chuck's father, and

Mildred Kerr Cobb, his mother, were from a long line of central valley ranchers. Elvan was a fourth generation Californian and attended Stanford University. Among other things they owned a very fashionable dress shop in Fresno, which Mildred ran for many years. From some genealogy work that Chuck has done, he has found definitive proof that his early ancestors landed near Plymouth, Massachusetts, shortly after the Mayflower's arrival in 1620, and many Cobbs were laid to rest in the Cobb Hill Cemetery in Barnstable, Massachusetts. Chuck had one sister, Pat, who was five years younger, just enough age difference that I did not get to know Pat well until several years later when she married Captain John D. Veatch (West Point '60). My boys called their paternal grandparents "Pop" and "Mommer." I felt privileged to know these sophisticated, but down to earth, loving grandparents who proved to be such powerfully positive role models for the boys and, in fact, for me.

In 1965 Chuck accepted a position in the Office of the Treasurer of Kaiser Aluminum, headquartered in Oakland in the East Bay. In 1966 we bought our first house on Orchard Road in Orinda. I was still a stay at home mom, playing tennis, being a Cub Scout leader, but I now lost my two little playmates. They had started school; Chris was in first grade and Toby in a nice pre-school. I was embarrassed early on when it was my turn in the mothers' carpool to pick the children up after school and I forgot them. Not infrequently, I'd just be late. I loved my sons, but if it was a great match 4–6, 7–5, 4-all in the third set, I simply had to play on. Chuck was their soccer coach those years. We managed our lives like all young families – the best we could.

As soon as the boys could walk, I got ski boots for them that were five or six inches long and skis about twenty-four inches long. I made the boys walk in their boots and skis on the carpets in our house so that they'd get used to wearing skis.

*Chuck with his sister, Patricia Cobb Veatch, and parents,
Mildred and Elvan Cobb, Alexandria, Virginia, 1969.*

*One of Chris and Toby's first trout fishing lessons,
in the High Sierras, near Truckee, California, 1965.*

As soon as I could, I took them skiing. On the weekends during the time we lived in Orinda, I sometimes taught skiing at Sugar Bowl for the kindergarten to fifth grade age, mostly so my sons could ski free. We were a happy threesome. Sometimes, Chuck was with us, but it really just wasn't his "thing." When he did come, he would get really mad when we had snowstorms and he had to put chains on the car tires. Everyone hated that!

One of Chuck's most important jobs was to manage Kaiser Aluminum's investments in real estate, including some large pieces of property that Kaiser had purchased in California. The aluminum companies in the '60s had considerable liquidity and had turned to investing in real estate. However, they didn't have knowledgeable real estate finance employees, so Chuck quickly learned real estate finance and management. Before he was thirty, Chuck was in charge of Kaiser's largest developments, including 90,000 acres of property in Southern California south of Riverside and north of San Diego surrounding a very tiny town called Temecula. What to do with all this property? Even then in the late '60s, due to its location and California's growth, it was of considerable value. However, there was not yet a ready market for this land, so Chuck learned how to master-plan communities for orderly growth over time. The land became known as Rancho California. Kaiser first created sufficient infrastructure to provide access for potential farming opportunities. Initially, they sold parcels for large horse ranches and for acre upon acre of avocados, then they gradually began to bring people to the area by building homes and townhouses. Today, Temecula is the center of Rancho California; the 90,000 acres is fully developed and diversified with homes, vineyards, farms, golf courses, lakes, and other amenities.

Chuck also was in charge of building a shopping mall and office buildings in Santa Ana, California. We moved from Orinda to Laguna Beach in 1967 to be closer to the Southern

California projects. In Laguna Beach we lived in a community called Emerald Bay. I loved two-man beach volleyball, a popular sport on the beaches of Southern California. With an extraordinarily good male partner, we won the Southern California mixed doubles beach volleyball championship and, of course, I continued to play tennis. My son Chris remembers of his childhood:

> We lived in about five homes in the ten years that I lived in California. Every two years we moved so I remember better some of the later homes when I was six or eight. As little kids in Emerald Bay in Laguna we'd go to the beach every day. We'd play in the sand and we'd play in the surf. The Pacific was pretty cold. My Mom and Dad played volleyball on the beach with their friends, then we'd end up staying into the evening. The sun would set, they'd start a big fire in a fire pit that was on the beach, someone would bring food and drinks and we'd have a picnic dinner there in the dark, on the beach, before going home. It was a lot of fun. You know, as a child you didn't really know how good it was."
>
> Christian McCourt Cobb, September 23, 2017

Emerald Bay was rightly described as a pretty exclusive enclave, and in truth it was an unusually idyllic life. During that time, I was one hundred percent mom, paying close attention to my two young children and participating in whatever they were doing. I had taken up running when the boys started school in the mid-'60s and continued to run nearly every day for the next fifty years.

Most of my women friends were similar in age, similar in background in a general sense, financially secure for the most part, and were married to professionals, doctors, lawyers, and businessmen. We all had young children, so we would either be at the beach or we would be at the tennis courts just chatting about life, and about what life might be for us. A lot of the women, like me, really didn't know very much at that age.

Sue McCourt Cobb, Emerald Bay, Laguna Beach, California, 1968.

The young Cobb family enjoying the beach at Emerald Bay, Toby, Sue, Chris and Chuck, 1968.

We had been to college, we had some academic learning, but most of us grew up in a sheltered environment with limited vision. It was in Emerald Bay that I met Shari and Bill DuBois. They had two boys, Bill and Rich, about the same age as our sons; for many years we met every Christmas to ski at Alta, Aspen, or Vail, and later, Telluride. Shari and Bill became forever friends, even though they remained in California their entire lives.

Emerald Bay: idyllic and unchallenging. I decided to improve the "wives" groups' intellectual exposure and started a book club in Emerald Bay. We studied the existentialists – Kierkegaard, Heidegger, Paul Tillich, and others. We dug deeply into Solzhenitsyn's *The Gulag Archipelago*. We read mostly non-fiction and a few novels and got seriously into philosophy and psychology, subjects I had not studied. I thought of psychology as short-term problem solving and philosophy as long-term structured thinking – the architecture of a stable life. Gradually, relying on the writings of these consummate teachers and to the extent we had not consciously done so before, we developed our own individual philosophies of life.

Close to Laguna, at the University of California Irvine, there was a well-known professor teaching Abraham Maslow's theory of a human's hierarchy of needs. The psychologist Maslow believed in self-actualization. How do you get the most out of the talents that you have, to find a rewarding, fulfilling life? My women friends were invested in these subjects and we all took the Maslow course. I'm not certain, but I think we all profited from those studies. Meanwhile, I ran, played volleyball and tennis, and watched over Chris and Toby as they grew to ages five and six.

Sadly for me, in late 1969 we were called back to Northern California by Kaiser. We moved into a nice suburban area in Lafayette (adjacent to Orinda) on a beautiful street called Upper Happy Valley Road. No more beach. My boys went to the local public school – Chris in second grade and Toby going into first grade. To occupy myself while the boys were in school, I decided to lay new tile in our very large kitchen's floor. It was hard work, but I found it strangely satisfying. One day Toby came home from school with a picture book that had just three to five-word sentences at the bottom of the page, "Jack sees Bob jump," or whatever. The book was twelve or fifteen pages long and he was very excited. He told me he could read and wanted me to listen. We sat down on a couch and he started on the first page, showing me the pictures, turning the pages, telling me what was happening. We got to about the tenth page and he made a mistake. The words at the bottom were not what the picture was showing nor what Toby said. "Wait a minute, Toby. I don't understand. This doesn't make sense. Let's go back to the last page."

We turned back a page. On that page he relayed what was happening, but the words were in the wrong order. Then I suggested, "Let's go to the first page and start over." When we went back to the first page, it was clear he did not have a clue as to what the words said. He could not read any words. Toby had memorized the entire book at school, but the smallest change threw him off track. It was then that we learned Toby had dyslexia, a term which had only recently come into common conversation. Shortly thereafter, *Time* magazine had an article on dyslexia. That's when Chuck realized he also had a measure of the same problem, but it wasn't really named when he was growing up. Dyslexia is now referred to as a learning disability. It certainly did not stop Chuck. Nor did it stop Toby, who mastered economics at Southern Methodist University, graduated with an MBA from New York University's Stern School of Business and has gone on to have an admirable career in finance. Christian probably had a lower level of dyslexia, too, but it wasn't a hindrance to him. He graduated from Tulane's School of Architecture and received his MBA from Harvard.

In our Lafayette years, I was in my young thirties, still being one hundred percent mom, devoted Cub Scout leader, and diligent Boy Scout leader. I met with each of the boys' teachers and went to their schools' activities. And I continued skiing. One weekend I was racing in a slalom course against my former high school students when I broke my clavicle. (Of course I pushed too hard, because I didn't want to lose to them.) Although it required a full upper body hard cast, it was a minor nuisance. I was always an "all out" skier. I don't know why this was true, but I had no fear. Falling was of no concern whatsoever. I knew that I had the strength, the skill, the mindset, and I could do anything that any others, including the male ski racers, were doing at Sugar Bowl. And if it didn't work out, I knew my bones healed in six weeks (at least in those years).

This was also a time from which I have many happy memories of skiing with Toby. He loved skiing and he loved his mommy. He was then almost nine and I could easily get down to his level of humor and non-responsibility. We were two little kids in a land of snow and fun. We were as silly as we could be. All these years later he would say in an interview, "My mother has an almost unknown silly side to her," and he backed up that statement with recent examples, not to be printed here because they are secrets that belong only to Toby and me.

Also, now in his early 50s, Toby is a very gifted, nearly professional level, skier. I'm happy that he and his wife Luisa have passed our love of the sport to their three sons – Luis, Charlie, and Sebastian – all beautiful (though a little reckless) skiers.

In the spring of 1971, I was skiing at Sugar Bowl with the schoolgirls, and we happened to ski onto a run that had a racecourse set up. Nobody was there, so we decided to ski the course. Unbeknownst to me, a small group of people was near the bottom by some trees chatting. I didn't notice them, but as I

Chuck and Sue with Cub Scouts Toby age six and Chris age seven,
Lafayette, California, 1970.

exited the course, they called to me and asked where I had been training. I told them I wasn't a racer and was not "training." It turned out they were a group of master skiers who held races all over the United States. They invited me to join them to ski the Sierra master series races in the 1971–72 ski season. I was excited about that and did dry land training that summer and fall.

Chuck came home for dinner one night in the late summer of 1971. We had been married for twelve years; the boys were then seven and eight. Chuck said, "I had a really interesting discussion today with Victor Palmieri. There is a job prospect that I think is something that would be of interest and I want to tell you about it." He started talking about the potential new job. "It's managing a very large amount of separate properties owned by the same company. That company plans to get financing to expand and build on several properties around the country." He went on and on and on and said there were circumstances in which he could really be the leader of a successful company because he would be the CEO and, of course, it had a lot of upside potential and a wonderful salary. He carried on for at least forty-five minutes. All of a sudden, I thought: something's wrong with this. Why is he selling so hard? I'm thinking maybe we're going to move back to Southern California and he's afraid I won't want to do that because of my skiing. Finally it occurred to me that I should ask just where this great job was headquartered. He said, "Miami." I replied, "NO WAY! I AM NOT GOING. I'M KEEPING THE CHILDREN. HAVE A NICE LIFE IN MIAMI."

Two years before, in 1969, I had gone to meet Chuck at a conference in Miami where the accommodations were part of the package, though not airfare. That was the first and only time I'd been there. I flew to Miami from San Francisco on a red-eye because we didn't think we could afford a daytime transcontinental airline ticket. On arrival early in the morning, my eyes were hardly open. Chuck had arranged a room for me at the Fontainebleau Hotel, a big fancy hotel in Miami Beach. I got a taxi, went directly to the hotel and directly to bed. I was exhausted, slept until 11:00 a.m., woke up, and looked around my room. It was beyond ornate – mirrors in gold frames all over the place, even the ceiling, crystal dripping from chandeliers in shiny gold reflectors. It startled me. It was all completely unnecessary for what I wanted most – a comfortable night's sleep.

After dressing, I went to a café by the pool where I had been told that I could order breakfast or lunch. As is normal, people were sitting around the pool sunning. Suddenly music started to blare. I glanced around the surroundings. Adjacent to the pool was a large wooden dance floor. Soon, people started getting up from their chairs and lounges and coming out from the hotel doors – many somewhat rotund men and women in bathing suits. Some of the men had hair, most didn't. They were not young men. The women wore glittery bathing suits and high heels, the men were wearing tight little Speedo type bathing suits. They started dancing. They were dancing! They were dancing like people danced in the '50s and '60s, holding each other, sunscreen mixing. I just thought it was unreal. I could not believe my eyes. It was the middle of the day! Why weren't they working? This wasn't normal. I disliked the whole scene, the hotel, the dancing mid-day, the town, and entire state (even though I had seen nothing of it). That was etched into my memory as "Miami." So, that night in 1971 when Chuck uttered the word Miami, I just flatly said, "No!"

Finally, he said, "I know that you're adventurous and it is a very good opportunity for our family, so we should go there – the kids are flexible – we should go for one year and see what happens and then we'll come back." As simple as that he swayed me. This was a logical argument, so I said, "Okay." And everything changed. We never went back to California. We've been in Miami now for nearly fifty years. It is a unique and fabulous town!

In the fall of 1971, Chuck moved from our house in Lafayette to Miami to start his new job while the boys and I stayed in California so that Chris and Toby could finish the school year. After Chuck moved to Florida, I got to participate in many ski races (boys in tow) and just seemed to have a knack for it. Several of my new racing friends were former Olympians, and I learned quickly from them. Ski equipment companies noticed and provided my equipment. Kneissi was the most generous. I did a lot of racing with the masters group throughout the Far West Division. Late in March of 1972, as I was preparing myself to give up skiing and move to Florida with the boys, I received a surprise phone call inviting me to Aspen for the Masters National Championship races. I learned that I had the second fastest time in the 1971–72 season for all the Far West States in what were essentially giant slalom courses. The top two skiers in each age category were selected from each geographical division across the country to go to the national finals in Aspen Highlands. The race was a two-run giant slalom "combined." I won by six seconds and was number one in the United States. Now this wasn't the Olympics – it was in an age group, and I was in the 27–35 group. But I was excited about it. Though excited, I remember clearly that I did not stay for the trophy ceremony. I asked the surprised officials to mail the trophy to me because I wanted to catch a plane to California to race the next day in a slalom race near Sugar Bowl. (I lost.) Nonetheless, I admit that I was very happy about being number one in the United States at anything. I guess it was not a bad way to finish my short racing career.

*Sue Cobb, National Champion, US National Standard Races
(age category: 27-35), Aspen Highland, Colorado, March 1972.*

Chapter Four

Toda aventura empieza con su sí.
Anónimo

"I'M KEEPING THE CHILDREN. HAVE A NICE LIFE IN MIAMI"

After I agreed that we could move to Miami for a year, I flew to Florida to have a look. This time I had a first-class plane ticket and Chuck arranged a gorgeous, huge limousine to meet me. I mean a GIANT limousine. I was not used to riding in a giant limousine, nor with the overly polite driver who took me to the Boca Raton Hotel and Club, about forty miles north of the City of Miami. Now that Chuck had become the Chief Executive Officer of Arvida, which owned the Boca Raton Hotel and Club, everyone there treated him as a big shot. Part of that treatment rubbed off on his family.

We were thereafter to stay in the hotel's executive suite, consisting of the entire top two floors of the hotel's stunning tower. The lower floor of our suite was a spacious area for dining and entertaining and equipped with a grand piano. The day I arrived, Chuck had a pianist come to play the piano so that music would drift softly up to me in our private quarters. I mean, he was doing everything he possibly could think of to make me enjoy the experience so that I would like Florida. The hotel probably never knew that the large lower floor of what became our new temporary home was used by my two young sons – ages almost nine and ten – for practicing soccer and tennis! I should have been horrified, but usually I just removed the exposed lamps and joined them.

Let me give you a thumbnail sketch of Arvida Corporation in those days. The name Arvida came from the first two initials of Arthur Vining Davis, the original owner of the corporation. Davis was the chairman and largest shareholder of ALCOA (the Aluminum Company of America) and also ALCAN (the Aluminum Company of Canada). Aluminum companies had significant reserves in the '60s and '70s and purchased almost twenty percent of South Florida land to essentially hold in a land bank. Arvida became a subsidiary of the Penn Central Corporation, a New York Stock Exchange (NYSE) company best known for its railroads. In 1969 Penn Central went into bankruptcy, one of the biggest bankruptcies in American history. At the time, Penn Central was known as the majority shareholder of railroads, several other industrial entities, and its land bank – Arvida.

While Penn Central was in bankruptcy, Chuck's friend from Stanford Business School, Victor Palmieri, was in New York helping to sort out Penn Central's varied assets. A decision was made to separate all the rail assets and all the non-rail assets. The rail assets became ConRail, owned by the federal government. The non-rail assets, including Arvida and all its real estate, were divided into separate operating entities to be managed by the surviving Penn Central Company. Victor Palmieri recruited Chuck from Kaiser to run Penn Central's subsidiary Arvida. At that time Arvida held properties in Florida, Arizona, California, Texas, the Bahamas, and elsewhere. This was the career opportunity Chuck had described to me over dinner in California: to become the CEO of Arvida Corporation, headquartered in Miami, Florida.

In June 1972, the boys and I joined Chuck in Miami. South Florida was still very much the Old South. From my perspective we lived in a gentile, quiet, southern outpost at the end of the world. It was a huge adjustment. It didn't help that it rained torrentially every day for the first three weeks of my Miami life.

We bought a house about ten miles south of downtown Miami in an acceptable suburb across from Fairchild Tropical Gardens. We paid $65,000 for what was essentially a remodel. To get our Snapper Creek Lakes house into livable condition required considerable work. We stayed in one bedroom while I supervised remodeling the remainder of the house. Of course we also arranged schools for our boys. The *Time* magazine article we had read on dyslexia had mentioned that one of the best schools in America to assist children with dyslexia was McGlannan School in Miami. They were happy to help Toby his first two years in Miami and did a remarkable job. But at the same time we learned of his reading difficulties, we began to understand that he was quantitatively brilliant, a precursor to his very successful years on Wall Street.

On a personal level, I desperately missed skiing, but channeled my athletic energy into competitive tennis. I never really loved tennis, but I really didn't have anything else to do while the boys were in school, so I just started playing again. After winning a few state tournaments, I invested in a tennis academy with a displaced Cuban businessman named Andy Garcia (not the movie star) and my neighbor, Donna Fales. I became vice president of the Andy Garcia Tennis Corporation from 1973 to 1975. Of the three of us, I was the worst tennis player. Our company was not going to have an award-winning financial return, but we enjoyed running our tennis camps at the old Sheraton Resort on Key Biscayne. The tennis academy was really an investment in having fun, in just doing something that we liked to do. Andy was a true tournament-level player and a top-notch instructor. Donna Fales remained a great player throughout her entire life, including winning many tournaments in every age group and world championships in the 60-, 70-, and 75-year-old brackets. Most recently, Donna won the 75-year-old world championships in all categories: singles, doubles, and mixed doubles. She's still playing internationally.

There was a weather phenomenon in Miami that was interesting. During the summertime we had a lot of rain coming into South Florida from the ocean, particularly in July through September and October. Rain would pass right over the offshore island of Key Biscayne (a barrier reef), which is flat and had only a few high-rise buildings. Key Biscayne would rarely get rain, but across the causeway in downtown Miami, from which heat was rising, rain fell copiously. So tennis courts in Miami and Coral Gables on the mainland were rained out much of the summer, but Key Biscayne, where our tennis academy was located, was not.

I was literally playing six to eight hours a day and did well in a lot of tournaments. I played at the Royal Palm Tennis Club near our home, or at our academy. Frequently, I would just practice all day. It was kind of insane. I was not going to play at Wimbledon, but I practiced 500 forehands down the line, 500 backhands down the line, cross-courts, overheads, and serves.

Every day I would stand at the net and Andy, or another strong player, would serve right at me. My job was to be fast enough at the net to volley those hard hit serves across the net and out of reach. After a couple of years, I figured out this was really kind of dumb. Clearly our family was going to stay in Miami. Our boys were in junior high school with many after-school activities of their own. I needed to do something that would help my chances of getting a decent job. With only a BA from Stanford, I had no real discernable profession.

I was a typical housewife and mom of that era, trying to support my corporate husband and taking care of our children. Chuck and I had started getting more involved in Miami and the broader Florida community. People with whom we socialized were typically older than we were and well steeped in southern traditions. I very much liked how gentlemanly all the men were. It did not occur to me at the time that might be because my young husband was now running one of the largest businesses in the state.

Chuck had become totally immersed in the business community, engaging with all the local leaders in the Miami, Dade, Broward, and Palm Beach counties and, of course, the state leaders, including governors. In the 1970s we became friendly with Reubin Askew, the Democrat governor of Florida from 1971 to 1979, enjoying his company and that of his wife, Donna Lou. He later became the first-ever United States Trade Representative (USTR 1979–81). When Reubin returned to Florida from Washington, he became a partner at Greenberg Traurig, Hoffman, Lipoff, Rosen, & Quentel, where I eventually worked. Reubin and I occupied adjacent offices. Later the firm became known simply as The Greenberg Traurig Law Firm. Now it's one of America's largest and most successful international firms. But I digress.

Another important leader with whom Chuck became friendly was Bob Graham who succeeded Reubin as governor of Florida, later becoming a United States senator. Though as Democrats, these governors' political philosophies were not always exactly aligned with ours, Bob and his wife, Adele, like the Askews, became lifelong close friends. As a Florida senator, Bob Graham was a thoughtful, thorough, and positive leader for our state and a leader in the Senate. Over the years, Chuck and I began getting more and more involved in political matters and in the governance issues of the day. Those interests provided further motivation for me to do something more productive with my time.

Mostly because of exposure to Chuck's business, I decided I would go to business school and get an MBA. I had one choice: The University of Miami (UM). However, the University of Miami Business School was young and didn't motivate me. As I read the university materials, I saw that the other professional liberal arts school available at UM was law. Never once in my entire life had I ever thought about law school. But I was looking for a professional degree that would lead me to an interesting job while the boys were in school. I wondered if I had any propensity for law.

Propitiously, just at that time I read about the new woman dean who had come to lead UM's law school, Soia Mentschikoff and her husband, Karl Llewellyn, then of the Chicago Law School. Together they had, earlier in their careers, reviewed, updated, and published the entire Uniform Commercial Code (UCC) of the United States, which was first published in 1952. Over the years, the UCC was adopted by every state with just a few distinct state deviations enacted by local legislators. This uniform application of commercial law solidified interstate commercial rules throughout the country. Soia, who was Russian, left the University of Chicago Law School in 1974 to be the dean at the University of Miami School of Law. I thought she was an amazing intellect, so I just decided I would sign up for the law school exam (LSAT) and find out if I had any propensity for law.

I didn't study for the LSAT because I was only looking for a hint of potential and was quite afraid that I would do terribly since I had been out of Stanford for fifteen years. That was also why I did not tell my husband or anybody else about taking this exam. I just signed up and showed up. There were five sections on the day-long test. The last section was called Data

Interpretation – all numbers, graphs, and charts. The student was supposed to figure out something from these graphs and numbers. I looked at them and thought, I am a liberal arts major. I really don't have a clue what these things mean. The answer boxes had five choices: A, B, C, D, and E. I didn't read the Data Interpretation questions. I just marked B throughout that whole section, figuring that I'd get at least some right. Then I got up and left. Everybody in the exam room just stared, because they thought I had finished the test early. Several weeks later, despite twenty percent of the test being a total guess, I received a grade that qualified for the University of Miami. It was good enough for UM, but it wasn't good enough for me. I proceeded to study a course in Data Interpretation so that I could retake the LSAT. My score went up by one hundred points, which was quite satisfying. It really didn't matter because I had already been accepted, but I guess the competition was a bit like my skiing and tennis – me against me.

When I told Chuck about the LSAT and being accepted to law school, he showed a little reluctance. He has always been my biggest promoter, so I was a bit concerned. I believed it was because he was still fairly new in his tenure at Arvida and was young for the job and the community positions he held. Also, at that point in time, 1975, it was still fairly unusual for women to be working independently, outside the home in professional capacities requiring advanced degrees. I was a "corporate wife." Corporate wives were expected to show up at corporate functions, host events in their homes, take care of the children, and be proper housewives in support of their husbands' careers. He was concerned and said, "You're never going to have trouble getting a job, so I don't think you should work too hard at law school, maybe shoot for all Bs and Cs." That was very uncharacteristic. I really wasn't offended by it. I understood his motives. But that would not have been me (or him). My boys were now at the stage that they were getting quite independent, my husband was totally occupied with his business activities and so I started law school in the fall of 1975 at age thirty-eight.

To be a good wife and mother, I felt I had to accomplish everything and do it well. I was constantly interrupting my classes and my studies to go to Boca Raton for Arvida events (and I still enjoyed the luxury of the Executive Suite). It's not that I didn't try very hard my first year, I did. But rather than studying with a study group like everybody else, I studied by myself when and where I could. Rather than studying for finals to be taken in January, I went skiing for two weeks with the family and did not even take a book. Consequently, my grades in my first year were not stellar, but during that first year I became truly interested in the law and all its ramifications. Then I studied more rigorously, focusing on two areas – constitutional law and economics. I loved constitutional law. How we, the United States and each state, had framed the rules governing ourselves and the foundations of those rules were fascinating to me. My grades improved. I had a wonderful opportunity to clerk for one summer after my second year for US District Court of Appeals Judge Peter T. Fay where I learned to love the appellate area. My son Chris remembers of that time:

I was in junior high school when Mom went back to law school. She studied hard. As high school came along, I was studying less and less, because I didn't like school. I was trying to go out every night with my friends, and my mom was coming home from school and studying into the night, even after she got a job at Greenberg. So there was no sneaking back into the house because she was there with her books. We had a midnight curfew, and by the time we were seniors we had a 1:00 a.m. curfew, but she studied or worked late into the night. That's a lesson you would have to take away. Even if they don't say it, lessons of action are always stronger than lessons of words.

Christian McCourt Cobb, September 23, 2017

I was forty-one when I graduated in 1978 and, unlike all my classmates, I wasn't looking for a job. I wanted to go skiing. For my graduation present from law school, Chuck agreed to take me skiing in Portillo, Chile, which has great mountains and snow in the middle of our summer. That was a great adventure. We went to Chile with a well-known, highly respected lawyer, Parker Thompson and his twenty-two-year-old son. We wanted to visit Machu Picchu on this trip, flying to Santiago and then to Cuzco, a charming village, sitting at about 4,000 feet in the Andes. From there visitors take a train, at least in the late '70s that is what everyone did. The train left from Cuzco and wound its way up the mountainside. We took a taxi from our hotel to get to the station to catch the one train a day up to Machu Picchu and missed it. But, not by much. The train was pulling out of the station as we arrived. Chuck quickly ran to re-capture our taxi and told the driver he'd give him US$50 if he could find a place where we could catch the train and get on it. Of course, the taxi driver spoke no English and we spoke limited Spanish, but from the driver I could understand that there was a place about an hour from the Cuzco train station where the train has to slow down to go around a big bend at the end of which was a wooden platform where if anybody was standing and waiting on the platform, the train would stop to pick them up.

Chuck, Parker, and his son think, "Great. We'll get ahead of the train, get to that little platform, they'll see us, and stop." So we quickly start driving up the hill and two times the guy's radiator starts spewing steam. Each time he stops, jumps out, goes into the trunk, grabs a bucket he keeps there, and runs to a river, which wound along beside the road. He gets water, puts it into the radiator and then we race along until the radiator starts spewing steam again. But we are, in fact, catching up with the train, because it had so many curves to make. Chuck and I are cheering our driver on, waving a US$50 bill until we get ahead of the train. Well, we reach this long wooden platform, and we can hear the train coming from down below. It is getting closer and closer. It's kind of warm and my three teammates decide to take off their jackets. The train comes around the curve, but it doesn't stop. I'm holding our four coats while they try to flag down the train. Suddenly we realize that while slowing, the train is not stopping. We are going to have to try to catch the train. I am still stuck holding four coats. Chuck starts running down the platform looking at where he might be able to grab a handle on the side of the train to get on. He forgets to watch where he's running and runs off the end of the platform. He quickly scrambles back up, so now he is closer to me, but he is still ahead of me, and grabs onto one of the cars. The other two, father and son, are also running down the platform trying to grab the metal handles on the train's side. I see what's happening, but I'm still holding the coats. People in the train start leaning out motioning and yelling, *"Danos los abrigos."* I start running along the platform handing the coats up to outstretched arms as I run. Finally, with my hands free, I make a leap to a passenger car as hands come out to pull me on. That is when the passengers all started clapping and cheering. It was such a fun ride with all the Machu Picchu passengers cheering. The ruins were everything the guidebooks made them out to be – totally fascinating. From there we made our way to Portillo, a tiny somewhat isolated resort on a ridge in the midst of the Andes.

One evening in Portillo we were talking about the history of Argentina and Chile, which share the nearby border. We learned they'd had wars and after the last war, when they restored a peaceful relationship, they agreed to take all the lead cannonballs from each army and melt them down. From the melted armaments, together they built a very tall statue of Jesus Christ to put on the border a few miles from a well-known path between the two countries (which later became a well-traveled highway). The historian in Portillo who was telling us this story said the statue was about ten miles from Portillo. A local ski instructor said, "I can take you there if you want to see it."

We began to talk about how to do that, because Jesus was not on any road. We would have to hike in from the pass a few miles away. Another local said, "Remember that tomorrow morning, about seven o'clock, the hotel garbage truck crosses the pass and takes the road over to *el depósito*." The local ski instructor responded, "Perfect. We'll get a ride with the garbage." Well, we did. It was an open truck, flatbed with some wooden railings on each side. We sat in the back of this flatbed truck along with the hotel garbage. When our instructor told us to, we grabbed our skis and jumped off. It wasn't ten miles, but it was a good long hike carrying our skis until we saw the absolutely awesome Christ statue – presumably exactly on the border of Chile and Argentina. A vast, deep canyon reminiscent of our Grand Canyon fell off beneath Christ's feet. The lead Christ stood about eighteen feet tall with his arms raised to the sky as huge Andean condors with ten to twelve-foot wingspans rode the prevailing winds of the canyon, coming up and over us, gliding back into the depths. It was just gorgeous, absolutely gorgeous. I will never forget the condors of the Andes (or Christ of the Andes).

Then we put our skis on and pointed them in the direction of Portillo. Of course, it was all off-piste skiing, as the Europeans would say. There were no trails, no markers; nothing except the condors gliding by, querying, spying on us from above. Fortunately, we had our friendly ski instructor with us who led the way. We skied a good ten miles back to the lodge at Portillo and counted it as another wonderful, extraordinary adventure.

Chapter Five

Whatever you can do, or think you can do, begin it,
for boldness has genius, and power and magic in it.

Johann Wolfgang von Goethe

MIAMI IN THE EIGHTIES: GREENBERG TRAURIG, MARIEL, AND THE COCAINE COWBOYS

In the fall of 1978, I came back from my ski excursion to South America. I had graduated from law school in May without having sent out any résumés or job interview requests. One night in September I was at dinner with members of the University of Miami Board of Trustees, one of whom was Mel Greenberg, the founder with Bob Traurig and Larry Hoffman of the small but already prestigious Greenberg Traurig law firm. Across the table, Mel asked me what I was going to do with my law degree. I told him I hadn't decided.

He responded, "Why don't you come and talk to me?"

I said, "Okay," and only half joking said, "What do you do?" Of course, I knew who he was and what he did.

He replied, "Well, I have a law firm downtown called Greenberg Traurig Hoffman. We have almost thirty attorneys and several departments. You can come to see if you would be interested in the kind of work we do."

This was extraordinarily fortuitous. Greenberg Traurig was a ten-year-old highly regarded and growing corporate firm. Ultimately it became one of the largest and most respected law firms in the world. I did not know it that night, but I was about to be employed.

Much later, Mel Greenberg confided that he could tell I had the right stuff to be a lawyer in his firm. What really convinced him was that he was at the Royal Palm Tennis Club one day and he saw me practicing mid-day in 90°F heat, hitting 500 forehands down the line, 500 backhands down the line, paying attention to every detail. He liked that and hired me the first day I visited the firm in October 1978. I was scared to death for the following eight weeks because Florida Bar Exam results had not yet been returned. I was now hired, but I could still fail the bar exam. Thankfully, all was well when I received good news in early January 1979.

The firm was known to be what we used to call a "sweatshop." Everyone worked hard. Where the average attorney work year might be 2,000 to 2,500 hours, ours were routinely 2,800, 2,900, 3,000 hours. Which meant working from dawn until late into the night. I did litigation and some appellate work, but the senior partners repeatedly told me that I should do transactional work, acquisitions and mergers, and negotiation of business arrangements. But I didn't want to get into the same areas in which Chuck was active. I did not want to be in a circumstance where we could have potential conflicts, or I could be viewed as having the job only because he was in those businesses.

Secondly, I had not studied enough finance and tax law to feel that I was qualified to be a business attorney. Before I went to law school, I truly did not understand that taxes are the one area that everyone cares about and that taxes are all about government policy. To me, taxes were numbers that you add up and figure out what the company or individual has to pay. Of course, by the time I became a lawyer, I did understand taxes are about government policy – levers used by elected leaders to implement desired policies.

Sue as a young attorney at Greenberg, Traurig and Hoffman, 1980.

In my first year as a litigator, I worked for one of our more senior litigators, a young partner whom I really liked. He was smart, handsome, and fun. It turned out he was also routinely under the influence of products that were not legal in Florida. We will call him Rob. One day Rob and I were finalizing a divorce settlement for a very important corporate client in Broward County (the firm usually did not do such personal matters). We had the final judgment hearing by the court coming up on a set date at ten o'clock in the morning at the Ft. Lauderdale courthouse. The judge was to hand down his order. Rob had prepared our own favorable final judgment for the judge so that when the judge ruled, assuming a ruling on our side, Rob would hand him the final judgment and it would be signed then and there. Case closed. Client happy.

On the appointed morning, I was to meet Rob at our offices in Miami. I went to the office, allowing an hour to drive to Ft. Lauderdale. Rob didn't show up. I waited and waited. He didn't come. He had all the papers relating to the case, including the prized final judgment. Maybe we had misunderstood each other, and he was going directly to the courthouse. I decided I better go to Ft. Lauderdale. Rob still did not show up. The judge called our case. I was soon sitting alone at my first-ever final judgment hearing without any documents relating to the case. Rob was a no show. Boldly, I moved into lead counsel's seat. In my briefcase, I had a file on another case that I was working on. I pulled it out, put it in front of me on counsel's table, got out a folder totally unrelated to the divorce case and opened it up. I told the judge it was an honor to be there, we felt that we had made our client's case, and we were hoping that his honor saw the matter in the same manner.

He said, "Young lady, I agree with you and I'm prepared to rule for your client. If you will just give me the final judgment, I'll sign it."

I had to say, "Your honor, I've just made a terrible mistake. I'm so embarrassed. I didn't bring the judgment with me. I'm just really, really, so embarrassed. I wanted to make a good impression on you." I was saying whatever I could possibly think of, and added, "I can get it here. I can get it to you within ninety minutes." (Unsaid, that would be at unlawful speeds to my Miami office and back to Ft. Lauderdale.)

That worked. The judge said, "Fine."

I called the Miami office, said, "Get a new final judgment prepared," and quickly raced to Miami. The paralegal ran it down to my car and I raced back to the judge's chambers. He signed. Meanwhile my senior partner Rob, it seems, had interests other than our client's and didn't show up for three days. He was not forgiven and was quickly dismissed from the firm. What a learning experience for me! It was also a learning experience for Rob, but a bad one. Latin American drugs had migrated to Miami and cocaine was readily accessible. Rob had somehow fallen prey to the scourge of Miami's Cocaine Cowboys, and he paid dearly.

My first and only jury trial was in my second year at the firm, for a very important bank client. The amount in controversy was $300 (that's why it was given to me). It involved a conflict between Florida statutes and the Uniform Commercial Code, most of which the State of Florida had adopted. At the time of the trial, I did not realize it was a case of first impression (i.e., the particular issue had never been tried or ruled upon in a court of law). I did realize that juries do not favor banks over nurses. Here's the scenario: a debit created an overdraft in Defendant Nurse's account. Bank Plaintiff sued Nurse to collect. Nurse counterclaimed for wrongful payment of a check over a stop payment order and requested a jury trial. I picked a jury and made a powerful (in my mind), but unavailing argument to the jury. We lost. To add insult to injury, the jury awarded Nurse

$10,000 in punitive damages. Utterly crushed, I was afraid to return to my law firm.

To my surprise, Bank wanted to appeal, and the CEO specifically wanted me to argue the appeal since I was familiar with the case. I argued. The three-judge appellate panel took a year and a half to deliberate the case before handing down a ruling. Case reversed. Bank wins! (Capital Bank *v.* Schuler, 3d D.C.A. No 81-92, Oct. 26, 1982.) It was pathetically satisfying. I felt sorry for Nurse. The arguments in my case were about whether or not Nurse had put on the stop payment order all the proper data that is required by Florida Statute under the UCC to effectively stop payment. Under Florida law, one must provide banks more specific information about to whom the check was payable, the date of the check, the specific amount of the check, and proper signature. The justices of the appellate court found that the specificity of a stop payment order under Florida law exceeded those of other states under UCC common law. Nurse had failed Florida's rigid specificity. It was a precedent setting ruling.

While I was absorbed in litigation, real life was unfolding outside our doors in the City of Miami and in Dade County (Miami-Dade County since 1997). In addition to the arrival of the Cocaine Cowboys (mostly Colombians), Liberty City and Overtown, Miami's largest Black communities, erupted in riots. Haitian immigrants also arrived in large numbers, and a new wave of Cubans overwhelmed the city.

Cuban professionals started coming to Florida in large numbers in 1959 and 1960 when Fidel Castro took over Cuba. There are many stories of someone who was a physician or a dentist or an attorney in Cuba who came to Miami due to the repression of Castro, but arrived with none of the requisite licenses or degrees to practice their professions in the United States. To earn a living they became taxi drivers or small entrepreneurs or carpenters and plumbers. They would sell fruit at street corners, open a little storefront shop, or do anything to feed their families. You would find a veterinarian or business owner in Cuba who had to take a job as a waiter or a roofer or mechanic to survive in Miami.

Cubans remaining on the island were worried about their children, particularly about their sons being conscripted at age fourteen, as was Castro's practice. The Catholic Church put together a big operation called "Pedro Pan" in which young men and boys, largely aged twelve to eighteen, were sent out of Cuba to US shelters to avoid conscription into the Cuban army. Parents typically followed as soon as they could, but many boys spent years without their families. Castro began cutting back on emigration, but the influx of 1959 and during the 1960s into Miami was largely a well-educated, professional group of people. Many thought they were going to be able to return to Cuba in just a few months, or a year or two. That did not happen. Instead they banded together in Florida and grew into a strong political force. In the late 1970s and early 1980s, the Cubans began to elect congressmen and women, as well as senators and other federal officials. Ultimately, those legislators responded to their constituents with very tough legislation relating to the communist island of Cuba. The primary vehicle was the Helms-Burton Act, which includes the embargo. All these years later, much of Helms-Burton remains US law today.

Those who came in the 1959–62 wave, the early years, remained angry beyond words. It is hard to describe, but you would have to put yourself in their shoes, watching soldiers entering your home and at gunpoint saying to you: "You are leaving now and you're never coming back." There was no choice. One of my Cuban friends told me this: "I was out in my yard when the Jeep arrived at my ranch. I asked the man with the machine gun if I could just get my boots to put on. He said, 'No, you're going barefoot!'" My friend lost everything. Everything his parents, grandparents, and he himself had worked for was no longer theirs. The family is to this day, understandably, very emotional about the subject. The children of the first generation of Cubans, in many cases, absorbed that anger and were indoctrinated into that tragic history. Nonetheless they grew up in an American society where not everybody felt the same way. Gradually over the years, the depth of the hurt was attenuated in the younger generations. I learned a great deal about Cuba and the psyche of the Cuban generations from Toby's wife, Luisa Salazar, who is a first generation Cuban-American. As everyone knows, politics is always in play and the future of US-Cuban relations remains unsettled.

In 1980, along with the Cocaine Cowboys, Miami experienced the arrival of another wave of Cubans in what became known as the Mariel boatlift. Telling folks in Florida they could come pick up their relatives without prohibition, Castro then released Cubans from his jails and mental institutions. A huge flotilla of boats navigated the Florida Straits and made their way to Cuba in anticipation of picking up their relatives in the port of Mariel. Along with family reunifications, Castro forced all boaters to pick up his prisoners and mentally unstable to take to Florida. The 1980 refugees were called *Marielitos*. The boatlift created a severe humanitarian crisis when a reported nearly 150,000 Cubans arrived on Florida shores.

During the Mariel boat lift, with boats arriving in Miami from April to October of 1980, I was in my second year as an associate at Greenberg Traurig. While in my office one day that spring another attorney came running to my office door and rather frantically said, "Mr. Greenberg is trying to reach you. He said to tell you that the White House is calling for you." My thoughts: "Geez, what is this?" The voice said, "He wants you to come to his office right way." I did so.

Our CEO coolly said, "The White House is on hold." I learned that it was Victor Palmieri calling. Because migration from Vietnam had been so important, President Carter had created a cabinet level position with the rank of ambassador, called the White House Coordinator for Refugee Affairs. Carter appointed Victor Palmieri to that post. The same Victor Palmieri who had been involved in the unwinding of the Penn Central bankruptcy and, you may remember, had recommended that Chuck be recruited to Miami to run Arvida. Victor, a prominent West Coast lawyer and television personality without a Florida network was calling to ask if we had any knowledge of boats serendipitously coming in or going out between Miami and Cuba. Of course, we did. Ambassador Palmieri was coming to Miami the following week and wanted to set up a meeting with our friend Governor Bob Graham. Since Chuck was tied up, could I help him arrange this meeting and accompany him to Tallahassee to meet with the Democratic governor of Florida to discuss what was unfolding? Of course, I could do that. But, for me as a "young" associate at my law firm, the fact that the White House called the head of our firm looking for me, was just – let's say – a huge PR boost. I was silently saying to myself: "Thank you, Victor!"

I arranged for Ambassador Palmieri to meet with Bob Graham, his team, and me. Collectively we devised a course of action. It would start with immediately putting together a planning committee in South Florida to begin addressing all the incipient problems, particularly how we would house and feed an influx of basically indigent humans. The private sector business leaders would be the think tank – the policy planners for how the citizens of our state could manage the crisis. This also meant pulling together the governments of Dade, Monroe, Broward, and Palm Beach counties, the City of Miami, and the thirty other incorporated cities within what is now Miami-Dade

County. Of course, the biggest impact was on the City of Miami and Miami-Dade County (separate government entities). We were able to build a public-private partnership, including leading Cubans who maintained contact with relatives on the island. Chuck and I were both heavily involved coordinating the city, state, and federal governments impacted by the crisis.

Most of the *Marielitos* were not picked up by relatives. The city and county authorities opted to use the Orange Bowl stadium and tent cities under freeway overpasses for the overflow. City/county elected officials had the heaviest burden of caring for these hundreds of people – some of whom truly were mentally incapacitated and some of whom were just bad guys. According to later data analysis, during the Mariel boatlift (which lasted approximately six months) approximately 130,000 Cubans arrived in the United States – mostly in Monroe and Miami-Dade counties. The exact number of "undesirables" who arrived in the 1,600-vessel boatlift is disputed, but estimates range from as low as 7,500 to as high as 40,000. The majority of refugees were ordinary Cubans who proved to be worthy citizens of our state and of the United States.

The able refugees were distributed around the large local Cuban community. Many also went to the Tampa and Orlando areas into the arms of the now large Cuban population extending across the central part of Florida. Some other states agreed to take *Marielitos*. Eventually we received assistance from the federal government. We finally got everyone who came in the Mariel boatlift to Florida settled in one way or another.

To compound matters during the boat crisis it was also the time of rampant and massive drug trafficking in and through Miami, causing violent clashes with Cocaine Cowboys who were dealing their drugs and fighting for turf in Miami streets. Additionally, it was a time of violent confrontation between the citizens of Liberty City and Overtown and local law enforcement authorities caused by racial tensions and unjust treatment of Black men. Several days of rioting caused eighteen deaths and $100 million in damages. These events in the early '80s is why *Time* magazine posted Miami on its cover and labeled it as "Paradise Lost." Between the Cocaine Cowboys, the Liberty City riots, and the Mariel Boatlift, the 1980s was an emotional and transformational time in Miami.

Chuck and I kept working hard, while enjoying our sons and doing our civic duties. We were over one hundred percent occupied because we were very active in the community and in many charitable roles throughout the 1980s. On the side, I was also responsible for building our small condominium complex in Telluride, Colorado. One of our other projects was helping to coordinate the move to Key Biscayne of what became known as the Lipton International Tennis Championship. Chuck and I were involved because the tournament's previous site in Boca Raton was built and owned by Arvida. I was unintentionally the tournament's very first attorney because I just happened to be on the grounds in the very first tournament when a player was injured. The Key Biscayne International Tennis Tournament became a major attraction in Miami-Dade, remaining on Key Biscayne under different sponsorships for thirty-two years. After the 2018 tournament, new sponsors moved the tournament to Hard Rock Stadium, home of the Miami Dolphins football team.

As Arvida CEO, Chuck created a great team of young real estate and financial professionals and built a company operating in several states. In 1982 he was asked to move to New York City and assume a much larger role at the head office of Penn Central, which as a public company still held the controlling shares of Arvida. Of course, he was eager to do a job that had forty thousand people throughout the world reporting to him. Because of the boy's school and of my job, I did not want to move to New York, although I recognized that this was another big step for my husband and our family. Chuck moved into the Carlisle Hotel in Manhattan where he was well taken care of. Chris was a freshman at Tulane University in New Orleans. Toby, then a junior in high school, and I continued our lives in Miami.

In 1983 Mel Greenberg came to my office and said, "We always thought you should be a transactional lawyer. We know you don't want to do corporate work. This is related but it's different. We want you to start a public finance department."

Public finance is frequently called bond work, but if you tell many non-lawyers you are a bond attorney, they think you are handling bail bonds to get criminals out of jail. However, in this case bonds are highly structured financial arrangements subject to numerous legal constraints. Bonds are simply citizens buying the integrity of a city, county, or state government (or government-backed entity) by loaning the government private funds for which the lender receives a promise to repay in the form of a legal document (a bond). Public projects are often funded by thousands of people in $1,000, $5,000, or $10,000 denominations. Bonds are paid back to lenders over time with negotiated interest rates and are generally considered to be very safe.

In the early 1980s, almost all the public finance legal work in the fast-growing state of Florida was done by New York and Chicago law firms. Florida was growing by one thousand people a day and needed money to build additional infrastructure, roads, bridges, schools, and hospitals. Miami-Dade County began to issue more bonds than it had in the past. Greenberg Traurig was very interested in earning it's own bond fees in this growing dynamic market.

Bond financing requires the analysis of a nationally rated municipal bond attorney to sign off on all legal aspects of the transaction. However, a law firm could not hold itself out to be a nationally rated municipal bond firm unless the firm was in a book known as the Red Book. But no firm could get into the Red Book unless it had closed a bond deal. It was a conundrum. A group of mostly New York lawyers had captured this business and were protecting their franchises with published rules of engagement. My law firm was now asking me to find a way to get into the Red Book. Marvin Rosen, a partner, and I, then still an associate, went to our county elected officials and said, "Look, we have as many smart attorneys here in Florida as the law firms in New York. Local law firms need a chance to be able to work on these public transactions." We persuaded county officials to pass a resolution that in essence said: any bonds issued in Miami-Dade County must include among the managing attorneys, one of four named Florida law firms. Of course, Greenberg Traurig was named. Now the out-of-state firms were forced to accept us as "co-counsel" because they didn't want to lose all of the income from the lucrative bond work.

Suddenly I was a bond attorney heading a legal department in which there were no attorneys knowledgeable in a subject matter for which I was definitely not yet qualified. Marvin's highest and best use was as the rainmaker he was. I started studying and we quickly hired experienced bond attorneys. My firm soon became co-counsel with a qualified out-of-state bond firm on a bond transaction and was immediately admitted to the Red Book. From its 1983 start, the Greenberg Traurig Public Finance Department grew rapidly and was an outstanding financial success for the firm, which is probably why I became a partner in 1984.

In 1985, with the collaboration of my Greenberg Traurig friend, Marlene Silverman, I took the opportunity to be sworn into the United States Supreme Court Bar. I was already a member of the Florida Bar, the Colorado Bar, and the

Washington, DC Bar (i.e., licensed and recognized by those individual state legal authorities), but the Supreme Court Bar has its own practices and procedures. My swearing-in was a special moment because at that time there were four justices on the Court who were alumni of Stanford University: Chief Judge Warren Rehnquist and Associate Justices Sandra Day O'Connor, Anthony Kennedy, and David Souter. In quite a treat they provided a unique solo appearance and swearing-in before the full court. Justice Kennedy was a friend who in 1989 led the swearing-in ceremony for Chuck as ambassador to Iceland. Later, he invited us to be guests in his personal box at the Supreme Court for oral arguments in important cases such as the final arguments in the case that became known as "Obama Care".

I enjoyed the challenges of those years immensely. I met local, state, and national public officials along the way. In that manner I gained useful experience in fairly sophisticated financial transactions. Toby went off to SMU and with both boys in college and Chuck mostly in New York, I routinely worked fourteen to sixteen hours a day. At the time of bond closings, it was not unusual to do "all-niters." Basically I worked ungodly hours those years. I'm really not sure how I, or any of us, had the fortitude. One night (morning) at 3:00 a.m. I was reading bond documents and took a break to check my personal mail. In the mail was a letter that changed my life irrevocably. I did not know it at the time, but Mt. Everest loomed in my future.

When I joined Greenberg Traurig in 1978, there had only been one female partner, Susan Lytell, who moved to New York before I was aboard. Marlene Silverman was a litigator and the second woman partner. I was third. Marlene was my mentor and became a dear friend. As Greenberg expanded to its current nearly two thousand attorneys, many more women became part of the practice. While I was at the firm, there were many opportunities to guide younger men and women lawyers. For the women, I think my impact was more as a role model (recall that having graduated from law school at age forty-one, I was much older than most of our young lawyers). I had life experiences and contacts that the younger women had not had time to develop. I worked hard in my legal practice and tried to comport myself in a manner that might warrant the respect of the younger women. Raquel "Rocky" Rodriguez was one young woman who expressed her appreciation and later played an absolutely instrumental role in Florida's state government. She is a brilliant attorney and was Governor Jeb Bush's general counsel for four years (2004–2008). Rocky became a lifetime friend, and I needed her help desperately in the 2000 national presidential election.

In the media there is unending talk about sexual harassment to meet the public's insatiable appetite about the topic. If I were asked today, I can honestly say things were different in the '80s, at least at Greenberg Traurig. Maybe it was because I was older, maybe it was because I was crystal clear about who I was, but I have no "me-too" stories to tell. I could perhaps report "advances" in and out of the office, but what I read about sexual harassment today was not an experience I encountered. Inequality of women in the workplace? Lesser pay? I see that all the time and always have. Help other women? Yes. Focus on women's inequality exclusively? Not my style. Can I be proud of those women I have been able to help? Absolutely – and I have wonderful examples to share, both here in the US and in Jamaica, of women who have made enormous and unequivocal contributions in civic affairs, in business, and in professions, on whom I may have had a little influence. Who knows?

In response to direct questions from job applicants about what difficulties a woman would encounter at our firm, here is what I wrote in 1986 when I was head of recruiting (and I would say the same now):

First of all, I wouldn't concentrate on difficulties. The "traditional male work force" is not the enemy. Concentrate on what great opportunities are going to open up; on the sheer excitement of being at a time and place in our society's evolution that young women can do anything they want; that while these professions are still somewhat of a new frontier for women, one of the great pluses, it seems to me, is that these areas are filled with intelligent men who have interests in common with yours, who have a high degree of curiosity about the world – which will make them exciting company – and, who will more often than not, be very helpful to you. I personally have never had anything against working with a high ratio of men. The best advice I can give to young women on this subject is to do your own job professionally and to the best of your abilities, keep a balanced perspective and a sense of humor, and let the real or imagined problems and prejudices of your co-workers, men or women, take care of themselves.

During the Greenberg Traurig years I also served on the Federal Reserve Bank (Fed) Board of Directors in Miami, part of the Fed's Atlanta Bank. I was appointed first in 1982 by the Washington Board of Governors to fill a one-year vacancy on the Miami Branch Board. In 1983 I was appointed by the Fed's Atlanta Bank for a three-year term, and in 1986 I was again appointed by the Fed Board of Governors in Washington for a second three-year term on the Miami Board. Thus, I had an unusual seven years of service, three years of which I served as chair of the Miami Bank.

As directors, one of our most important jobs was to contribute to the Beige Book published by the Washington Governing Board eight times a year in conjunction with the eight Federal Open Market Committee Meetings. We directors observed local, state and regional economic data, talked to business leaders, and sought to divine what trends seemed to be affecting the economy in our region at the time. We presented our findings at our monthly board of directors meetings in Miami to be relayed for analysis to our regional headquarters in Atlanta and then sent on to the Fed Open Market Committee in Washington. The end results were published in the Beige Book for national and international consumption.

Atlanta-based freelance writer Don Bedwell tagged me as "The Fed's Eyes in Miami" and reported in the *Southern Banker* in September 1986: "Sue Cobb is the central bank's star performer in South Florida." And noted: "Not just anyone invites Federal Reserve Board Chairman Paul Volcker to drop in for a visit – and receives an acceptance. But then Sue McCourt Cobb is used to unusual challenges. The result of Sue's invitation: Chairman Volcker came to dinner with Sue and a small group of her guests." This flattering article served to both introduce me to a large number of readers in the financial circles of the Southeast United States and to explain to that audience the role of regional and district reserve banks. Paul Volcker then accepted an honorary degree at the University of Miami.

I loved the Fed job and learned a ton over the years. I also had very good relationships with both Fed Chairmen Paul Volcker and Alan Greenspan, as well as other Washington directors. In 1984 and again in 1991 I was nominated for an open seat on the Fed Board of Governors in Washington. Each time I was a finalist but lost out to real, qualified economists. I remain, as the bank says of all its directors, one of the "Fed Family," a group I feel extremely honored to have joined. Paul Volcker became a lifelong friend.

Developing and writing my Fed monthly reports (usually about five or six pages) was difficult to fit in with my bond work, but it was very important to me and I simply made sure I got it done. It just became part of my ongoing juggling act. At the time, I was also on the board of directors of several voluntary organizations, including the United Way, Goodwill Industries, the Zoological Society of Florida (now Zoo Miami Foundation), and other Florida charitable entities. At Mayor Maurice Ferré's request, I was chair of Miami's Super Bowl Committee for five years, from 1983 to 1987. Every year our committee would arrange hotels, transportation, entertainment, and figure out benefits we could offer to lure the National Football League (NFL) to come back to Miami for its extravagant Super Bowl. We made Miami's pitch each year at the annual NFL Owner's Meeting. It was fun to meet all the NFL owners and coaches, but four of the five years we were not successful. Finally, at the 1987 Owner's Meeting, Miami was awarded the 1989 game. But I did not see our work unfold. By 1989 I was on to new challenges and our great friend and civic leader Dean Colson took over the Super Bowl Committee.

Now how did I meet all these commitments in the '80s? It was largely because both Chris and Toby were away at college and Chuck had moved to New York to be vice president of Penn Central. Chuck and I scheduled our lives to be able to be together on weekends, basically meeting wherever he needed to be the following week. I remember long weekends in Caracas, Bogotá, Costa Rica, Europe, or later China. Sometimes a Penn Central plane would drop me off back in Miami, sometimes I would fly commercially. Somehow it worked.

We kept up the same crazy pace when Chuck bought Arvida in an "unfriendly" leveraged buyout, an LBO (the seller did not want to be purchased on the buyer's terms). Then our pace picked up. I was still in full legal swing in the mid-'80s running Greenberg's bond department and attending to the Fed and to civic responsibilities, while Chuck orchestrated a dramatic purchase of Arvida from its Penn Central owners. After the purchase, Chuck returned to Miami and along with key Arvida partners began to figure out how to manage all the debt, personal and institutional, that had been incurred in the

LBO. This is Chuck's story, but in quick succession, he found and structured the required financing, did an unfriendly LBO of Arvida, moved back to Miami from New York, restructured the debt, then found the Walt Disney Company looking for real estate talent in Florida to help with a secret project they were developing in Orlando, Florida. Within a year of the LBO Arvida had a wedding with the Walt Disney Company; Chuck went onto the Walt Disney Company Board of Directors and was charged with running all eighty-eight Walt Disney real estate projects. He commuted between offices in Miami, Orlando, and Burbank. It remained a fast-paced life while Chuck was president of Disney Development and oversaw Disney projects in Orlando and around the world.

Basically, in the mid-'80s, Chuck focused on his work and I focused on my work. It was rewarding and it was fun. But it was also lonely. I missed Chuck and my boys and normal family activities. I remember getting kind of depressed, but I did two things about that. I was a runner, which really helps to stay mentally strong. While I was practicing law, my friends would go out to lunch, but I didn't like spending an hour and a half eating and chatting. It just was not my thing. I would go run during the lunch hour summer or winter and in either case come back to the office a bit on the sweaty side. It was rather unusual, but I was intent on running. It is hot all year in Miami and perspiring was unavoidable. So, to run around in the Brickell area I had to find a place where I could change clothes. Our building was then at 1401 Brickell Avenue. There was a side street with a little house next to our office garage entrance. One day I saw a young man coming out of the house. I'd never seen anybody there before.

I said, "Hi, do you live here?"

He answered, "Yeah, I live here."

We chatted, and I explained, "I work next door. Are your parents or your grandparents here?"

He said, "No, it's just me."

"Well, you must have roommates."

"No."

So I came out with it, "Can I rent a room from you?"

In surprise, he responded, "What?" and then added, "Well, maybe."

"Well, I don't really need a room, I just need a bathroom."

"Oh?" I'm standing there in running clothes sweating. Suddenly, he gets it, "Oh, maybe I'm understanding this now. You need a place to change clothes."

"That's exactly right."

"Well, yes, I can do that," he agreed. "I'm an artist. I have my work studio inside but there's an extra bedroom and bathroom. However, I'm sorry about this, but I have to charge you."

"That's only fair – be happy to pay," I said.

"Well, it's gonna be a dollar a day."

"I can manage that," I told him, hoping he would not sense how elated (and smug) I felt about this high-level negotiation.

I must have looked awful! It was all absurdly funny, but now I would at least be able to clean up and change clothes. This arrangement worked very nicely. I always went to run right around the lunch hour, so people wouldn't know what I was doing. After a run, I did not often shower. I went to my new room and just used the sink and a face towel, washed down my legs, my arms and changed clothes, both coming and going. I would pull myself together best as I could, go back into the office, and close the door like I was in a meeting. Then about an hour later I would be able to put on my hose and walk around outside my office. I got a lot of work done because nobody would bother me if my door was closed. That went along fine for several months, then one of my colleagues, a tax attorney who liked to ride his bike to and from work, came to my office.

He said, "I've heard about what you're doing."

"How did you hear about that?"

"People know things, they always know things. I like to ride my bike in the morning to work and home in the afternoon, so I would never bother you if you would let me share your room."

I said, "Paul, I'm not sure you can afford it. It's gonna cost you fifty cents a day." He laughed.

The two of us used the house for another year, but then the artist told me he was going to move. With the prospect of losing the house, I was on the lookout for what I could possibly do next. I was running down Brickell Avenue one lunchtime shortly thereafter and saw the president of Swire Properties, whom I had met at one of Chuck's real estate functions. Swire had built three apartment buildings on Brickell Avenue. When I saw him, we both stopped to say "Hello."

"Charles, how are you? What are you doing out here in this heat?"

His response, "What in the world are you doing out here on the street?"

"Well, I have to go out and run during the day because it's the only time I have."

He said, "You're kidding me."

"Well, I do," I replied. "That's just what I do, but it's kind of hard because I get so sweaty."

He responded, "We just built these buildings," gesturing toward the adjacent apartment buildings, and continued, "Between these two buildings is a swimming pool and a women's locker room. Why don't you use them? Of course, it will be complimentary."

It was so fortuitous. I eagerly accepted and used those

facilities for two years to relieve the pressures of work and my absent family.

My second depression avoidance action was not as healthy. I drank more Pinot Noir than was necessary on nights I was not working. But mostly I was working. I would only be at home at a reasonable hour if the boys were home. And I did continue taking ski holidays, which did not always turn out as planned. I remember Christmas one December in Aspen, Colorado; I broke my left shoulder, which could have turned into a problem, but after four days I was able to get out on the slopes again. Actually, it was just a hairline crack of the clavicle, and I have a high pain tolerance, which I believe is as much mental as it is physical. That mindset probably came from my mother's Christian Science teachings.

The absence of my family followed a particularly difficult time for me personally because while my father died in 1967, my mom lived another fifteen years, until 1982, living with her dogs and having just one or two friends. She definitely did not have a big social circle. She had broken her hip in 1978 – that was the start of my self-imposed guilt trip. My brother Peter called and said that Mother's hip surgery was going to be in two days. I was in my third year at law school, and we were in mid-year finals. The rule of the professor in my business association commercial class was that there would be no make-up exams for any reason whatsoever. Students must be there for the exam on the day and time of the exam or take the entire course over again the following year. If I went to California, I would have had to stay another year at the University of Miami. It did not make sense to miss the exam, but I felt horrible because my mother was having serious surgery, and I couldn't be there.

After that surgery, Mother had two or three strokes that were fairly minor and for the next year or two I was flying out to see her in California once a quarter. Her last stroke took away her ability to speak and put her in a wheelchair. It was a very painful time. In her last two or three years, I went there a lot more because I knew she was dying. Due to my law practice, I would fly out to Los Angeles about one weekend a month on the Friday night after work, and Sunday night I drove from Chino back to Los Angeles and took the red eye back to Miami. On arrival I drove from the airport to my law office and went directly to work. It was hard. The end came in early 1982. Chuck and I were at some conference in Palm Springs. I drove to Chino to be with her. She couldn't speak. She was inert in bed. I knew that this would be the last time I would ever see her. Her birthday was the day after she died. She would have been eighty-two.

My support group with respect to my parents had always been Peter and his wife Suzanne. Suzie and I have been great friends since the second grade. She is totally different than me, but the thing I liked most, she was very smart and physically capable of doing the things that I liked to do, which as we got older most women our age either weren't interested in or simply weren't able to do. But Suzie and I would get on our bicycles in the San Fernando Valley and ride south to Hermosa Beach, through the Valley, Venice Beach, south by Los Angeles Airport (LAX) to the house our family owned in Hermosa. That ride was approximately fifty miles. Pete would not do it, none of our friends could do it. During those times when my mother was dying, Suzie and Pete took care of everything – driving out to the ranch to see my mom – and I felt terribly guilty. That was one of the low points of my life. I was three thousand miles away and I knew she needed me. I'm not sure what Toby and Chris were experiencing, but here is what Toby said:

One of the toughest things that I ever saw my mom go through is when my mom's mom was dying, and my mom's mom had a terrible series of strokes that left her without speech and in a wheelchair.

That was really, really hard for my mom because my mom so looked up to the strength of her mom, and to see her mom incapacitated and incapable of caring for herself, I think, has left my mother with a very, very strict belief or demand, almost, that she not be in that same spot. To her, almost the worst thing in the world would be the inability of taking care of herself, or to be a burden on others. To her, that weakness would be intolerable.

I mean, if there is any weakness in the woman, it would be in her inability to accept any weakness. She just doesn't want to admit – And I don't mean that she's not humble, because I think she is incredibly humble for someone who has attained the levels of success that she has attained – but even today, if you suggested to her, "I'll carry your bag, Mom," that would be almost insolent.

Tobin Templeton Cobb, November 7, 2017

It was also during the '80s living in Miami that I decided that I must have a ski-in/ski-out residence in Colorado. I convinced Chuck that it would be good asset diversification. I made up a little saying, "The family that skis together, be's together." We had discovered Telluride and I purchased three acres on the San Miguel River that runs through town. My land backed up to the ski mountain and included a short trail that would allow us to ski into and out of our to-be-built mountain cabin. We eventually built two private residences, six townhouses, and a caretaker unit. Our home there has served as a wonderful family retreat for over thirty years.

One side benefit I found from building our ski home that I had not anticipated was the considerable amount of time I got to spend with my son Chris, and later with Chris and his entire family. While Chris was not as crazy about skiing as Toby and I were, Chris really loved Telluride. In 1986, right after he got his degree in architecture from Tulane, Chris moved to Telluride and worked for the construction crew completing our complex. I think that is when he learned that while he liked to build things, he did not like pouring cement and hammering nails in

-30°F weather on winter mornings in the mountains. However, he thoroughly enjoyed the independence of being a twenty-three-year-old bachelor living in Telluride.

We had a number of adventures when I visited him: climbing a nearby 14,000-foot peak and skiing down it; nearly killing ourselves on our self-guided rafting trips down the San Miguel River; jeeping the harrowing, dangerous dirt passes over the San Juan Mountains; mountain biking the precipitous single-track bike trails. Once I visited and needed Chris to give me a ride to Montrose – seventy miles away – to catch a flight to Miami. He had a fair-size motorcycle at the time (I am told it was a Honda CX 500). I said I was fine riding on the back of his bike to Montrose. We decided to stop for lunch and a beer at the True Grit Café in Ridgeway, not far from Ricky and Ralph Lauren's ranch. We sat and chatted until we realized I might miss the flight in Montrose. We took off. I missed my flight by just three or four minutes, and there were no more flights out of that airport that day. I made some calls and found that the only flight available out of Southwest Colorado that day was an hour and a half later out of Grand Junction, sixty miles away. Chris was okay with continuing our journey, as long as I paid for his gas. We made the flight with easily four minutes to spare – 130 miles from Telluride on the back of Chris's bike.

In the fall of 1987 Chris returned to Miami to intern on an apprenticeship program with noted architects Andres Duany and Elizabeth Plater-Zyberk. Chris's passion turned to boating, but he never lost his love for Telluride. Chris, his wife Kolleen and their children, Fred, Nick, Cassidy, and Ben all acquired the taste for Telluride and together we have had many times, summer and winter, enjoying our now over thirty-year-old house. With inexplicable foresight, one of the largest rooms in our ski house is an office. We all have work to do. Kolleen, a very highly respected attorney (and fabulous cook), is general counsel of a large complex group of companies based on the East Coast. With three to four personal stations in our office we all work as hard as we play in Telluride.

Chuck and Sue at their Telluride, Colorado home on the San Miguel River, 1988. By Barry Staver, a noted People *magazine photographer.*

With President Ronald Reagan, 40th US President (1981-89) and Nancy Reagan, Disney World, Orlando, Florida, 1984.

Chapter Six

Life is like riding a bicycle –
it is when you stop pedalling that you fall.
Anonymous

NEW ADVENTURES
ON THE HORIZON

On New Year's Eve 1985, I said to Chuck, "Would you like to go to the Andes for three or four weeks early next year on this really interesting trip we're invited on? I told you about the guys from Wyoming. I don't know them well personally, but they are known as good people and competent mountaineers. I know we can at least go to the base camp of the mountain they plan to climb. It's called Aconcagua, the highest mountain in the Western Hemisphere." His response, "No. I don't want to go. But if you want to, go ahead." That invitation was in the mystery letter that changed my life, the one I opened at 3:00 a.m. when I was all alone, working on bond documents as though my life depended on my success as a lawyer. I'd always hiked in the mountains with my father and brother and this trip appealed to me. I was able to go because President Reagan's Tax Act of 1986, which commenced on January 1st, quashed all bond transactions in the first quarter of the year.

So on January 12, 1986, at 10:00 p.m., I went to the Miami airport and met five strangers, led by Courtney and Bob Skinner, the Skinner Brothers as they were known, for their Skinner Brothers Outdoor Wilderness Camps, from Pinedale,

Wyoming. More of the team were coming from different directions. They intended to climb Aconcagua, at 22,841 feet the highest mountain in the Western Hemisphere. From Miami we flew to Buenos Aires and from there to Mendoza, Argentina. I did not know any of the group, except for Courtney Skinner whom I had met once. I did not know any of the routes they were talking about. I did not know what was involved in the climb. There were four other women, all much younger than I. The only equipment I had was what I had accumulated in Colorado, which was something a little better than tennis shoes, but not much. I did not have the right gear. They sent me a list of things to bring, so I brought a down jacket, a backpack, a sleeping bag, and a pair of hiking boots.

We stayed a couple of nights in Mendoza, which is beautiful wine country, well known now, but not so much in 1986. We got a bus, which took us to a pass on the highway over the Andes from Argentina to Chile. We were dropped off at a rather basic hotel with bunkrooms for our overnight stay. In the morning, we were directed to a trailhead and then hiked for eighteen miles to the 14,400-foot base camp of Aconcagua, Plaza de Mules, carrying our full packs and gaining 5,000 feet of elevation – a substantial first-day hike.

Our hotel was at about 9,000 feet, so it was not a steep climb, just a long gradual one. I had not been exercising as much as I would have liked because of office work, but fortunately I was up for the long hike. I will never forget Plaza de Mules, rocky debris on glacial terrain over which we pitched our tents. I thought it grim. En route we had to cross a river, which on our return required the help of some mules and rigged lines. Going over, we all held hands in a long line to offer stability and in case someone fell. We could wade through, but in some spots, it was above the waist. Hiking back out the challenge was bigger because there had been a month of snowmelt, so the river ran higher and faster.

The thing about mountains is that each mountain is different. You should know what to expect when you tackle big mountains. Aconcagua at almost 23,000 feet is very near the Pacific Ocean in the Andes range. The mountain experiences extremely strong ocean winds and the wind chill can easily drop to -80°F. As the tallest mountain in the world outside of Asia, it is one of the seven summits that climbers talk about, each continent's highest point. Aconcagua has the highest death rate of any mountain in South America. Conditions on the mountain were such that our leaders, the Skinner Brothers decided to stay at Plaza de Mules for a couple of days and teach mountaineering classes before the team attempted an ascent. That was perfect for me, because though I had climbed some Colorado 14,000 footers, I had never had any formal training. We went over proper use of an ice axe, what type of crampons to use in different conditions, when you need to have fixed lines, how to do front pointing correctly, and other techniques. I was strong, I was having fun, and I was game for climbing a steep, snow-covered mountain; but it was a very good thing for me to have a little training before the climb.

Courtney and Bob were similar in age to me, so I sort of hung out with them. There was also a doctor from Miami our age and a couple of other "adults" as we called them. Then there were six or eight guys and gals in their twenties, plus a Bolivian lad who joined us at our base camp. Our guys just struck up a conversation with him because they were trying to get cocoa leaves to chew, quite acceptable in Bolivia. I tried a little tiny leaf, but I did not like the taste. The kid from Bolivia called Courtney, me, and our small group "the old people of the USA." I was a little offended, being only forty-eight. Anyway, I got to know Courtney and Bob well on that trip and liked both a lot.

Much of their advice and admonitions reminded me of my dad. The Skinner Brothers were also straight out of the Old West, the heritage I had grown up with on our ranch.

We finally had a weather window allowing us to start the climb. It was steep, some parts harder than others. We reached our campsite at 18,000 feet. Our next goal was a camp at 22,000 feet. A couple of the twenty-year-olds went up, came back, and said it was quite doable for all of us. I was pleased, because that included me. Just as they got back down that afternoon, a huge storm rolled in off the Pacific. We were a group of about fifteen and now knew we were going to have to bivouac (stay overnight) at this 18,000-foot camp. It was late in the afternoon and very cold. I began to feel a little chilled, but not really too bad. I tried to help the group set up tents, but quickly got colder. I was moving slowly at our 18,000-foot elevation and decided to sit down on a nearby rock for a rest. There I felt comfortable and satisfied. Indeed, I felt happy and very warm, so I took off my down jacket. This was around 6:00 p.m., about 5°F, and getting very dark. The storm was turning into a blizzard, and I was sitting on a rock with my down jacket in the soft snow near my feet.

A teammate saw me and recognized the signs of hypothermia, a deadly killer in cold mountain or water environments. Courtney was concerned and instructed two of the young guys to get me into a tent, get all three of us into sleeping bags, and put me in the center bag between them. Now, if it were a case of near death, we would have been near naked and they would have put their bodies next to mine. In this case, sleeping bags and substantial body warmth from these two men would do the job. They were keeping me warm, rubbing my hands, arms, and back until soon I warmed up. Courtney and Bob did not want me to try to go any higher. In fact, as that trip turned out, the team got no higher than 22,000 feet due to that storm. Time ran out on Aconcagua. Lessons learned.

Definitely a great deal of lessons were learned on that trip about climbing, about people, and about myself. I was forty-eight years old, I climbed to 18,000 feet, and except for getting hypothermia because I did not know what I was doing, it was easy for me. I did not have any kind of acclimatization problem and did not find the climbing too difficult. The Skinner Brothers observed that. So at the end of our trip as we hiked back out the many miles to meet our bus, they told me about the permit they had obtained to climb Mt. Everest in 1988, and invited me to go. I immediately said, "No, I can't do that, because I have a job, and I have a family, and I have a husband and I seriously like all three of those things."

They said, "Well if you won't go, would you be a member of our advisory group?"

I replied, "No, I can't be on your advisory group. I don't know what I'm doing myself, let alone advise you."

And they replied, "We're going to create a board of governors for this Everest expedition and we're going to work with the National Science Foundation (NSF) in Washington to do some scientific work." In fact, Courtney had previously done scientific work with the NSF in Antarctica. "We're going to do some scientific work while on the mountain and we need to raise a sufficient amount of money to take a large number of climbers. Our permit is for the fall climbing season of 1988 using a route on the Tibet side of Everest."

They explained that the Tibetan routes had been closed for almost forty years by the Chinese government and added, "We would be only the second American team to be allowed to go to Everest through Tibet since its re-opening in the mid-'80s." It was odd in a way that on the first US team allowed to go to Everest through Tibet were two friends of mine – Dick Bass (who built the Snowbird Ski Resort and on a later expedition summited Everest) and Frank Wells (a senior executive of the

Walt Disney companies who later died in a helicopter accident heli-skiing in Nevada). Dick Bass and Frank Wells later wrote the foreword to my book, *The Edge of Everest*.

The Skinners told me that the climb would be in honor of the State of Wyoming's Centennial anniversary and on their board of governors would be Wyoming Senators Malcolm Wallop and Alan Simpson, both of whom I knew well, and the congressman for their region in Wyoming, Richard Cheney, who later became vice president of the United States under President George W. Bush. The climbing team would become known as "Cowboys on Everest."

That same year, 1986, Chuck and I had planned to take our sons on a trip around the world. Chris had just graduated from Tulane School of Architecture and Toby would soon graduate from Southern Methodist University (SMU) in Dallas, Texas. One night at a family dinner, Chuck just casually said, "Everybody pick one city or country you would like to see."

Chris chose Bali. Chuck had two choices, Bangkok and Moscow. I chose Kathmandu. Toby chose Paris. When we got to Bali, I figured out why Chris wanted to go there. It was not for the Indonesian culture or to learn about the Hindu religion. He was twenty-three years old, not married, and had heard from a buddy that many young Australian women vacationed in Bali and did not bother to wear their bathing suit tops! He wanted to go to the beach where the Australians frolicked. We stayed in a beautiful Oberoi hotel and had a very educational and interesting stay in Bali. We even had the chance to go scuba diving in the Bali Sea. Despite the many diversions, we all learned a little about the Hindu religion and the Indonesian environment before flying on to Thailand.

In Bangkok we stayed at what was then the number one-ranked hotel in the world, the Bangkok Oriental, which truly was fabulous in every way. Years later, I made it a point to return to the Oriental en route to Nepal for another Himalayan climb.

On this trip we had two "learning experiences." We had agreed on no checked luggage, and we had not washed our clothes since leaving the States. I frequently wore a comfortable, washable skirt, top, and flat shoes rather than heels for our fast-paced excursions. I could easily wash and dry them in a shower, but at this stop everybody wanted to get something laundered. Toby and Chris were in a suite adjacent to ours. We filled out the laundry slips at the Oriental, put all our stuff in the hotel bags and left them to be picked up and laundered when we went to dinner.

We wanted to see another nice location, not just the beautiful Oriental, so we decided to go to dinner at the Shangri-La, another high-end hotel on the Chao Praya River about four or five blocks from the Oriental. Our hotel staff cautioned us that between the two hotels was a district that tourists should not enter. They knew it was tempting to walk along the river but maintained that we would be targets if we did that. The message was clear. We got a taxicab from the Oriental to the restaurant at the Shangri-La, went to dinner, and when we left the restaurant Chris declared, "I want to see this area that they said is unwise to walk in. I'm sure I'll be fine. I'll meet you at the hotel." He walked away.

Now, there were three of us. We were waiting for a taxi in front of the Shangri-La when an open air tuk-tuk pulled up. This is basically a platform seat on the back of a three-wheeled motorcycle – common in the Orient. Toby, Chuck, and I hopped into the tuk-tuk and off we went back onto the main street. We knew exactly where the Oriental Hotel was. At a couple of stoplights, the driver stopped. At the fourth stoplight, he did not stop. He just kept going straight and faster. We knew that if he had turned left, we would have run right into the Bangkok Oriental. Chuck was trying to talk to the driver. I am sure he knew what we were trying to tell him, but he pretended not to understand. There is no way he could have missed the message. We were pounding on him and pointing, "This way, this way!" At that point, we knew we were being taken for what was going to be an unpleasant ride.

It is a typical tourist danger: a driver will direct or escort tourists to a location a little bit off the beaten path and his buddies are waiting at a predetermined spot with knives or guns or some kind of weapon. We understood that was what was happening. We went several blocks on the one main street before the driver turned to the right onto a little smaller street. Chuck and I were whispering back and forth; Chuck said, "You take my wallet."

Why should I take his wallet? Because he would be the logical target. I took his wallet. He said, "Take my watch, too." He was wearing a gold Rolex. I took his watch and put it high on my arm under my sleeve. We were communicating with each other quietly, Toby on one side, Chuck on the other, I in the middle. We were looking for the first opportunity to jump and run. The driver was forced to slow down to turn into a small alley. As he slowed to make the turn, we instinctively knew this was our chance. We were instantaneously out of there, running as fast as we could back to the main street. Imagine if I had worn high heels to our elegant dinner!

Once we were on that main street, we hailed a taxicab and headed towards our hotel talking to each other about how upset Chris was going to be that we had not gotten home yet. He presumably had reached the Oriental and was worrying about us, calling the concierge, and asking what he should do. We went to our double suite and there he was – in bed sound asleep. Worried about the family? Guess not!

The next day we went sightseeing, came back late in the afternoon, walked into our rooms, which had all been made up nicely of course, and on our bed were twenty to twenty-five small white packages wrapped in different colored ribbons with an orchid entwined in each bow. I was delightfully surprised and exclaimed, "Chuck, look. They brought us some gifts." We opened the first gift box, unfolded the tissue and found a T-shirt that Chris had packed despite having a ripped left sleeve and a big stain right on the chest. The next box held a pair of Toby's socks, which probably started out white and long ago turned tan. We kept opening these beautiful packages. All turned out to be our laundry – our underwear, cotton shirts, jeans, and soiled travel clothes. It was funnier each time we opened a box. We all just started laughing uncontrollably about it.

When we saw the invoice, US$350, we stopped laughing. Chuck turned to the boys and said, "Throw all used T-shirts away. In the future we'll buy the $2 ones we've seen down on the streets," and that's what we did.

Next stop was Kathmandu. We were going there because I wanted to see the Himalayas, and also because one of Chris's high school friends had joined the US Peace Corps and was stationed there. We found Chris's friend, Omar Shafey, who was a great tour guide. We chartered a plane to go up as close as possible to the Himalayas, including Mt. Everest. I am telling you, I was very excited. Chris and Toby later told me that when our plane approached the highest mountain in the world, I got out of my seat and was jumping up and down and pointing, "Did you see that mountain? Did you see that mountain?" To me the sight was just breathtaking.

From there – normal people do not do these things – we took river rafts down the Bagmati River to India, spending one night in makeshift tents on a beach in Nepal. Our goal was Tiger Tops, an elephant-tiger camp on the border of Nepal and India near Chitwan National Park. Once at Tiger Tops we met our personal elephants and riding atop them set out searching for tigers in the long, tall grass – literally taller than our elephants' backs. Chris and I were on the same flat platform, strapped on the back of an elephant with a small four-inch rail to hold onto. The trainer, or *mahout,* sat astride the elephant's neck. All *mahouts* carefully train their own elephants. We enjoyed the ride and were intently scouting for tigers. In this tall grass we rounded a corner near a river and at first did not see the very large rhinoceros emerging from the water, trailed by two baby rhinos. We were face-to-face about four or five feet apart on a little fifteen-inch wide path. At this incredibly close range both our elephant and the mother rhino were startled and reacted quickly. Trumpeting, the elephant reared. Both its front feet went into the air. The rhino stopped in a defensive posture and wailed a sound I had never before heard.

Chris and I held on as best we could (as though there was any other choice). The animals glared at each other. The *mahout* spoke quietly to his elephant. Chris and I were frozen – we were lucky one of us had not fallen off during the initial surprise encounter. If these large animals went after each other, if they started fighting, what in the world were we going to do? Fortunately, after a minute or two each backed slowly off. What a scary, scary moment, because we had zero control over anything. We did not find a tiger that day, but we survived to search another day.

Next stop Moscow. Chuck was not yet in government service, but the Soviets watched us like hawks. We were followed everywhere we went, including inside our hotel. Our every move was monitored. They searched our room and personal property while we were out. We were assigned a guide and got a very rudimentary and superficial tour of the city, followed by a basic meal of mostly potatoes and what we assumed was some kind of meat.

We moved on to St. Petersburg to explore the Hermitage Museum. Now that was fabulous! Being in those two Russian cities motivated me to read, *Peter the Great* and later *Anna Karenina*. I am very glad I did. Those books gave me a much broader perspective than I previously had on Russian history and culture. Robert K. Massie's version of Peter the Great, in many ways, illuminates the Russia we know today.

One of my goals in Europe was to get to Stuttgart, Germany for a very specific reason: I knew what kind of car my son, Chris the new graduate, wanted to buy when he started his work life in Miami. He wanted a white Audi, then made by Porsche. So prior to our departure from Miami for this round-the-world trip, I arranged to buy a white Audi and to stop by and pick it up at the factory in Stuttgart at the end of our journey.

Chuck told the boys we were going to Stuttgart because their mother insisted on driving the Porsche track at the factory. That actually would have made sense to them. The ruse was that it was just for older drivers who might want to buy a Porsche. The boys could not drive the track, so I would go over first thing in the morning from our hotel to test a Porsche. My real goal was to make sure that the Audi was ready. It was beautifully set up on a revolving stand in a grand showroom. I scurried back to our hotel and said, "Actually I think you guys would really enjoy seeing the Porsche factory and track." Chuck wisely said, "Sure, let's do that." The factory staff was all in on this, of course. I had the keys to the Audi in my pocket when the four of us returned to the factory. We first walked through a long hallway, then stepped into the designated very large showroom with the revolving white Audi. The salesman said, "We are just going to cross this Audi showroom and go through the hallway on the other side." As we walked across, Chris stared at the white Audi on the revolving stand. He was looking at every part of that car.

The rest of us were near the appointed exit when I called out, "Come on, Chris." His response was, "I really like this car." Chuck and I stalled a couple of minutes, then walked back and said, "Okay, you can have it." I pulled the keys out and held them towards Chris. His jaw dropped nearly to the floor. That is how Chris and I got to Paris. Chris drove the car right out of the showroom and off we went to Paris in his new car. He was beyond thrilled. I guess I was too and told him his dad and I felt he had earned it, going from average grades to straight As and president of the student body of Tulane's School of Architecture.

Chuck and Toby met us in Paris and three of us left Europe for home. Chris stayed and drove around France and Spain in his Audi. It was a special surprise and certainly a memorable trip for all of us.

Later that year, in the fall of 1986, President Ronald Reagan, whom we knew from California when he was governor, asked Chuck if he would come to Washington and serve the two remaining years of the Reagan administration as assistant secretary or undersecretary of the US Department of Commerce where, among other things, he would be in charge of United States Travel and Tourism.

At that point I began thinking, this is crazy. My husband is going away again. This time to be in our nation's capital meeting interesting people and doing interesting things and I am going to be sitting here in my law office at three in the morning reading the fine print of bond documents. This was not making sense to me. I had been working really hard since I started law school in 1975 and now my boys were away; I decided to take a timeout and ask for a leave of absence from the law firm to go to Washington with my husband. The law firm was amenable to my plan. Chuck would be at the Commerce Department from '87 through '89 and I would enjoy meeting new people, leisurely visiting all of Washington's museums, and being close to US government policymaking. Definitely, I wanted to go to Washington with Chuck and support him in his newest career. In March of 1987, I walked out the doors of

Greenberg Traurig. The firm kept my office exactly as I left it for twelve years expecting my return to the practice of law. I would stop by from time to time, but life had changed irrevocably.

Chuck was scouting DC to find a place where we might live. I loved Georgetown and it's tall, narrow colorful townhouses. I told Chuck that I wanted to live in one of those houses, and then I would be perfectly happy. But he did not find one he liked. He found a quite luxurious penthouse apartment right on the Potomac in the heart of Georgetown in a building called Washington Harbour near the infamous Watergate complex. He liked it and wanted me to see it. As a very private person, I could not see myself living in even a very small condominium building. I agreed it was quite nice, but I really just thought I would not like living in a condo.

Obviously, I did not know Washington very well at the time and I did not appreciate the advantages of being in that building in that location. For Chuck, it was about three minutes to the Commerce Department. The towpath that runs along the Chesapeake & Ohio Canal provided a perfect bike and running path for me, and all the Georgetown shops were within a couple of blocks of Washington Harbour. But I was stubborn and asked Chuck to keep searching. He then found a lovely house in Kalorama, one of the upscale residential areas of Washington that has fine homes on a third to three-acre properties. Chuck thought I would like it – not too big, not too fancy, not ostentatious, but clearly very elegant.

I flew to Washington to see the Kalorama house and the Washington Harbour penthouse. Unbeknownst to me, Chuck had the sales contracts in his briefcase for both Kalorama and Washington Harbour. The Kalorama house contained a collection of antique furniture, largely British – Victorian, and Edwardian. I loved the antiques, and that attracted me to the house. The sellers intended to put the antiques at auction, so I suggested to the wife, "Let's just look at each one you plan to auction. You tell me what you think each is worth. Show me what your appraisal is and if it's agreeable, I'll buy them directly from you." I picked out many that I was very keen on. It took this woman and me over an hour to go piece by piece through the house and agree on the price of each antique. Meanwhile, her husband was entertaining Chuck. Finally, all four of us met in the kitchen as we closed in on a final agreement. Suddenly, the man said to my husband, "Oh, Chuck" – now they're friends – "Chuck, I forgot to show you one of the best things. You've got to see this."

They go from the kitchen out a side door into the garage, which was beautiful, like the ones you see in sales brochures, clean as a whistle, with shelves and places to hang all necessities. The man is saying, "Here, I'm going to be leaving all these tools as well, and this I particularly like. It's a handsaw but it's sharp and really does a nice job. But the best thing of all is this brand new snowblower."

He points happily to the machine and Chuck says, "Snowblower?"

The man replies, "Yes, we do get snow in Washington."

Chuck responds, "Oh yeah, I know that."

The man says, "The driveway to the garage, you're going to have to have somebody take care of that for you, unless like me you love to shovel yourself."

Chuck came back in, motioned to me, and said, "Excuse me I want to talk this over with my wife for a moment."

We step outside and he whispers, "He has a snowblower. I'm supposed to blow snow off the driveway. I can't do this. I just can't do this."

"Oh," say I. He opens his briefcase, pulls out the Washington Harbour contract and signs it on the spot, on the hood of the car. We walk back in and tell the soon to be clearly stunned couple that we have decided on a condominium. They could not believe it. We were embarrassed but escaped straight to our new condo at Washington Harbour. And that is how we bought Senator John Warner and Elizabeth Taylor's Penthouse in Washington, DC. And though I didn't want to live in a condominium…well I had been totally wrong…I loved it!

A highly respected DC designer had started an interior plan for the Warner apartment. I think she stopped the planning because the owners decided to divorce. I thought to myself, "If this designer is good enough for Elizabeth Taylor, she's going to be my designer." Her name was Carol Lascaris and she and her husband, Climas, became our good friends. Both are talented people and did our new home beautifully. Climas was of Greek heritage, and they were simultaneously doing several homes for diplomats, as well as several homes in the Middle East.

During the time when Chuck was assistant secretary and we were living at Washington Harbour, we had reason to go to Ankara, the capital of Turkey. The US ambassador invited us to stay at his residence. We made our way to Ankara and had just arrived at the ambassador's residence. We were exchanging greetings with our hosts when I heard a phone ring in an adjacent room. In short order, the butler stepped into the room where we were chatting with the ambassador and his wife and whispered to our hostess, who turned to me and said, "It's for you, Sue."

I had just landed in the country, just arrived in Ankara, just arrived at the ambassador's residence – nobody could know where I was. This was totally puzzling. Of course, I took the call. It was Climas Lascaris who said, "I heard you were in Ankara. Carol told me you would need some nice oriental carpets for your Washington apartment. She thought it might be a good idea if you and I just bought a few things while you are here." I was excited about that prospect and responded, "That sounds like a good idea to me, but I don't know the town. Chuck has a meeting in fifteen minutes, where should I go?"

Climas responded, "This is not going to be a problem. I'll just meet you and we'll go together." He was in Ankara! "We'll meet and I'll show you the right places to look."

I said, "Listen I just got here. I don't have a car. I don't want to impose on my hosts for a solution."

"Oh, Sue you don't understand. This is no problem. I know you are at the ambassador's residence. I am across the street at the president's house. I'll be right over."

Together we drove into town to a tall office building and took an elevator to the seventh floor. Suddenly we were amidst hundreds of carpets. What an experience! Before we entered, Climas said, "Do not say a word, just look. After they've gone through all their sales pitches, I will tell you what you want to buy, and you will say "yes." I bought seven beautiful carpets of various sizes that day in Ankara with Climas.

Shortly thereafter, Carol and Climas finished the apartment for us, we moved in and we loved it. We kept it for about ten years and then, not knowing how much time we would spend in Washington in the future, we sold that beautiful spot. My highest priority at that time was to make sure the carpets came safely to Florida with me.

Washington was a wonderful experience in many ways. As an assistant secretary and then undersecretary, Chuck was one of the top officials at the Commerce Department. His first secretary was Malcolm Baldrige Jr. Within a couple of weeks of Chuck arriving at Commerce, Secretary Baldrige was thrown from his horse and tragically killed. His successor as secretary was Bill Verity, the former chairman of Armco Steel. Chuck and Secretary Verity worked well together. Those were productive years for the Commerce Department.

We visited the White House several times and also visited Vice President George H. W. Bush at the Naval Observatory where he and Barbara were living. There seemed to be an immediate compatibility between George H. W. Bush and Chuck. They had an excellent relationship, which was initially purely a working relationship, particularly on matters of trade. I instantly liked Barbara; who wouldn't? She was an extraordinary person and a particularly important role model for me. We just had some commonalities among the four of us that lent themselves to a warm relationship.

Over the years, in several contexts, we developed a strong friendship, amplified by the Bushes' sons, Jeb and George. Sadly, in April 2018, we mourned with the nation on Barbara's passing. Chuck and I journeyed to Houston on April 20, 2018 and the following day gathered with the capacity crowd at St. Martin's Episcopal Church for the beloved former first lady's life celebration. The service was beautifully performed to reflect her life's dedication to faith, family, and friends. Barbara left us in the manner of her choosing – peacefully and with great dignity. Jeb represented the family with a beautiful eulogy. Chuck and I continue to be loyal trustees of the President George H. W. Bush Library Foundation as well as supporters of the Barbara Bush Literacy Foundation. Soon after Barbara's death we were faced with the loss of President George Herbert Walker Bush. Chuck and I joined many friends at the magnificent services in President Bush's honor at the National Cathedral in Washington. President George W. Bush presented a moving eulogy. For those of us who served in the administration of Bush, the elder, it was a time of deep reflection and recognition that this loss was the end of an extraordinary era.

Meanwhile, back to living in Washington in 1987. Chuck was absolutely thriving. I was enjoying the experience, but after I had visited every museum in the city and run on the towpath to the state of Maryland and around the DC mall too many times to count, I was getting bored. There were calls from the Everest Board of Governors and I tried to think of ways to help the team raise money, but that process was not very fulfilling. Then Courtney called with a suggestion: "Why don't you think about coming on one of our US training climbs? We'll be doing Mt. McKinley (Denali), then Mt. Rainier near Seattle, and a winter climb in January 1988 of Gannett Peak and a later climb of Orizaba, in Mexico." Gannett Peak at just under 14,000 feet is on the continental divide in Wyoming's Wind River Range, while Rainier is 14,410 feet in the Cascade Range near Seattle, Washington. The average temperature in January in the Gannett area is roughly -17°F. I said, "Hmmm," while jotting down the dates. I knew I couldn't go on the McKinley climb, but Rainier was just a commercial flight away and a time commitment of less than two weeks. It was a possibility. Well, okay, within twenty-four hours I said, "Yes" to Rainier. Unbeknownst to me, my decade-long high-altitude mountaineering career was underway. Summiting Rainier was not difficult. I signed up for "Winter Gannett." That was a different story.

Federal Reserve Director and Greenberg, Traurig, Hoffman Partner Sue Cobb on balcony of her Miami office, Southern Banker *magazine, 1986.*

BUSINESS SOUTH FLORIDA

Sue Cobb

THE FED'S EYES & EARS IN MIAMI

BY DON BEDLOW
PHOTO BY DENNY CODY

The highest mountain in this hemisphere is throwing a tantrum. Aconcagua has surprised a party of climbers with a blizzard that is quickly burying the tents they hurriedly pitched to provide shelter from 100-mile-an-hour gusts and 40-below temperatures. Huddled in a sleeping bag, a chilled Sue McCourt Cobb is thawing out after a case of hypothermia. Still shaking, she is exhausted from two weeks of trying to claw her way up the icy mountain.

Less than a year after that February, 1985 blizzard aborted her effort to climb the peak in the

Sue repelling off 13,776-foot Grand Teton above Wyoming's Gros Ventre Valley after successful summit via the Exum Ridge route, 1995.

Federal Reserve Miami Director, Sue Cobb, Washington Federal Reserve Chair, Paul Volcker and Charles Cobb, University of Miami, Board of Trustees, 1984.

Grand opening of Telluride's free gondola between Town of Telluride (8,750 ft) and Mountain Village (9,545 ft) with retired General Norman Schwarzkopf and Joyce Allred, 1996.

With NBA superstar Michael Jordan on a visit to Telluride, 1997.

Preparing to climb the 2,000-foot face of the North Col, Northeast Ridge Route, (aka the North Col Route) Mt. Everest, September 1988.

Crossing the North Col's bergschrund (frequently called a crevasse but typically much deeper and more dangerous) using our 'homemade' ladder of flexible climbing rope and three-foot ice picks, October 1988.

A teammate at our 25,500 ft camp on the North Ridge. After almost three months and 13,000 miles, the peak was within reach.

Sir Edmund Hillary visited Telluride when I was a director of the Telluride Mountain Film Festival, 1991.

Ambassador Charles Cobb and Mrs. Cobb, official residence, US Embassy, Reykjavik, Iceland, 1990.

Renowned Icelandic painter, Erikur Smith, in Coral Gables, painting Iceland's Order of the Falcon onto Sue's gown in "The Portrait of Ambassadors," 1994.

With president of Iceland, Vigdís Finnbogadóttir, (1980-1996) to date the first and longest serving elected female head of state in the world, 1991.

Reception at Tahiti Beach, after the wedding of son Chris Cobb and Kolleen Pasternack, Coral Gables, Florida, February 1994. On left is an identical replica of "Partnership," the sculpture created by Pëtur Bjarnason and dedicated to Iceland by the Cobbs as our farewell gift to the nation.

Toby Cobb and Luisa Salazar at the alter to be wed, Church of the Little Flower, Coral Gables, Florida, September 4, 1992.

Elizabeth Pasternack and Dr. Fred Pasternack, patriarchs of our new extended family, with Chris and their daughter, Kolleen, 1994.

Luisa with her parents, Margarita (Tota) Salazar de Armas and Eduardo Salazar Carrillo, formerly of Havana, Cuba, now of Coral Gables, Florida, 1992.

*CEO and Secretary ad interim of the Florida Lottery,
Sue Cobb, 1999.*

Chapter Seven

Everyone has an Everest inside. It may not be a mountain peak, or a raging river, or a deep ocean, but we all have our challenges. It is reaching beyond our grasp, striving to go further than we ever thought we could that makes life worthwhile.
Courtney J. Skinner

CLIMBING MOUNTAINS: EIGHT WEEKS ON MT. EVEREST

Chuck was totally engaged with all the matters he had undertaken at the Commerce Department. Going occasionally to the White House and to important events was fun, but during the day my life was so unlike the fast-paced, multi-faceted life that I had been leading, I was completely bored. So, I called the guys in Wyoming and said, "You're still going to Everest, right? And they said, "Yes." "Okay, am I still welcome to come?" "You bet you are!" Those were Courtney's exact words.

So, it was time for a discussion with my husband. The evening's dinner conversation was a little difficult. I think I started with, "You're enjoying your job and you're very busy, do you mind if I leave for three months?" Chuck responded, "What are you planning now?"

I explained about Everest, how the group in Wyoming led by the Skinner Brothers had the second permit ever given by the Chinese government to allow Americans to go through China and Tibet to climb the north side of the mountain. At the time it was not possible to buy any kind of passage to climb Everest other than from the governments of Nepal or China who granted few permits. Later it became possible to purchase a place from a guide, and that was a popular way to access the mountain. In the '80s it still took several years to get a permit, and for many years this mountain could only be reached through Nepal. After seizing Tibet in 1951, the Chinese government had closed all climbing by foreigners from its north side.

Of course, no husband or wife could possibly want their spouse to simply leave for three months, let alone undertake climbing Mt. Everest. But Chuck is a "doer" and a competitor who recognized what kind of unusual opportunity this was. No woman from the United States had ever reached the summit of Everest. While he did not like it, he did not say, "I really don't want you to do that." In fact, he said, "I will support you all the way. I wish you weren't going to do this, but I understand it." Despite his reluctance and his urging friends to try to discourage me, I made up my mind to go. I had finally figured out one thing about why I kept doing things that were always challenging – and this is applicable to Chuck, too – we just like challenges. We like difficult challenges. We were not looking for rewards, we would always walk away from anything that looked like an award ceremony. It was never about getting something at the end of a venture; it was the challenge of a difficult problem, figuring out how to manage it, how to deal with complex situations, how to reach for the highest goals and to help others be successful. That was the intriguing part to us, and that was true of almost everything we each undertook. Certainly Everest.

The Wyoming Centennial Everest Expedition was scheduled for late summer and fall of 1988. The governor of Wyoming declared me an honorary citizen of Wyoming. Once I had become involved with the board of governors, I was hooked. Courtney told me about the process of selecting their team – seeking out strong climbers who had what he called an "expeditionary personality." That is, those who were strong mentally, tough physically, and potentially capable as high-altitude climbers.

In my case they also saw some ability to help with the team's fund-raising. In their minds I was a logical choice, though not necessarily in anybody else's mind, including mine. But that was okay with me. And, of course, the Skinner Brothers knew something about me from Aconcagua. An article in a California newspaper quoted Courtney as saying, "I was impressed with Sue's gung-ho approach to life. It was Cobb who kept their spirits high when climbers were pinned down for three days at 18,200 feet with temperatures approaching 50 below zero." To have a "gung-ho" life, you have to stay alive, and Courtney later told me that while I was "gung-ho," it was my calm, reasoned approach that would be my best asset in the challenges to come.

The January 1987 training climb of Gannett Peak took place near the Skinner Brothers' guest ranch in Pinedale, Wyoming. Just under 14,000 feet, Gannett is known to be one of the coldest places in the United States in the winter. The approach to the base camp requires three days trekking in on skis, pulling a sled with your own gear and a portion of the team gear. Climbing uphill on skis pulling the weight of the sled was hard physical labor and it was, as predicted, extremely cold. By the end of the excursion, I had frostbite on my toes (but not badly). The climb accomplished the purpose of thinning out aspiring Everest climbers who could not handle tough circumstances. We had one aspirant who got pulmonary edema, caused by fluid leaking into his lungs as a result of the air pressure influencing fluids in his body. Increased fluid in the brain leads to swelling which results in cerebral edema. Both are fatal unless the stricken climber can get to a lower altitude. We stopped the climb around 12,000 feet and put up a tent to let him rest and keep him warm, but he kept getting worse. His cough was getting to where he could not breathe. It was imperative that we take him to a lower elevation. We attached two plastic sleds together, put him on the makeshift litter, bundled him up, and added ropes to the litter to try to control this sled bed while skiing him out.

But he was not going to make it out of there alive at the rate of our controlled descent. He was too sick and the going was too slow. Courtney opted for an emergency evacuation and called in a rescue helicopter.

Team members traded off attending the ropes on each end to restrain the sled on our downhill run until finally we found a flat area, an ice-covered lake, where a helicopter might land. But there was one hundred percent cloud cover that day and the chopper could not land. Courtney was on the radio with the pilot as he circled above the clouds. There came a moment when the pilot said he thought he could get through a break in the cloud cover for just a few minutes. He wasn't going to land, but he was going to hover right above the ice, and we were to rush this young man onto the helicopter. As we executed that maneuver, another aspiring Everest climber came racing up behind us, dove into the helicopter and said, "I'm going home." We got our sick team member in and this other guy had just leaped aboard and moved out of reach. He obviously couldn't handle the intense cold as well as the work of carrying heavy loads and pulling sleds. This is one of the reasons teams have training climbs – to see who can handle the really hard stuff. He had not said a word to any of us, just ran and threw himself into the chopper. He definitely did not have an expeditionary personality! The pilot ascended quickly to get above the clouds and suddenly the helicopter with two climbers was gone. Our near-death climber recovered, later rejoined the team, and made it to the Everest base camp that fall.

Our team was now well known as "Cowboys on Everest." We did two training climbs in 1987 on Mt. Rainier. The first Rainier climb, we summited with no difficulties whatsoever. It was not hard for me at all. The second climb we did not intend to summit. We camped in an area that had many crevasses and trained on crevasse rescue (which came in handy for me later on

Everest). We also were coached on various self-arrest techniques for stopping (hopefully) or at least impeding a fall on snow or ice. Instruction on the skilled use of equipment mixed with character assessment by the leaders were the Rainier goals.

Over the years I had learned knots, but not much about the use of ropes, which are critical for high altitude climbs and crevasse protection. Each day our mountaineering knowledge increased with the help of several teammates who were already highly skilled. As part of our "training" we lived together for a week or two on each trip and got to know each other a little better. Normal life in Washington, DC, as part of any administration includes extensive social life, embassy events, and diplomacy related activities so I could only do dry land training while home in DC. Somehow *People* magazine heard about my joining the Cowboys on Everest climb and called for an interview. Frankly, I think they questioned my sanity, but they apparently also thought this would be an interesting story. They came to Colorado and to Washington for interviews and photos, later publishing an article noting:

> *Saying that Sue Cobb is a late bloomer is a little like saying Mike Tyson can punch....To date, more Americans have sojourned in space than have strolled to the top of the planet's 29,028-foot tallest peak....A serious climber for fifteen years with limited expedition experience, she runs three to six miles a day, lifts weights and jets off periodically for altitude training on peaks from Canada to Argentina....Once on Everest, according to trip organizer Bob Skinner, the Wyoming climber who selected her, "Cobb's age and attitude certainly will be an advantage. She's tough and ambitious and stays with a climb," Skinner says. "She is more likely to reach the summit than any of the younger women. We feel there is an excellent chance to put an American woman there. Sue is the ideal candidate."*

> People, July 25, 1988, by Ned Geeslin,
> with Linda Marx in Miami.

A book publisher saw the *People* spread and wanted me to do a book about my climb of Mt. Everest. I said, "No, it's a serious business. I'm going to have to be totally focused on the preparations and the climb."

They countered by offering quite a large advance for rights to a book. It immediately occurred to me that mountain climbers generally do not have a lot of financial resources, so this would be a big monetary boost for an enterprise such as ours. We needed to raise at least a million dollars to cover the project. The rest of the team was reaching out to contacts, selling T-shirts, begging, selling their souls for financial support. The advance for a book would go to the team and was simply too good to turn down. So I told them I would do a diary. I would take a Dictaphone with me and when and where I could, I would relate what was happening on our expedition. If I was in a safe place, generally at night in my sleeping bag, I would record. They agreed. Obviously, the publishers thought the two most likely scenarios were that I would either be the first woman from the United States to reach the summit of Mt. Everest, or I would die. I disappointed them. I missed getting to the top by a short margin due to the weather. And I didn't die.

I have a strong memory of the night before I was to start up the North Col to be in position for our final summit attempt. That night I was in a safe camp at 22,000 feet. Climbing the imposing glacial face to reach the saddle was a huge and frequently very dangerous climb of 2,000 vertical feet of ice, snow, and rock. One memory still brings a lump to my throat. I gathered up all the tapes I had dictated since leaving home, wrapped them in waterproof layers and placed them in my tent where they would be found…just in case.

My diary, *The Edge of Everest*, was published by Stackpole Books in October 1989. The book relays from my perspective the entire experience of our travels and the climb as it unfolded.

While you can read my experience in that book, in the years that followed, I learned more about the trip. Here are some recollections of Courtney Skinner some three decades later.

The opportunity came to get the permit to China in 1980 not long after Richard Nixon and Henry Kissinger's early '70s journey to China and the "opening" of China. The north side of Everest was our goal. It was not the South Col route in Nepal, but Tibet where we wished to go. The Nepal approach through Kathmandu simply was not the option I wanted. I wanted the early historical route that the British pioneered in the 1920s. In 1980, I put in the Tibet application to Beijing and never a word was heard until 1984 when the Chinese gave permission to climb the Northeast Ridge route in the fall of 1988.

Wyoming, called The Equality State, has always been on the front of women's rights. One of my goals within the expedition was to take many young American climbers to gain experience in the Himalayas and another goal was to put the first American woman on the summit of Mt. Everest. Sue was one of two women designated to be on our summit team.

Sue had worked diligently two years on the board of governors, as did all the board of governors, which included then Representative Dick Cheney and Senators Alan Simpson and Malcolm Wallop, to get us to the position to go to China. Sue had a very hard road. Some of the team members were immediately skeptical, thinking, "She paid her way onto the expedition." She had to overcome the obstacles of attitude and altitude, to say nothing of the difficulties of the North side route and the pressures of being a woman. She had to overcome the skepticism of those other climbers who were saying, "Well, why does she get to go to the summit when I am a better climber, or I am more experienced?" Over time those questions receded, but the fact remained that our journey from beginning to end was a picture of hardship.

Everest has a tendency to captivate climbers. One of the features of the North side of Everest is that from the base camp you see the whole mountain in all its bulk and majesty. You can see the summit and much of the route, and you can feel the history of Mallory and Irvine's death climb of 1924. I could envision the British trying to get into Lhasa and taking along their bayonets in the late 1800s, marching with all of their troops into Lhasa, and the Tibetans rolling rocks and ashes down to impede their advance.

Most every successful ascent of Everest had been done in the spring, the pre-monsoon climbing season. This was a fall, post-monsoon climb, on the north and coldest side of Everest.

As it turned out, Sue probably was the only person to have climbed the entire Col alone in the dead of night and reach the top of the North Col (a saddle between peaks). We were initially climbing together but I stopped to pick up bottles of oxygen to put in my pack, while she was leading up ahead. We went into the wee hours of the night. I don't know what time we finally arrived at the top of the North Col, but I do remember my brother, Bob Skinner, trying to reach Sue by radio to tell her to come down. Unknown to us, Sue did not have a radio. We thought she had one and had turned it off. To me that was an amazing feat. None of the men were climbing at night and I don't know if I would have been able to have made it to the top of the Col without her having been in front, knowing that she was finding the route.

On the Col we were both living in a small and old British tent just off the Northeast ridge and steps away from a gaping crevasse. The tent was very low, the fabric was not insulated and didn't breathe. Outside it was forty below zero. Icicles were hanging down right above our chests and our mouths, inhibiting breathing. We couldn't move. It was absolutely the worst feeling in the world. If I hadn't been an environmentalist, I'd have thrown that tent off the cliff. We're spending time at forty below zero in that tent with those icicles right in our faces. I don't know how either of us survived that. The next day Sue and I rigged up a belay system [a climber's safety system] to retrieve company gear. Sue belayed me and she helped save me when I descended forty-five feet into a nasty crevasse to retrieve team equipment that had blown into it. At that time, she probably in many ways saved everything. All our climbers had been exposed at altitude for too long. It was very cold, very cramped, and most of our equipment had blown off the mountain. Sue was calm, steady, and optimistic.

By the next day Sue had become hypothermic and unable to speak well. It was critical that she descend to a lower elevation. Even if a climber is in good shape the descent off the Col is treacherous. She and a young climber, Jim Burnett, had to go down. I was able to go with Sue past the most difficult spots near the top. Then she was on her own again to conclude the 2,000-foot drop off the face to the Advance Base Camp. I'm sure she mentioned this in her book.

Probably one of the major challenges that Sue conquered even more than climbing the mountain was the interaction with the younger climbers, the ability to become a part of the team of mountaineers. In the end, Sue won their support, and their hearts, and their dedication. She certainly did mine. She did it by that grit, that heart, and by the ultimate recognition that she cared more about the other people, her rope mates, her tent mates, and those that she was going for the summit with. I thought she of all the women mountaineers in America would be ideal to be the first woman on Everest because of her grit.

Sue used to describe Bob Skinner, my older brother, as John Wayne, and myself as Gene Autry, the romanticist. I want to say her grit and her caring deeply for not only teammates, but people. I don't know quite know how to put that, but the caring about people equally or more than herself. Only a few of the heartiest were on the Col and it had really boiled down in the end that the team of Sue Cobb and Courtney Skinner were among them.

Courtney Skinner, January 2, 2018

What Courtney did not say was that it was really he who saved my life the night of October 13, 1988 by cooking retorts (dried food in compressed packs) and melting snow for water, making me eat and drink, checking the emergency oxygen tank he gave me that kept me alive. As I relate in *The Edge of Everest*, the next day I descended the Col to reach our camp at 22,000 feet. What I did not know was that our team doctor told others that night that in his judgment, I had about four hours to live. I did not learn about it until many months later. Without Courtney's extensive experience and recognition of my deteriorating state, I know I would not have lived through that last night on the Col.

Courtney also reiterated tales of our difficulties with the Chinese and the challenges of traveling from the US and across China and Tibet. It was just such an amazing adventure. We first flew from California to Dover, Delaware on a US Air Force C-5 training flight, picked up a helicopter to deliver to Lhasa, then flew to Anchorage, Alaska. From Anchorage we flew to Okinawa. On arriving in Okinawa, it was announced to the team that while the Chinese were happy to receive the plane and the helicopter, they were not going to allow the mountain climbing team to land in Beijing. The plan was California, Anchorage, Okinawa, Beijing, and Lhasa. Lhasa was where we were to pick up our trucks and venture on to what should have been three days of driving to the Rongbuk Base Camp to start our climb. The Chinese said, "No" to flying to Beijing. We were stuck in Okinawa with thirty-five climbers and thousands of pounds of food and equipment.

In a fortuitous twist, my husband had decided that he, in his role as undersecretary of Commerce, needed to visit China. He was to be in Beijing the very next day to meet with China's tourism minister. At the time, Chuck was in charge of the United States Worldwide Travel and Tourism. I called him from Okinawa before he left Washington and told him, "The Chinese are saying they are not letting us come; can you call the minister of tourism or talk to the foreign minister and see if you can get this cleared up?" We spent one day in Okinawa with phone calls trying to get our team travel to Beijing approved. In the end my husband agreed to put up $25,000 as a "loan" and guaranteed a much larger amount to get a permit for us to land in Beijing. We thought that once we got to Beijing, we would be able to talk them into letting the team go with the plane to Lhasa. This was not to be. So, we agreed in Beijing that team members would do their best to get to Chengdu in Sichuan Province as soon as possible, and we would meet at a particular hotel.

My two sons were able to be with Chuck and me in China. Toby had flown with me on the Air Force C-5 and Chris flew commercially with Chuck. With the team's delay in Beijing, our family took a day's side trip to Xi'an to see the underground Terracotta Warriors of the Qin Dynasty, which had only been uncovered in 1974. The terracotta army had been buried in 209-210 BCE and since we visited in 1988, only fourteen years after its discovery, there had been very little excavation of the necropolis. The history is absolutely fascinating. The four of us returned to Beijing and managed to arrange flights to Chengdu. The journey was a great adventure for my then college-age sons. We searched for giant pandas and marveled at Chinese rural life in Chengdu, then a relatively small city. At dinner Toby decided to try the chicken head soup only to find that, yes, there was a chicken head (with a long neck) in his soup. We spent a couple of nights in the designated hotel waiting for everybody to gather. Team members came one or two at a time. We had already lost almost a whole week. Chuck and my boys declared that they could go no further due to various commitments and time constraints. Chris was to be in a wedding in Guam, and Chuck was making a Commerce Department appearance in the Philippines. Toby just said the food was not to his taste. They left me in Chengdu. The parting was emotional because no one knew who from our team was going to get back alive, and it was brief because none of us wanted to be the first to cry. I carry with me an indelible image of the three of them, backs to me, walking out the door of that hotel in Chengdu.

Meanwhile, the team leaders were trying to figure out how we were all going to get from Chengdu to Lhasa. They decided we would have to again split up and get to Lhasa in any way we could manage. We agreed to meet at Lhasa's well-known Chinese-owned Holiday Inn. Chinese officials were completely unhelpful. My supposition is they really felt that at least some of us were spies, and they did not know who. They openly displayed total suspicion and barely hidden opposition, assigning three men whom they said were members of the Chinese Mountaineering Association to be with us at all times. And yes, they stayed with us the entire time including at our base camp. They spoke almost no English. Fortunately for us, Ethan Golding, a young Stanford graduate who spoke Mandarin, was on our team; he became our invaluable interpreter.

We stayed in Lhasa for a week. Lhasa sits at approximately 12,000 feet. This was an acclimatization step and an opportunity to round up some additional supplies. We were being watched all the time, but we could walk around Lhasa, see the town and famous Potela Place. When we would go out to walk around town, our belongings left at the Holiday Inn, both team and personal goods, were thoroughly searched. The whole visit in Lhasa was laced with tension, but nonetheless, totally fascinating. We could also see the ways in which Chinese soldiers were really cruel to the Tibetans. The soldiers yelled at the Tibetans and routinely pushed them aside with gun butts. We tried to avoid the soldiers, while engaging with the Tibetans.

Our team had arranged six big lorries with bulbous canvas tops to carry fifteen tons of gear on the expected three-day drive between Lhasa and the Rongbuk Valley. The team was assigned a really finicky, really uncomfortable, really old bus. On leaving Lhasa, the top of one of the lorries hit some low-hanging electrical wires, probably because we had piled gear on top of the canvas tops. The Chinese police (under the control of the army) pulled us over and machine guns in hand, took all of us to a Chinese army compound. The soldiers rustled us out of the bus and lined us up against a concrete wall where we could see bullet holes in the wall behind our heads and blood on the wall where people had been executed. We were made to stand there for about an hour waiting while our leaders were taken into a nearby building. We did not really think they were going to shoot us. It was more like they wanted to scare us and give us a hard time all the time. Eventually they let us go and, I am sure, went right back to work on getting rid of the Tibetans, their religion, and their culture. Due to monsoon rain, flooding, and rockslides, the alleged three-day trip from Lhasa to the Rongbuk Valley, detailed in *The Edge of Everest*, took us two weeks. We did not reach base camp until August 26. The Chinese have now built a road into the Rongbuk Valley, and climbers can drive directly to the Rongbuk Everest Base Camp. I was sorry to learn that.

As for being a woman on the expedition, I think there were minor disadvantages simply by physical characteristics. Climbers are scrupulous about hygiene, cleanliness, and healthcare. There are no courtesies extended on the mountain. You have to take care of yourself. The hygienic circumstances are more difficult for women and one of the interesting things I noticed was that in our base camp where all of us could survive relatively easily with our personal tents and a big dining tent, our latrine area spouted an "on/off" flag system. We had dug latrines, maybe 100–150 yards away from the camp itself, in an area that our three Chinese minders indicated we could use as a bathroom area. We were very careful to maintain normal decorum at 16,900 feet.

However, when we were higher up the mountains, there were no choices. Above base camp level, if somebody had to step aside to relieve themselves, your only duty was to continue very slowly or to just turn your head and wait a few steps further away. You had to just step off the trail somewhere. For the men the smallest chore was easier than for the women. Mountain climbing suits provide a rear "flap" that can be released and let down. That was useful when necessary, but still awkward.

One day when a few of us were on the trail between camps, we heard this huge rumbling. The earth shifted, groaning loudly. It was either an avalanche or a monumental rock fall in our proximity. One poor guy had stepped off the trail and his pants were around his ankles. At the noise, he struggled to run away from the area of potential danger with his pants around his knees. Of course, we all turned around and had a good laugh. He had reason to run because it was, indeed, one of the not infrequent rock falls. A Japanese climber had been killed earlier in the year in the same area by wildly flying boulders.

While at base camp we hired a few Tibetans who owned yaks (a sign of wealth) to take some of our gear to the next higher camp level, but their availability and capabilities were quite limited. We did not have money to hire guides, Sherpas, yaks, or herders; so while we retained a few yaks, each of us carried all of our own and some part of team gear as we ascended. It does not sound like much, but if you are carrying forty pounds at high altitude going up a steep mountain it feels like eighty pounds. For me it was really hard. More than once, I just sat down on the trail and started crying because it was so hard. But I would never let any team member see me crying.

We got into shape on the mountain by carrying these loads of gear to each higher camp. Teams set up camps at different elevations and acclimatized along the way. Expedition style climbing is kind of a hopscotch system where you take a load of food, for example, to the camp that is 1,000 feet higher. You drop it there and go back to a lower elevation to sleep. The next day you take sleeping bags or blankets or whatever and you may climb 1,500 feet, drop your team gear, and then descend to the 1,000-foot camp. And repeat until the appropriate gear is distributed at the appropriate camps along the fifteen-mile route.

The experiences of that excursion helped to prepare me for many more things in life. It was undeniably physically difficult, but the way in which it was hardest surprised me: it was extraordinarily difficult psychologically and emotionally draining. Physically we knew it would be extremely harsh, we expected that. We anticipated extreme physical strains, but most of us were not prepared psychologically for the degree to which we would have to absorb the mountain's challenges without normal support systems. We could not even call home. This was a team drawn from around the United States, not necessarily all of those we had trained with earlier. We did not know each other very well when we gathered in California to start our trip. The nature of our travel had not provided time to meld into a real team with acceptance and allegiance to our friends and leaders. I have always been strong, mentally and physically. What I learned is that when you get into life and death situations and there is nobody nearby that you really know or that cares about your survival or that you believe you can really trust, you are compromised. It becomes a very heavy psychological load.

We were totally isolated under severe physical pressure in constant life and death situations. It would be absolutely nothing to a soldier who had been in Afghanistan, for example, but for the rest of us, unaccustomed to living day to day in a constant life-threatening environment without any kind of emotional support, the stress was unexpectedly difficult. In the final analysis, it made me stronger. There was simply no choice.

I knew Chuck was worried the whole time. At our base camp, we had phone communication via the Indian Ocean Inmarsat Satellite that we could only use on exceptional occasions, because it was ghastly expensive. At a more moderate price, my husband could call to the base camp and find out if I was still alive, where I was, and what the team status was. I talked to him very briefly only once. A second time he called I was at the base camp in a meeting but was not told of the call until later in the day. I was heartbroken. I left camp to sit in the makeshift graveyard to cry.

As October came upon us, I became among the last climbers high on the mountain. In the end, I knew I was somewhere above 24,000 feet, but I did not know where. The plan was to move up to 25,500, then to 27,500, and be ready to make our final ascent. The peak was clearly visible right above us. I felt I could almost reach out and touch it. We really thought we would make the top. In the end, we had eight climbers on top of the Col, including me. All were weak but intended to continue climbing until the Polar Jet Stream dismantled our well-laid plans. Word was passed up the mountain by hand-held radios that an incoming storm was extremely serious. Courtney and Bob called for "an orderly retreat" to get all Cowboys away from high-altitude exposure. All team members were required to descend. The day our last climbers descended, a team of four Czechoslovakians on an adjacent ridge decided to stay one more night. Their tents were blown away and they all died. To get as close as we were to the summit was a mind-bending experience, but we all knew it was too late in the season to try again. The game was over.

I think back on the trip often. I can see myself, standing on the North Ridge. I was alone on that narrow ridge somewhere between our 24,000 to 25,500-foot camps, sad that our climb was over. I stopped ascending and turned to look for the first time at the scenery below. Some of the highest mountains in the world were under my feet. As I looked down to my right, I could see into Tibet and China; and to my left, into Nepal and India. There were hundreds of snow-covered mountains below me.

I was just a tiny speck in an immense universe. I was stunned by the scene yet curiously elated. It is difficult to describe the feeling after climbing that high. Oddly, Edmund Burke, the Irish leader after whom my grandfather Ed was named, in the treatise "A Philosophical Enquiry into the Origin of our Ideas of Sublime and Beautiful" (1757), after ascending a high mountain in Switzerland called the feeling "sublime...a curious amalgam of fear, serenity, exhaustion, and awe." That seems right to me. I had looked down and felt the immensity of infinity and the wonder of life. It was a transcendent experience.

The only time I ever even really thought about death on the mountain as possibly being applicable to me was the night before my last climb on the North Ridge, knowing we had to descend in the morning. In my sleeping bag that night, with the knowledge that the adventure was at its end, I thought to myself how ironic it would be if this were the night that an avalanche breaks loose or a rock fall thunders down to our pathetic little camp. Maybe this is the night that something bad will happen, and I knew that neither I nor our remaining completely drained climbers had the strength to manage any kind of crisis. That night, I desperately wanted to live.

Three days later in our Rongbuk base camp, after we knew all the Cowboys were alive – a pretty exhilarating thought – Julie Cheney (really our best woman climber) said, "Well Sue, it's really disappointing not to get to the top, but we were very, very close and maybe just putting your foot on the last rock doesn't matter so much – we basically climbed that whole mountain. Besides, we can always come back next year." I looked at her and said, "Julie, you're nuts. I'm fifty-one years old. You can come back next year, I've done Everest, this is it, this is over!" Julie was killed in a climbing accident two years later. She was thirty-six years old. Bob Skinner, our John Wayne, the consummate mountain man, died of natural causes in Pinedale, Wyoming in December 2006. He was seventy-seven years old. Courtney, the Gene Autry of my book, is alive and well, living in Wyoming and planning his next adventure.

One of the themes of our lives, Chuck's and mine, is the willingness to assess what the opportunity value is versus the known negatives of ventures under consideration. We assess probabilities and study exit strategies. When the Arvida job came up for Chuck in Florida in the 1970s, and I clearly did not want to move to Miami, it was a tough decision for him. In fact, he did not want to leave California either. He is a fifth generation Californian. I am fourth generation Californian. All of our family, all of our friends, our college life, everything that we knew was in California. But we decided the opportunity was worth testing, at least for a year or two. The Everest decision was similar in a way. I have always thought of Everest as a metaphor, as a symbol of man's highest aspirations, for aiming high, for going for the top, for getting as high as you can in whatever you are doing then. I had the totally unexpected chance to go for that magical summit, which included the unique opportunity to travel across China and Tibet. Why not try? Well, the downside in this case was pretty bad. Still percentage wise it was not too bad a balance. There was nearly an eighty percent chance I would come home alive. Together Chuck and I have looked at many choices life has to offer. In nearly all cases, our lives have been enriched by saying the word "yes."

Our son Christian had his own take on my Everest expedition:

My parents have had fantastic careers and they are ginormous shoes to fill. Probably not possible. You talk about the sports I mean Dad was an alternate on the US Olympic Team. I didn't play college sports. And Mom deciding in mid-life to go climb Mt. Everest, would have been the first American woman on the summit. How did I feel while she was doing that?

You know that was after my college years and before going to Harvard for my MBA. I was working for an architect. I was pretty fit, playing club sports regularly for fun, so the age thing I didn't yet understand. I didn't understand what a fifty-year-old body felt like. Now I know, so I have much more respect for that component of what she did. But I'm sort of used to them making audacious goals and then going after them so that didn't surprise me.

My father was much more worried during the climb because he was much more analytically understanding the associated risks. I forget the numbers, but it's something like one in fifteen people who go to Everest die. I'm thinking that's a low percentage and he's thinking, "But why have that percentage at all?" So, I wasn't as afraid as he was. Because he was going to be losing his life partner. I, of course, would be losing my mother, but she had already given me the vast majority of the lessons I was going to learn. I didn't think about it all that way, but I wasn't as worried. And, of course, I knew she would make it home safely.

Christian McCourt Cobb, September 23, 2017

October 17, 1988, I left the Everest base camp in a sweatsuit carrying one small duffle bag, which contained only another sweatsuit. I had both a Tibetan and a Nepalese visa. I decided to exit through Nepal. Earlier from base camp, I had been able to arrange a car to pick me up in the Rongbuk basin and possibly a car to meet me when I got through Nepalese immigration on the other side of the mountains. Another climber, a wonderful friend and great climber, David Frawley, was the only other person who had a visa to get into Nepal and at the last minute he decided to go with me. We had to cross a 17,000-foot pass to reach the south side of Everest and descend to Kathmandu. I felt badly about not staying to help reload our excess gear, at base camp, but I had warned Courtney this would happen.

Our exit from Tibet and arrival into Nepal was an adventure in itself related in full in *The Edge of Everest*. The car took David and me part way, then we had to walk on foot, crossing the 17,000-foot pass at night, then scrambling down a steep river gorge toward Nepal. I finally got to sleep in a real bed in a rented room just short of Nepalese customs – the first night since mid-August I did not have to crawl into a sleeping bag. The following day David and I reached the Nepal immigration station. To our amazement, we learned the car I had tried ordering on my scratchy phone call from Tibet was waiting for us on the Nepalese side of the Friendship Bridge which marks the Nepal-Tibet border. In a temperature of about 75°F, we had a joyful ride to the Yak and Yeti Hotel in downtown Kathmandu.

The following day I was to meet Chuck at the Excelsior Hotel in Rome where he was on official US government business. At the Kathmandu Airport David and I split up and I made my way via Dubai to Rome. When I finally reached the Hotel Excelsior and went to check in, they just stared at me. I was gaunt – I had lost thirty pounds – I had no luggage, and I was still in the same sweatsuit I had on when I left base camp in the Rongbuk Valley. They could not believe I was the wife of The Honorable Charles Cobb who I knew was at a meeting outside the hotel. With my US passport, they let me into our room.

Later that day, I went to a nearby department store and bought an appropriate wardrobe. Then I met Chuck on the Spanish Steps – alive and well, but thirty pounds slimmer. We flew from Italy to the Hungarian People's Republic. Chuck was to be one of the featured speakers at the World Tourism Organization Conference. Sir Edmund Hillary, the first man to climb Mt. Everest, was the other speaker on the program. Having been on Everest only a few days before, it was a great pleasure and a privilege to be seated with Sir Edmund and to converse together. We reconnected years later when he visited Telluride.

Of course, the Everest trip was one of the most memorable events of my life and it has been with me every day since I walked off the mountain. The thirty-year residual is not easily explainable. The feeling of absolute awe I had standing alone on the North Ridge is still crystal clear to me. The wonder continues to live inside me. That absolute awe was a gift, which remains with me every day of my life.

It is quite true that I never had any desire to go back to Everest. But I was not quite done with the Himalayas. As far as climbing was concerned, I took a detour to engage in another unanticipated and extraordinary experience: living in Reykjavik, Iceland while Chuck served as the United States ambassador. Well, of course, every country has its highest mountain to climb. On Iceland, that amazing volcanic island, the highest peak is called Hvannadalshnúkur on the top of the Öræfajökul volcano covered by glaciers and riddled with crevasses. The summit is just under 7,000 feet. The challenge of this peak is that it sits on an island in the middle of the North Atlantic and is regularly subject to high and extremely unpredictable ocean winds laced with ice.

I summited Hvannadalshnúkur with two Icelandic climbers on what turned out to be a beautiful, cold day in March 1990. We had agreed to ski both ways, all the way up and all the way back down. We started the route at about 2:00 a.m. Using skins on skis and climbing diagonally up in a left-hand angle, then switching and climbing up at a right-hand angle, we were able to keep a more or less direct route. It took twelve hours to reach a fairly flat spot about 300 meters below the peak, near the edge of the volcano's caldera. From there we abandoned our skis and roped up (I was in the middle) for a steep, approximately 1,000-foot climb to the peak. It was a good thing we roped up, because we hadn't gone fifty yards before I stepped right into a crevasse up to my armpits. Experienced climbers that they were, my two friends thrust themselves flat on the snow in opposite directions tightening the rope, while ramming their ice axes into the snow for a firm hold. The effect of their action was efficient, tightening our rope until I popped right up like a mechanical doll to a height at which I could swing a leg up and over the edge of the crevasse and climb out. No harm done.

We ascended to the peak and were lucky with the weather. There was not a cloud in the sky. We enjoyed a 360-degree view of mountains, glaciers, and the Atlantic Ocean. We down climbed, retrieved our skis, removed the skins, and began our ski descent. The only instructions I had been given were "watch for crevasses and keep your skis perpendicular to them." We had a total of about fourteen hours climbing to the peak and an exhilarating forty-five minutes skiing down, then returned directly to our tiny hostel late in the day. I was surprised to see Guđrun there cooking dinner, as she had fixed our breakfast at 2:00 a.m. "Guđrun," I said in surprise, "When do you sleep?" She quickly responded, "I sleep in January and February when there is no light."

We left Iceland in 1992. While living in Reykjavik, we were simultaneously building a new home in Coral Gables, Florida, with the help of our architect son Christian. It was basically finished shortly after we returned to Florida. We took up residence in March 1992, just in time to participate in Hurricane Andrew, August 24, 1992, one of the most devastating hurricanes in US history. There was tremendous damage in South Florida causing huge trauma for the region. Our new home on Biscayne Bay, like many others, had extensive damage. We had to move out for almost a year.

In the turmoil after Hurricane Andrew, after we had done what we could to help, and since we could not move into our home, Chuck and I decided to take some time to travel. We were holding an invitation to visit from the US ambassador to Kenya, Smith Hempstone Jr. and his wife, Kitty, so we decided on a short East African safari in 1993. We had not planned exactly what we would do after our visit in Kenya with the Hempstones. In Nairobi, as we pondered what to do next,

Chuck suddenly decided he wanted to go see the pyramids in Egypt. At the same time I realized how close we were to Mt. Kilimanjaro. I said, "I'd like to go south to Tanzania and climb Kilimanjaro." He said, "I don't want to do that. I'm going to Egypt." He got on a plane that day and went to Egypt.

Kitty helped me find a DHL bus to Arusha, Tanzania, and then dropped me at the Norfolk Hotel in downtown Nairobi to wait for the bus. I got a front row seat and could not help but notice that I was the only white person on the vehicle. The bus driver seemed a little anxious when I boarded. I could tell because he had me sit right behind him and a man who was clearly a friend of his was seated next to me. When we got to the crossing from Kenya into Tanzania, all passengers had to get out of the bus, go into a building, and present a passport. The plaza around the immigration office was filled with people, and it was a bit of a raucous scene. The bus driver asked me for my passport but would not let me get off the bus. His friend sat with me while everybody else got off and went into the border station. Maybe he just did not want me exposed to all the people trying to sell their wares. When the driver returned, my passport was properly stamped.

In the five-hour drive to Arusha we passed many Masai with their herds of cattle and goats. The Masai were all very tall and absolutely elegant in their red robes. An embassy contact met me in Arusha and drove me to the town of Moshi where I was dropped off at a farm with exquisite small cottages overseen by a charming elderly German woman. My cottage hotel was just lovely. I had my own little house and the chickens liked my area of grass, so they kept me company pecking away outside my window. I really just enjoyed being there. The following day I signed up for the climb and learned that I was required to have three porters go along with me. One carries the firewood, the second carries the food and cooks the meals, and the third is the guide who supervises the others. The only word I learned in Swahili was *pole pole*, slowly, slowly. My guide kept saying it to me on our five-day hike to the mountaintop. I learned later that my porters had a bet with the other guides on the mountain as to how old I was. Apparently, they thought I was somewhere between thirty and forty, because of the fact that the average life span of a woman in Tanzania at that time was fifty. I had just turned fifty-five. My personal guide won the bet by being closest. He guessed forty, so when I left I gave him the sleeping bag I had bought in Nairobi as his prize.

I really enjoyed the climb. First, because climbers travel through five different ecological zones with ever changing flora and fauna. The beginning was almost forest-like. Then, you go through four different levels with associated climate changes. It was a horticultural education. I loved it. On the Marango Route, climbers stop along the route at three camps to overnight prior to reaching the large base camp of Kibo. The distances each day are short, but each day you are ascending. The three established camps had rather small wooden huts with peaked roofs and two bunks on each side. As there are a number of other climbers on the same route, when you arrive at a camp you are simply assigned to a bunk that follows that of the person that got into the camp just ahead of you. The person who comes behind you, may come to your hut, or if it already has four people, then that climber would go on to the next nearby hut. As a solo climber, every night I would be with a different group of people. As it happened in every case, I bunked with three solo men of all different nationalities. The one I remember best was a priest from the Netherlands who gave me a little black Bible to make sure I got on and off the mountain safely. I still have it. I met a few women, but all had companions, and none were compatible with me in hiking. By the second day, I could see that if you watch with whom you are entering a camp (always random, set mainly by pace) you could decide if you want to be in a little hut with that person overnight or not, and if necessary change your pace to arrive with someone else. The fourth overnight is in Kibo Hut, basically a huge bunkroom sitting at 15,200 feet. Many people cannot adjust to the rise in elevation at 15,000 feet and return to a lower hut.

Bedtime at Kibo is early. You are called to start for the peak ascent at one in the morning. You carry a lantern and hike up a steep trail of "scree" (tiny rocks the size of marbles which are frustrating because as you walk up, you slide down a bit with every step). I don't know what the percentage is, but there aren't a high number of people who actually make it to the real summit of Uhuru at 19,340 feet. Most climbers stop at the caldera edge, which is lower. About ninety percent of climbing Kilimanjaro is walking uphill. From Kibo up the last section of the climb, you are in a jack-o-lantern parade of about forty or forty-five people and the climb is steep. You are climbing quite a precipitous, rocky, uncomfortable section in the dark. The climbing is not terribly hard but it is just not easy. My guide was leading the jack-o-lantern parade, so I was second in line. I did not find it very hard, just dark and cold. It took us five hours to reach Gillman's Point, the caldera edge, at 18,345 feet. Due to the altitude, people were dropping out at every turn as we snaked up the mountain traverses. Almost everyone stopped at Gillman's. Only three men (and my guide) walked with me from Gillman's 'false summit' around the crater to the real summit at Uhuru Peak (19,340 feet).

I assumed my cook and the other porter were at Kibo waiting, probably hoping I would turn around early like most of the climbers. There was a lot of snow on Kilimanjaro that year, so it was quite beautiful with spectacular views. The whole experience was enjoyable. Descending by this short cut to Kibo is a little hard to visualize. It is quite steep and all on scree, those small marbles. As hard as it is climbing up on scree, it is great fun going downhill. There is no snaking, traverse style side-to-side down the mountain. You simply go straight down. The technique is to take a long downward stride, place your heel into the marbles and balance on the implanted foot as it slides. The marbles keep rolling down, under your planted foot for up to about thirty-six inches. When the planted foot begins to grip and to stop, you take the next long stride downward with the opposite leg and foot and plant that heel. With alternating heel planting strides, you slide smoothly down the mountain. Oh, it was so much fun. Using this technique took me about an hour to get back to Kibo from Gillman's.

After our descent, my guide and porter were very happy because I gave them the sleeping bag, parka, boots, and other provisions purchased for this unplanned climb. I sure wasn't going to carry all the stuff home from Tanzania. So, I just gave everything to my three helpers. They were thrilled. The whole expedition from when I left Nairobi on the bus to the international airport in Arusha took seven days and was a wonderful adventure.

Five years later, in 1998, one of the most recognized women ambassadors in the State Department, who became a good friend of mine, Prudence Bushnell, was serving as US ambassador to Kenya leading the embassy team in Nairobi. That was the year terrorists attacked our embassies in both Nairobi and Dar es Salaam, Tanzania. Having visited Embassy Nairobi I could visualize exactly what had happened and had tremendous sympathy and respect for Ambassador Bushnell and her colleagues. Ambassador Bushnell published her account of that terrible disaster in which hundreds of people died: *Terrorism, Betrayal, and Resilience: My Story of the 1998 U.S. Embassy Bombings*. I highly recommend it.

After the Kilimanjaro climb, I returned in 1995 to the Himalayas. David McNally, one of my Everest teammates, called and asked if I would like to join a small expedition to Kangchenjunga in northeast Nepal on the Bhutan border. I was fond of Dave. He is a superb high-altitude climber, skier, mountain guide, and also a very talented and successful artist. Dave did a portrait of me at the Everest base camp that I think is more realistic than any photo I have. To me, it is exactly me. Though Dave's subject matter is broad, he is so talented at portraiture that I later commissioned a full body portrait from a photo of Chuck in Iceland for his seventieth birthday, which I think is superb.

Kangchenjunga, the third highest mountain in the world, is considered one of the most difficult 8,000-meter peaks to climb. I immediately said, "Yes" to Dave; but since I would then be fifty-eight, I settled for the climbing team's fourteen-day trek to the north base camp at just under 17,000 feet. The peak itself at 28,169 feet looms imposingly over the base camp. This area around Kangchenjunga is known to be one of the most untainted and unspoiled parts of Nepal with a mind-boggling variety of flora and fauna and an equally large variety of wildlife. Our route was extremely remote and at that time not widely used.

I talked my lifelong friend and sister-in-law, Suzanne McCourt, also fifty-eight years-old at the time, into accompanying me along with eight former Cowboy teammates. I knew Suzie's character and knew her to be an experienced, regular High Sierra hiker and camper. She had never done any mountain climbing, so it would be a victory to just reach the 17,000-feet base camp, which we did. Neither of us would be climbing the higher tougher stuff. Even without our mountain adventure it was a great trip: Seoul, Bangkok, Kathmandu, Northeast Nepal returning through Saigon, Hanoi, Bangkok, and Seoul – an exciting, educational itinerary and fun for two "middle-aged" American women.

After arriving in Kathmandu, Suzie and I made our way to the small town of Britnigar, to a noisy hotel with, let's just say, bad facilities. We were on the fourth floor of a four-story building. We were not told that parts of the roof were missing. It rained that night. We got wet. We were afraid to eat dinner or anything else at the hotel. The next day, I recalled that it is perfectly safe to eat street food – even if you did not know what it was – if it has been in boiling grease. We got something quite tasty to eat and caught a ride to Dhahran, on the edge of the Terai region of India, elevation 1,000 feet, to meet our team and take a helicopter to the 3,000 feet starting point of our fourteen-day trek.

Our helicopter turned out to be a giant orange-colored Soviet Sikorsky made to transport goods and people using little metal benches for about fifteen to eighteen occupants and their gear. The helicopter was to drop us on the playground of a small school in a little village called Taplejung. But the helicopter had failed to deliver two diesel generators that had been promised to the villagers two months before, so the villagers, upset, sent a message that if the two generators were not on the next helicopter coming to Taplejung, the villagers were going to shoot it down with their machine guns. The Soviet pilot spoke only Russian, so we could not tell what was really going on. We decided to get on the helicopter that the villagers were threatening to shoot down, even though we could see there were no diesel generators on board. That was a little unnerving. We went anyway. There were no machine guns. The villagers were nice to us and we were nice to them, though none of us understood what the other's nice words were saying.

We joined our teammates and without further drama started the two-week hike to our base camp on Kangchenjunga. The countryside was more beautiful than any of the many beautiful places I had seen in Nepal. Our route sported exaggerated foliage and fauna at every turn, with many rivers to cross. It was raining the day we landed in Taplejung and it did not stop raining for the next fourteen days. As we would pass through small villages at lower elevations, we had been told that the proper protocol in this region was for Western women climbers to wear skirts. Suzanne and I each brought two cotton ankle length skirts. We camped out every night on our route, so every night we tried to figure out how to get something at least a little dry to wear the next day. Now if you sleep in a sleeping bag in a wet skirt, that will dry it, but it is certainly not very comfortable. When we got higher where we knew we were not going to have more villages to walk through, we changed to climbing gear: pants and jackets. I rolled up my two skirts and left them in a duffle bag that was stored at one of our low camps.

Not only were we quite wet day and night, we attracted leeches. These are horrible parasitic worm-like creatures that attach themselves to exposed skin and suck your blood. They were ghastly and had to be detached with great care – unless you just let them get their fill of blood. Then they would fall off on their own. But it was extremely unsightly to have a three-inch worm hanging off your face or neck. Oddly, since they were not really harmful, they became rather tolerable. It struck me as a perfect example of a "new normal."

Unlike Everest, we had Sherpas on the Kangchenjunga trip. What a luxury! They would set up tents and build a fire so we could hang clothes and blankets nearby. Nonetheless, almost every day for fourteen days as we gained altitude to our base camp it rained.

We were in exceedingly rugged terrain with what I would call evidence of a trail, but not like the hiking trails of Annapurna or other places in Nepal where many tourists go. There were no tourists on our route. One young Sherpa named Pemba was "assigned" to be sure Suzie and I got through the toughest and most dangerous spots, like the river crossings. Many memories have stayed with me. Once, when we were getting close to our base camp, we were ascending a glacier. Pemba was rushing us along to be sure we got to the camp before dark. I happened to glance over on the edge of the glacier about forty yards away and saw something on the snow that looked like a blanket. Then I realized there was somebody underneath the blanket.

"Pemba, Pemba, look, who is that?" It was clear a person was lying there, though we could not see his face.

Pemba replied, "Yes, I see, that's Norbu. He is resting."

"But Pemba, we have to get him up or he won't get to base camp before dark."

"No, Sue, Norbu is resting forever."

Base camp was our goal that day. In high altitude climbing almost all base camps are at 16,500 to 17,000 feet because that is where oxygen deprivation starts to cause your body to fail. From base camp the stark, bald face of this very steep mountain confronted us, leading to a difficult to obtain summit. Before we reached our camp, we came upon members of a French expedition. I do not know how many were on the French team, but one of them had died the previous day of pulmonary edema. The French were now trying to get a second of their team members to a lower elevation. They had attached a straight-backed wooden chair to the back of one of the Sherpas so that the ill man could be strapped into the chair, facing uphill, as the Sherpa carried him downhill. They passed us just before we started the last pitch to camp. Later we asked about the ill man we had encountered. He had died. When we got to the base camp, we were told that the French team had further trouble on the mountain and another climber had died in a climbing accident. Kanchenjunga, the third highest mountain in the world, is known to be difficult, but arriving to this news was definitely sobering.

At base camp, Suzie and I had a tent together. During the first night at 17,000 feet, I could hear Suzie's breathing. She would wake up periodically, which would wake me up, and I knew something just was not right. The next day Suzie had even more trouble breathing and began repetitive coughing. She was demonstrating signs of pulmonary edema. I couldn't leave Suzie's side. It became clear that I had to get her down at least 1,000 or 2,000 feet. The following day she and I descended. We knew a couple thousand feet below us was a large and beautiful meadow. We carried gear and camped in the meadow while the rest of the team set out to summit the mountain. In our meadow flowers were blooming, everything was green, and the sun was shining. It was totally gorgeous. We were able to get water from the nearby creek, wash our hair, and put on some clean clothes. Being at 15,000 feet had become very comfortable. Suzie improved immediately.

We spent the next three days comfortably camped, saying prayers for our climbers. Members of the French team, one or two at a time, filtered through our meadow. Suzie's French is perfect, so we learned of dire circumstance on the mountain, but, thankfully, no real problems on our team. Though I pined to go higher on the mountain, when the French team came through and told us how many people had died, I became relieved that Suzie and I were safely ensconced in the meadow.

It was October when the Polar Jet Stream descends and the winds were starting to wail. Team leaders became leery. Our climbers had made it part way to the summit but encountered very high winds and dangerous surface conditions with significant deterioration in snow stability from the summer's heat. Our climbers turned their attention to helping the French team evacuate. Sooner than Suzie and I expected, our teammates started to come down, their plans for climbing Kangchenjunga aborted.

We all descended together, and the challenge was again to get to an overnight camp far below before dark. When we approached the end of our retreat, Suzie, one Sherpa, and I were dragging behind. Knowing that we were going slowly and could not make camp by dark, the team members ahead of us set up a little camp for Suzie and me to stay overnight so that we could descend the next morning in daylight.

The rest of the team rolled on downhill toward a small cabin known to be a couple thousand feet lower. I was taught that you always stay with your team, so I refused to stay at the "interim" camp. It was very dark, and the trail non-existent. Our Sherpa was beside himself, conscious of his responsibility for our safety. I said firmly to Suzie, "We are not staying here. We are going to walk down that creek bed, which I am confident will take us to wherever our team is. You just put your foot exactly after mine every single step of the way." We turned our headlamps on as we slipped and slid down the steep wet ravine. We just more or less carefully stumbled along. It took us a long time. Finally, we could see the lights of the little cabin and could hear music and laughter.

Suzanne said she will never forget this in her entire life: when we walked in the door of the cabin filled with climbers and villagers, the music stopped! Everyone in the room leaped up and a loud cheer erupted. We were engulfed by clapping and hugging as though we had conquered that dreadful mountain. It was one of the most spontaneously exhilarating moments I ever experienced. Our teammates had gotten to this little shack, had a big fireplace going and villagers close by had come to see the Americans, sit by the fire, sing, and drink the local beer. They had been singing and drinking beer for about an hour and a half and were just stunned when Suzie and I walked in. They started cheering and shouting in several languages, "Yeah, yeah Sue, yeah, yeah Suzie." Cheering and putting beers into our hands. Understand, we were in this really remote location in the northeast corner of Nepal about thirteen thousand miles from home. We had a pretty raucous night with music on makeshift instruments and enthusiastic singing, albeit way off key, which brought joy to everyone and sounded wonderful to our ears – an experience that could only happen once in a lifetime – but would remain sealed in our memories for the rest of our lives.

It was early November, our six-week Kangchenjunga excursion was over. The airstrip was a day's walk away to meet a plane to take us to Kathmandu. That is when the porter gave me the duffle bag in which I had packed my skirts. I opened it and pulled out a skirt with some small inset lace trim. Grass and flowers were growing in the lace inserts. Yes. In the rainy days while walking in, we brushed against different kinds of plants, and the seeds attached to our clothes. Part of climbing trips is the unexpected things that happen; this was certainly one of them. In that nice warm bag for a couple of weeks, my damp clothes were in bloom.

We boarded our small, chartered two-engine plane, and that night we were back in Kathmandu at the Yak and Yeti enjoying a hot tub and phone service. Suzie and I felt like we were just in the lap of luxury. The next day we walked around Kathmandu being tourists. Suzie saw a sign in French Basque on a little shop. Having grown up speaking the language in her home, Suzie went in and started speaking Basque to the amazed shop owner. As I said, odd things happen when you seek mountains to climb. My brother told me later that Suzie had never imagined how hard this climb would be. She was in good shape, always an athlete, but she just never imagined what the experience would be like. That was 1995, my last mountaineering expedition in the Himalayas.

It was basically the end of my decade of high-altitude climbing, though through the '90s I continued to climb the "fourteeners" around Telluride and enjoyed a memorable climb up the vertical rock face of the Grand Teton, summiting via the Exum Ridge route with my Telluride-Dallas friends Jack and Annette Vaughn.

Mountain climbing is an inherently dangerous activity and there are clearly down sides. What I did learn in my decade of dedicated high-altitude climbing is:

- Climbing is a choice.

- Adventure and meeting people around the world is fun.

- Danger is exhilarating and trains the mind to focus intently.

- Many climbers report experiencing transcendent moments.

- Aiming high is rewarding, because you learn that you can do more than you ever thought you could.

- Unexpected incidents happen, good and bad, and must be resourcefully managed.

- In the end you learn that it is not really about a peak at all. It is about the journey.

- The memories are lasting.

- Your family will still love you.

And then there are the nearly dead – those people leading lives that, but for the merest of circumstances, should have already ended. Anyone who has been through a severe storm has, to one degree or another, almost died, and that fact will continue to alter them long after the winds have stopped blowing and the storm has died down. Like a war or a great fire, the effects of a storm go rippling outward through webs of people for years, even generations.

Sebastian Junger
The Perfect Storm: A True Story of Men Against the Sea

Chapter Eight

I am not sure we've absorbed the full impact, the full import of what happened. But communism died this year...by the Grace of God, America won the cold war.

George Herbert Walker Bush, 1992

CHARLES E. COBB JR., UNITED STATES AMBASSADOR TO ICELAND 1989–92

Knowing my husband as well as I do and knowing the successes he has had as an athlete, corporate CEO, community builder, university chairman, and high-level United States government official, why would I be surprised early in 1989 to learn that we would soon be moving on to another extraordinary experience?

While I was away in the summer of 1988 climbing Everest, Chuck had been working with President Reagan's potential Republican successor, Vice President George Herbert Walker Bush, on the vice president's 1988 presidential campaign. As the world knows, George H. W. Bush (hereinafter 41 or GHWB) was elected president of the United States in November of 1988. After Chuck's successes at the Department of Commerce in the Reagan administration, he was on President Bush's list of candidates for another high-level position in the GHWB administration. The job of ambassador to Canada was of interest to Chuck, primarily because he had played a role in creating the United States-Canada Free Trade Agreement, and he has always had interest in NATO matters. Of course the fact that Chuck is not multi-lingual and Canada is primarily an English-speaking nation also made the post attractive. President Bush had promised that position to another colleague and told Chuck he would like him to be the ambassador to Iceland because it was also a NATO country and was strategically important to the United States. This was a logical fit for Chuck. Chuck accepted the honor to be the United States ambassador to Iceland. The language was no problem because nearly every Icelander speaks perfect English.

Our country was still fully engaged with the Union of Soviet Socialist Republics (USSR), Russia, in the Cold War in 1989 and we understood the importance of Iceland's strategic location. Iceland sits on the Mid-Atlantic Ridge, which juts up in the North Atlantic from the ocean floor. The sides of the range flow downward, like foothills do in mountains around the world. The USSR submarine fleet was forced to come close to Iceland because the Soviets' only warm water opening to the Atlantic was from its port in Murmansk. This meant NATO forces (with its large complement of United States forces) could monitor, from the air, from the sea, or from ground facilities in Iceland, all the Russian subs that came into the Atlantic Ocean. When we arrived in Reykjavik in the fall of 1989, the United States had several thousand troops at the NATO base in nearby Keflavik, while the USSR had nearly a hundred KGB operatives living in and around the Russian embassy, located just blocks from the United States ambassador's residence in Reykjavik. As most everyone knows, the KGB was the main intelligence/security agency for the Soviet Union from 1954 until its collapse.

With a United States Navy admiral in command, the US had an excellent position for submarine surveillance headquartered in Keflavik (today the location of Iceland's international airport). Admiral Tom Hall and his wife Barbara became close friends. We shared with them some of the most dramatic moments of post-World War II history. As United States ambassador, Chuck's primary assignment was to expand our military presence and to secure Iceland's permission for the United States to build an alternate airfield in the north of the country. He went diligently to work on that assignment, but within six weeks of our arrival, that assignment dramatically changed.

At the time of our arrival in Reykjavik, the Berlin Wall, constructed in 1961, continued to separate East and West Berlin. After several weeks of civil unrest and the erosion of its political power, on November 9, 1989, a radio commentator for the German Democratic Republic (GDR), the East German government, announced that all GDR citizens could visit West Berlin and West Germany. On that night of November 9th, we were in Reykjavik at the home of the Swedish ambassador enjoying the annual black tie dinner for all diplomats accredited to Iceland. In the midst of this event, seated at our tables in all our finery, we noticed one or two diplomats slip out to take phone calls, which was highly unusual at such a formal affair. Soon fellow diplomats began excusing themselves. Each one would get up, excuse him or herself from the table, then come back, excuse themselves from the dinner and race out the doors heading to their respective embassies. We all did. We were learning that 1,500 miles away, the few East Germans crossing through the gates had rapidly become thousands. The "Fall of the Berlin Wall" was underway. Chuck was in immediate and constant contact with Washington.

The next day, Admiral Hall proceeded with a pre-planned lunch at the NATO base for all ambassadors representing NATO countries. I was seated next to the West German ambassador, Hans Haverkamph, dean of the Diplomatic Corps. Protocol dictates at such luncheons that the host, in this case Admiral Hall, stands, raises a glass and welcomes guests to the meal. Later as the event concludes, the dean of the Diplomatic Corps stands to offer thanks to the host on behalf of all. When Hans, a friend and frequent tennis partner, got up to speak, his words spilled forth haltingly, but eloquently, his facial expression was spellbinding. He thanked each ambassador representing a NATO country and their country leaders personally, by name, including particularly the United States and the United States ambassador for their respective efforts to free East Germany during the long and dangerous Cold War. He thanked Admiral Hall for the beautiful lunch and as he sat down, no longer able to control his composure, turned to me and burst into tears. Sobbing, he said, "Sue, you have no idea what this means to us." Intellectually I understood some of the ramifications, but certainly not to the depth of the man sitting at my side. I gently held my hand on his arm until he could control his weeping.

The fall of the Berlin Wall was the first step in the reunification of Germany in 1990. Even more importantly, it expedited the break-up of the Soviet Union in 1991. Chuck and I had the opportunity within just a couple of weeks to walk freely into and out of East Germany through Checkpoint Charlie with several other United States ambassadors serving in Europe. What an incredible experience to observe the Berlin Wall, as both East and West Germans hammered away with their axes, picks, and farm tools, still in the process of tearing down the hated barrier. I have in my home in Coral Gables a piece of the wall that an East German soldier hacked from the wall and handed to me. It was a very dramatic period of our life. I certainly never imagined that a similarly seminal moment in world history would occur on the very day in the future that I, too, became a United States ambassador in a foreign country.

But in Iceland I was an ambassador's spouse. From a personal perspective I got along well with the Icelanders who love outdoor activities and admire athletes. They knew that almost every day I would go skiing or, even in bad weather, running. They also knew I was interested in the United States-

Iceland relationship. Until 1989 the leaders of the government of Iceland and many citizens were concerned about the large military presence at the NATO base from 1940 to, eventually, 2003. Although other foreign nations had troops serving at Keflavik, the base had an abundance of male United States military personnel known to greatly admire the beauty of Icelandic women. This occasionally led to tension between the Icelandic population and United States troops, but it was a shock to Iceland when just a few weeks after the fall of the Berlin Wall Washington made a big change in Chuck's assignment: from building troops and a new north east airport, to negotiating a smooth future exit for United States troops and all their equipment at the existing NATO base. The economic and security consequences for Iceland were obvious.

The history behind United States involvement in Iceland is interesting. Early in World War II the United States was not in the war. By the summer of 1940, Hitler had worked his way up into the Scandinavian countries and taken control in Denmark and Norway. Iceland was a Danish protectorate and though the Nazis occupied Denmark, they were prevented from taking over Iceland's strategic surveillance location because British troops were stationed on the island. In mid-1940, as the German siege of London began, the Brits remained defending Iceland while simultaneous trying to defend their own capital city with everything they had.

Although the United States was not engaged at that time, Prime Minister Churchill asked President Franklin Roosevelt to send troops into Iceland to protect that strategic location, allowing Churchill to withdraw his British troops to help defend London. Even though Senator Taft and other United States leaders disagreed, Roosevelt agreed. So in July 1941, prior to Pearl Harbor in December 1941, the United States recognized Iceland as an independent nation and sent in the United States military. To respect Denmark, Iceland only declared itself independent in 1944, so in essence, the United States recognized Iceland as an independent nation before Iceland officially recognized itself!

The history of these changing events fascinated us. Because the State Department held its European Bureau meetings in different cities on the Continent, we were also able to spend time visiting United States embassies in other European cities. Iceland had more or less one foot in the United States and one in Europe. That is both figuratively and literally true, because just a few miles from Reykjavik, the western side of the Eurasian tectonic plate and the eastern side of the North American tectonic plate meet and grind against each other. The two plates are separating at the rate of about two and a half centimeters or about an inch annually. There are places in this rift where a person can actually have one foot in North America and one in Europe. There are wider places you can ride through the rift with a thundering herd of horses (which I did). The geological phenomenon, which has created a huge tourist attraction, is in the area called Thingvieller where settlers, in the year 930 CE, created the first democratic parliament known to man.

Icelanders are remarkable people to have survived independently in the environment in which they did, north of 64 degrees latitude. Most people know that Iceland was first settled by Norwegian Vikings in the late 874 CE. Icelanders have over a 1,000-year history of literature partially due, perhaps, to very long cold and dark winter nights. A strong oral tradition naturally arose with poetry and prose developing over the years, including stories recorded in the famous series called "The Sagas," written in the tenth and eleventh centuries of the Common Era. History, writing, love of music and art forms remain very important and are reflected abundantly in Icelandic culture.

As the world began to study genetics and genetic connections with various diseases, Iceland came under exquisite scrutiny. Because of long isolation Iceland maintained a pure genetic pool for centuries, unlike many countries where people intermix and intermarry so that races and cultures become scrambled together. Not only was the gene pool not mixed, the Icelanders are arduous record keepers. Essentially from the time of the Settlement (874 CE) a record of every life and every death has been maintained, a goldmine for medical science.

Nor was their language compromised. A type of Old Norse, which is almost impossible to speak by outsiders, has been carefully preserved over centuries. Icelanders, it seemed to me, were naturally self-composed and somewhat suspicious of outsiders. They didn't want others to disturb their language, their customs, or their lives. People were discouraged from intermingling. While we were living there, there was virtually no immigration and no tourist industry. Over the years, few outsiders ventured to visit or settle in Iceland. Just when we were leaving Iceland in 1992 the country for the first time agreed to take immigrants, five Vietnamese refugee families. Now Iceland, still a country of only about 350,000 people, is more culturally diverse and has a sophisticated and dynamic tourism industry. Nonetheless there remains a large percentage of the population who would not even consider marrying anyone who is not Icelandic.

The patronymic system remains the norm. Everyone goes by first names, even the president and the prime minister. A child's first name is chosen from the approved list of first names, often that of the paternal grandparent or a relative's first name. For the last name the child always takes the father's first name and adds the Icelandic word for either son or daughter. For example, my father's name is "Benjamin" so his son's last name would be "Benjaminsson." As for Benjamin's daughter, my last name would be "Benjaminsdottir," and my first name from the approved Icelandic list. A common woman's name is "Guðrun." I might have been "Guðrun Benjaminsdottir." A woman seldom takes the name of a spouse. She would normally keep her last name and be addressed by her first name. In the end there are a multitude of identical names. There could be ten men named "Bjorn Heinricksson," so the Icelandic phone book lists everybody by their first name, but also with the occupation of the person and his or her address. If someone is looking for a particular Bjorn, he could distinguish him from the nine other Bjorns in the phone book through location and occupation. Nonetheless, it was a bit of a shock to us as American diplomats to have someone we had never met walk into our embassy and say, "Good evening Charles." "Hello Sue."

In diplomatic receiving lines, several people would have the same name. You could never tell who was married to whom, if in fact they were married at all, because wives have different names than their husbands. And Icelandic names are hard. They are long and use extra letters that we do not have in our alphabet. Chuck and I struggled to figure out who was who and how to say their names, using titles if we could, such as "Mr. Prime Minister." It was an unusual immersion into Icelandic culture, but we got used to it fairly quickly. We hired a tutor, but never conquered the language, we just learned common greetings and exchanges.

Of course, the embassy protocol officer was very helpful and we promptly put names and faces together of our most important contacts. The prime minister, elected while we were there, was Davíð Oddsson. He and his wife, Astridúr Thorarensen, became our very good friends along with other ministers with whom we have remained in touch. It was all business while we were in Reykjavik and diplomatically formal, not unlike my experience in Jamaica, but you do just naturally make friends with people of common values and common interests. We have several friends of whom we are very fond from our Iceland days, as well as from our Jamaican tour. We go to Iceland about every other year or our Icelandic friends come to visit us in the United States.

Icelandic children are well educated and those attending college stay in Iceland though some travel to the Scandinavian countries or Great Britain, and to a lesser degree, to the United States. Prior to our tenure and the disintegration of the Soviet Union, some Icelanders were educated in Russia, but that had become unpopular by the late '80s. The University of Iceland is a fine university with a superb medical school, producing many outstanding researchers and physicians. The country has an excellent health system. Although they were totally isolated for hundreds of years, and proud of it, as World War II ended and the Cold War evolved, Iceland became more involved with the rest of the world in every sense.

Icelanders have always depended on fish and the fishing industry to support a large part of their economy. To them, the worldwide ban on whale fishing was unfair because the whales around Iceland are minke whales, which aren't an endangered species, and Iceland relied on whales in a number of ways. Iceland joined with Japan against the rest of the world in the whaling disputes causing diplomatic feathers to ruffle.

From my perspective, a very special treat was to go salmon fishing. It is just unbelievably exciting to catch and bring in one of the large salmon abundant in Icelandic rivers. Even though very expensive, salmon fishing is a big sport and a beneficial export for the country. Farmers whose lands touch a river are paid enormous amounts of money by avid fishermen from around the world for access to the banks of the most productive rivers. And every year the salmon return from the sea.

Another unusual topographical feature are the natural hot springs and hot spots that abound around the country due to Iceland's volcanic origin. If you are chilly outside, you can go into a hot pond to warm up, which undoubtedly contributed to the survival of settlers in the early centuries. Pipelines under Reykjavik have harnessed hot sulfur underground streams to supply heat to all buildings in the city. Originally the sulfur smell remained, but that is no longer the case. The Blue Lagoon, a famous hot water attraction near the Keflavik airport, roughly thirty or forty minutes from the center of Reykjavik, is an internationally well-known high-end resort and for many, the highlight of a visit to Iceland.

Of course we had not foreseen the dramatic events of the Berlin Wall that transpired, nor did we understand the beauties of the country to which he was assigned when Chuck was confirmed by the United States Senate as ambassador to Iceland. We left Miami in September 1989 and home became the United States Chief of Mission (CMR) official residence in Reykjavik, in this case directly attached to the United States Embassy. Most CMR residences are not in the same location as the Chancery (the ambassador's offices), let alone attached. This oddly was of high value to me. Chuck's commute consisted of opening a door on the second floor of our home and walking into the Embassy. I, too, enjoyed that liberty, but within about six months a new RSO (regional security officer) assigned to Reykjavik by the State Department said that since I did not have security clearance I had to go downstairs, outside, through the public entrance to the Embassy, and present my passport to the Marine Security Guards. I guess the RSO thought I was a big security threat to the United States.

Another benefit of the proximity was that Chuck arranged to have a high percentage of his diplomatic duties accomplished at the residence over lunch, not at dinners as is often the case.

This allowed Chuck and me to frequently enjoy quiet, private dinners together in our home. Since I was deemed to be such a security risk, I assured the RSO I would not even be in the house when these diplomatic lunches took place. I'm quite sure he checked up on me. Instead, I enjoyed a long run around the city, or I'd go out of town for cross-country skiing. Sometimes I'd drive to a nearby ski area for alpine skiing, but Atlantic Ocean winds often made wind-drift snow conditions icy and uneven and the runs uncomfortable and not infrequently, intimidating.

Another new experience was having Thanksgiving without our two sons that first November in Iceland in 1989. They felt the absence, too, and Chris wrote a long and thoughtful letter in which he reflected on my return from Everest and expressed his love and gratitude to his father and me for opportunities he'd had along the way. The following summer Chris and Toby, accompanied by two guests, came to visit us in Reykjavik and for the first time we met the two young women who were to become our daughters-in-law. We really challenged them. I didn't mean to do this, but I just naturally thought everyone would want to ride the Icelandic horses, go climb a glacier, and ski down it, so that's what I planned for our first day. I couldn't help that it rained that day as we rode up the waterfall trail to the glacier or that, bad luck, the rain turned to sleet. Our skis had already been taken by the guides to the top of the glacier so we quickly (more or less) got off our dripping horses, got into the skis and plunged down the mountain. I admit the visibility was poor on the unbroken snow with no trail for guidance. The girls were good sports and have been ever since. I learned only later that one of my sons got an ear full because his girlfriend had never ridden a horse and never skied before – but she did it. It's amazing that she married him! I was smart enough to figure out that our second day together probably shouldn't be to go scuba diving in a special place in the Thingvieller rift, even if we would have been among the first to ever do it!

As the ambassador's spouse, it was expected that I would manage the residence and frequently entertain large numbers of people. I wanted to be a supportive spouse, but when Chuck and I visited United States Ambassador Marc Grossman in Turkey a year or so earlier, he was not accompanied by his wife. I asked him how the entertainment and household chores got done, to which he replied, "Oh, the State Department has people at every Embassy that handle those matters." "Ah-ha," I thought and quickly requested that Ambassador Cobb make it known to the State Department that he would be an "unaccompanied" ambassador, greatly reducing expectations that there would be a diligent housewife at the United States residence. That worked out very well for me.

The truth was that since a United States government official at the level of ambassador has to forgo all business activities, I became the *de facto* head of all Cobb business enterprises, so that except for my daily hour or two of exercise, I spent a great deal of time in the office I created on the third floor in the residence. It was adjacent to the gym I organized in what used to be a guest room. After all, in mid-winter at peak twenty-two hours of darkness, I wasn't exactly going to go cross-country skiing or running the streets of Reykjavik.

The role of women in Iceland and the country's societal norms differed from the United States. Women were quite powerful in business and cultural activities and became so in politics when Vigdís Finnbogadóttir was elected president in 1980. Families were very close, and it was not uncommon at all for a sixteen-year-old to have a baby and stay with her family so the child would grow up with the mother and her parents. That was perfectly normal and probably descended from years in the past when there were isolated farms, or small farming communities around the periphery of the island with very little travel, the entire interior of the country being glaciated. So, children stayed in the warm heart of their family. Moreover, there was absolutely nothing unusual about having a child out of wedlock. In the days when I grew up in America that would have been very much looked down on, but not Iceland. As women matured, they worked outside the home, rather unusual in America until perhaps the Depression.

Vigdís Finnbogadóttir was president of Iceland while we lived there and for a total of sixteen years. As Icelanders always go by first names, the president was commonly called "Vigdís." In the late '70s Vigdís headed the National Theater Company. Music, dance, acting, all forms of individual and collective cultural activities were important elements of society. All could be done from youth to old age in a cold and/or dark environment. As the powerful head of the National Theater Company, Vigdís felt that Icelandic women, while they were working and taking care of their families, were not receiving the credit that they deserved from the men in the country. In her view, men undervalued women's work. So Vigdís organized a strike of the women in Iceland, saying simply, "Don't go to work on the date set for the strike, whether it's in your home, in a business, or on the farm, just simply don't do anything." Predictably, the strike resulted in a complete halt of all business and normal routines in the country to the great discomfort of fathers, sons, and husbands. For Vigdís, this proved to be a successful endeavor. She was drafted to run for president in the 1980 election and she won, becoming the first female president of Iceland and the first female elected head of state in the world. She was a virtuous leader, stepping down only in 1996.

We didn't get many well-known official United States government visitors in Iceland in those days, but we did have Vaclav Havel, president of Czechoslovakia and first president of the Czech Republic, en route to meet President George H. W. Bush in Washington, DC. President Havel was accompanied by Ambassador Shirley Temple Black. Havel had just been released from prison when he was elected in 1989. He stopped by Reykjavik because Iceland's National Theatre was staging a play that Havel had written while in prison. He had never seen it, so he accepted President Vigdís's invitation to stay one night in Reykjavik. When the president of a country travels to the United States to visit our president, the ambassador always accompanies, so Ambassador Black came along and stayed with us at the United States residence while Havel stayed at the president's residence.

Havel was impressive on the strength of his character and writings, but not necessarily as the president of a country. He had not grown into that stature yet and had been out of the gulag for less than a year. He was almost – meek is not the right word – shy is not the right word, but quiet and observing.

Shirley Temple Black, on the other hand, was a powerful force, a force of nature, sweeping through the country. She was not the sweet little, curly haired Shirley Temple that we knew from the movies. She was a hardened, hard core, acclaimed personality who knew who she was and what she needed to do. She knew she was idealized and revered. She didn't care much about maintaining any kind of veneer at all about that obvious self-knowledge. She simply didn't suffer fools or servants well.

I'm sure, under different circumstances, we could have had an enjoyable conversation and she would have been a joy to meet, but here she was accompanying the president of the country to which she was posted, whom she barely knew, and she was taking him to the United States president. It felt as if she resented the fact that she had to stop in Iceland because President Havel wanted to see his play. Of course, she didn't understand Iceland, or the people, or care about that component at all. To add to her obvious dissatisfaction, it was a miserably cold, snowy, windy night. She didn't like that either. She didn't like the fact that she had to walk from her car, about ten yards to the opera house entrance. It wasn't that she said anything. However, it was very clear. I would say she did not make a favorable impression on her hosts, or to the best of my knowledge, on the Icelanders whom she met. In her defense, she did treat President Havel properly and with respect, but we didn't see them much. We sat together, but they didn't talk. They didn't chat. They arrived. We had a cocktail. We rushed off to the play. Then she wanted to rush home, get to bed as quickly as possible so she did not attend a small Icelandic reception. They left the next morning. Meanwhile, President Havel and his play were well received. I know he was pleased. And that seemed most important to me.

In December and January Reykjavik has little daylight, as little as two hours and, if cloudy, none at all. But in June and July, during the summertime, there are more than twenty-two hours of light. Getting used to that big swing wasn't terribly hard, but it was odd for us. We observed that Icelanders would have dinner at their routine time in the evening, then they'd go out, play tennis, go swimming, or to one of the many local taverns. We followed suit and became accustomed to the patterns of the Northern Hemisphere.

One summer night after dinner Chuck said, "Let's just go take a walk." It was maybe 9:30 or 10:00. We did not have personal guards as I had later in Jamaica, so we roamed freely anywhere and felt no danger whatsoever. As we walked toward the harbor, about four blocks from our residence, we saw two quite large Soviet military vessels moored at the city docks. Chuck knew they had come in. We walked nearby and Chuck said, "Let's go over and talk to them." There was a young officer standing at the foot of the gangplank, so my husband said, "I am the ambassador of the United States and we would like to see your ship." The young man was flustered but knew enough English to respond, "Wait a moment please." He went up the gangplank and came back with a higher-level English-speaking officer who said he'd be pleased to welcome us aboard. They showed us everything on every deck, including their mapping room equipped to map the ocean floor.

We muffled our surprise. They did not appear to be hiding anything or guiding us to avoid any areas. We walked into the mapping room as machines were spitting out bright colored graphs with great delineation, showing the bottom of the ocean floor – the rises and falls – indicating distances from the bottom of the ocean – and displaying many other measurements. The graphs were actually pretty, intriguing in a modern art sort of way, and I said something like that to the officer in charge. "Well here," he replied, as he ripped off a three-foot piece of map and handed it to me, "Why don't you take this as a souvenir?" He gave me two printed maps. I rolled them up thinking, "I can frame these when I get home. What a good souvenir of Iceland during the Cold War!" Chuck and I genuinely enjoyed the visit and trotted off to our residence, maps under arms.

The next morning at 7:00 my phone rang. The embassy political officer was looking for me. I did not know at the time that the political officer also wore another hat. Nobody was supposed to know his other activities on behalf of our government. "Mrs. Cobb, some of our people noticed that you went aboard the Soviet ship last night." Unbeknownst to us, the United States had "eyes on" us the entire previous evening. Our people were watching us. He continued, "We noticed that you came out with some papers in your hand and we're interested in seeing what the papers are."

I said, "Oh?"

He said, "What do you think they are?"

"Well they are maps of the ocean floor that the Soviets were printing."

He said, "We must see those."

I said, "You can see them but I'm not giving them to you." Frankly, I was afraid I wouldn't get them back. Finally, he talked me into letting somebody come over and take them to the embassy. That was the end of that. I never saw them again. No colorful framed ocean floor souvenirs for me!

Displaying my naiveté, the oddest part of that evening I thought was that our people – not the KGB – were watching us, (well, the KGB was too). But even knowing the KGB was watching, the Russian officers let us aboard the ship without hesitation. This was a strange feeling. I wondered what else our own people watched the ambassador and his wife doing. Later I came to know the answer: everything.

I have been asked how my husband felt about being ambassador to Iceland. No one I know who is plucked from their normal life and asked to represent their country abroad has come back and said, "That was a terrible experience. I would never do it again." What most of us feel is that it is a truly great honor. It's extremely educational, it can be fun, and it can be stressful. It is certainly a huge responsibility. Most of us 'draftees' genuinely try our level best to do a good job in displaying our representative democracy, our values, and the policies of the elected administration in which we are engaged. And most love the challenges of the job. Chuck and I certainly did.

We had fascinating and educational experiences while living in Iceland and traveling in Europe. Chuck relates many of these in a great chapter in his 2005 book, *A Letter of a Grandfather on his 'Lessons Learned'*.

We left Iceland in early 1992 with very fond memories and several lifelong friends. As a gesture of appreciation to the wonderful people of Iceland and in celebration of the fiftieth anniversary of Icelandic-American diplomatic relations, we commissioned Iceland's best sculptor, Petúr Bjarnason, to do a bronze sculpture for a prominent site on the Reykjavik waterfront. Petúr's elegant fifteen-foot-high bronze called "Partnership" sits on pillars of Icelandic and American granite beside the bay near Höfdi House where Ronald Reagan and Mikhail Gorbachev met in 1986. Chuck and I liked the sculpture so much we talked Petúr into coming to Florida to do a replica for the new home we were building on Biscayne Bay in Coral Gables. The two partnership sculptures – one in Iceland and one in America – are forever connected by the endless flow of the warm waters of the Gulf Stream.

I had wanted a record, really for his dad, of Chuck being a United States ambassador. One night in Iceland, when we had to go to a very formal, diplomatic function, he was adorned in white tie and tails, and I was dressed in the nicest dress I could pull out of the closet. A well-known photographer took pictures of us at the residence. Then I decided we should have a portrait done by Iceland's finest portrait artist. Vigdís recommended the acclaimed Erikur Smith, who agreed for some not too outrageous sum to do a portrait of us in the same clothes we wore the night of the photograph. Of course, we took that portrait home to Florida when we left Iceland.

Later Vigdís came for a visit. Staying at our house in Coral Gables and coming upon Erikur's portrait she admonished my husband: "Ambassador, I'm so disappointed you're not wearing the honors that I gave you." The Order of the Falcon Grand Cross Knight is the highest award that could be given by the nation to a non-citizen of Iceland. The honor comes replete with a large sash and cuffs in Iceland's colors (red, white, and blue) and a couple of diplomatic decorations (fancy wearable medals). Before Chuck could respond, Vigdís said, "I'm going to call Erikur Smith right this minute and tell him he must come to Miami and put the decorations on your portrait." Chuck tried to explain that Erikur had done the portrait before she "knighted" him. He ended up just saying "Okay."

Erikur happens to be a golfer and was excited to come to Miami. He came, stayed at our house for two weeks, played golf, and painted all the regalia onto Chuck's portrait. About a year and a half later, I was getting phone calls at my office downtown, "Foreign Minister Benedict Ärneson is calling for you." I told our staff, "That call is not for me. It is for Chuck." He called three times trying to reach me. Each time, I told my assistant to give the message to Chuck. Finally, she said, "Well, he's getting really disturbed because he wants to talk to you not to Chuck!" I said: "Transfer him in." How embarrassing. He was calling to tell me that President Vigdís was conferring on me an Icelandic Honor, a lower level of the Order of the Falcon. That meant another call to Erikur Smith who was delighted to come back, play two more weeks of golf, and put the decorative medals onto my gown in our portrait.

I was just my normal self in Iceland, there to support my husband. I did most of the things that an ambassador's spouse was supposed to do except as mentioned earlier. I had my regular workdays, managing Cobb Partners' assets and pursuing outdoor pleasures. I was available for every diplomatic function that was necessary. It is appreciated when visitors like the country in which they are staying, and it was clear I liked Iceland. I did not expect to get rewarded for that. I really didn't deserve an honor for what I did in Iceland, but I was assured by the foreign minister that I was an "excellent representative of the United States."

It was the summer of 1993 when Vigdís was our guest in our Coral Gables home. We had planned a private lunch at the house when my son Toby and his wife Luisa called and asked to join the luncheon. Of course, we said fine. They came to tell us that we were going to be first-time grandparents. Luis Eduardo Cobb was born January 12, 1994. During the conversation over lunch, Vigdís dictated that we must use the Icelandic names for grandfather and grandmother, which are Afi and Amma with, of course, our first names. We had a little discussion. I thought Amma was too close to Mama. We finally settled on Afi Chuck and Ami Sue. And that's what our seven grandchildren and many of their friends have called us for years: Afi Chuck and Ami Sue.

I recall that as we were preparing to leave Iceland, Chuck and I discussed how very honored we felt, and humbled, to have been granted the privilege of representing the United States of America. We were grateful for the opportunity, for the education we received on the conduct of US foreign policy, on relationships with our European allies, and our introduction to a unique and beautiful country and its people. In addition to the "Partnership" sculpture dedicated to Iceland, Chuck also wanted to recognize those we had come to know as the hardworking Foreign Service officers (FSOs) of the United States State Department. In Washington on farewell rounds, Chuck met with then secretary of state Larry Eagleburger. They reached agreement on an annual State Department Award for the most outstanding career Foreign Service officer worldwide in the realm of economics and trade. The Charles E. Cobb Award for Initiative and Success in Trade Development has been awarded annually since 1993. The award is accompanied by a substantial monetary component for the successful officer and is highly prized within the State Department.

Chuck loved working for the honorable, self-effacing George H. W. Bush. We became close friends of George and Barbara Bush and shared many experiences with them over the years.

In 2018 the greatly admired George Herbert Walker Bush and Barbara Pierce Bush – as we used to say out West – departed for greener pastures. As I mentioned, Chuck and I traveled to Houston in April to bid Barbara a fond farewell and to the State Funeral at the National Cathedral in Washington for the glorious earthly departure of our forty-first president. We were fortunate to have them in our lives as steady, moral, humble servants of God and of our country.

It has been said that George H. W. Bush's greatest ambition was to be the best husband, father, and grandfather that he could be. That would also be Chuck Cobb's greatest ambition and I believe he has attained that goal magnificently. He likes to tell his grandchildren:

> *Never, never, never give up; give thanks to God each day for all your blessings; have fun, laugh, and work hard, and don't forget to apply your sunscreen.*

Chapter Nine

*There is no definition of a successful life that does not include
service to others.*

George Herbert Walker Bush

THE NINETIES:
HOME IN CORAL GABLES,
BECOMING AN INTELLECTUAL
PROPERTY ATTORNEY

Along the way Chuck and I acquired a lovely vacant lot on an island in Biscayne Bay, just south of Miami's Coconut Grove. It was to become a private community called Tahiti Beach. Arvida was the developer of the large community of Cocoplum and the separate private island of Tahiti Beach. Andres Duany and Elizabeth Plater-Zyberk, highly regarded architects for whom our older son Christian worked after architecture school, began drawings for our home which was to sit on a peninsula jutting into the bay. Chuck and I didn't know at the time that we would soon be living in Iceland. We decided to just keep moving forward with the house while we were in Reykjavik even though we wouldn't be nearby to oversee the project. That was a decision we might not have taken had Chris not been an intern with the Duany Plater-Zyberk architecture firm. Chris knew our interests in quality and function and, of course, knew our tastes. He was tremendously helpful in representing us during the entire process of designing and building our home and had a dramatically positive impact on the finished product. Even now when I stop to actually look at our home or some part of it, I think of my son Chris.

But I have to give full credit to Chuck whose vision for our own home was informed by his years of creating resort communities while heading Arvida Corporation. Chuck's career is well documented by the late renowned landscape architect Kalvin Platt in *Master-Planned Communities: Lessons Learned from the Developments of Chuck Cobb*, published by the Urban Land Institute in 2011.

We returned home from Iceland in 1992, moved into our beautiful new home on Biscayne Bay, and soon were faced with Hurricane Andrew, a vicious category 5 Atlantic hurricane. Winds up to 165 mph hit the Florida coast immediately to our south. It was the strongest and most destructive hurricane to come ashore in Florida in several decades. Chuck and I rode out the storm in an interior closet of our former home in Snapper Creek Lakes, inland a few miles south of Tahiti Beach. Chris stayed at our Tahiti Beach house on Biscayne Bay and later declared himself to have been "scared to death." Our bay front property had a twelve-foot storm surge while winds ripped off a portion of the roof allowing hurricane force winds to circulate fiercely and freely throughout the house. Although the basic structure did not fail, the whole interior was soddened and trashed and the recently installed landscape completely gone. The storm surge in Biscayne Bay had a high of thirteen-feet, pummeling its way so far inland that Chris said when he looked out from the third-floor window the night of the storm he felt he was adrift on the Titanic death trap in the middle of the Atlantic Ocean.

We were unable to live in our new house for almost a year. After helping neighbors and organizing federal help for South Florida, Chuck and I began to reintegrate into South Florida life. During the following decade we spent most of our time in three areas: private sector businesses; charitable and civic engagements; and state and federal governance matters. Chuck became chairman of the board of trustees of the University of Miami. I took over as president of Cobb Family Foundation and re-engaged with other philanthropic organizations in which I had a strong interest.

We also re-engaged with the real estate and resort development worlds, expanding our interests and investments from coast to coast. For me, there were too many interesting things going on to return to Greenberg Traurig. Anyway I had learned that once you become a lawyer, whether you want to or not, you practice law every day.

During 1992 Chuck obtained, among other things, all the remaining intellectual property assets of the bankrupt Pan American World Airway aka Pan Am. Suddenly, Cobb Partners had approximately 450 valuable worldwide trademarks. Cobb Partners did not have an intellectual property attorney who could manage these new assets, so quite unexpectedly I became an intellectual property rights attorney. The obvious first move for me was to hire a firm that had experience in this field and represented other large companies around the world. I located such a firm in New York and could easily work from our offices in Coral Gables with our New York firm. Becoming educated in this new field, I could rely on outside counsel as necessary. I monitored all the marks worldwide, tracking everyone to make sure that we were legally protecting important assets and not wasting money on others. The Pan Am logo and trademarks were valuable because of Pan Am's history and the length of time and breadth of their use over the years all around the world. We had no intention of trying to restart or create an airline. The concept that we had in mind when we purchased those assets was one of leveraging the well-known Pan Am name by branding another type of popular, marketable product, possibly a travel product, but not necessarily.

One idea was to gather together a group of small airlines to be called the Pan Am Alliance, with the goal of providing a smooth feeder system from smaller countries and smaller towns to access major airline hubs in New York, Boston, and Miami. Other major cities on the East Coast could be added as demand warranted. With the Pan Am name, we did not want to acquire airplanes, a notoriously difficult business to operate. However, as we were building the Alliance we were approached by the owners of the recently bankrupt Eastern Airlines. Eastern's newest owners did have airplanes and were interested in being in the airline business. They coveted our Pan Am trademarks as well as the Pan Am reservation system we had also acquired. Eastern had gained experienced airline personnel and a built-in management team. They wanted to join the assets of both companies to create a new Pan American Airline. We agreed to merge and on the insistence of our investors, Chuck was named chairman of the new Pan Am. There was a great deal of excitement on the launch of the new Pan Am, particularly from former employees of the two bankrupt airlines. We soon learned that while Eastern brought along their key managers, they were not very good at management. In relatively short order, they too, went into bankruptcy and all the Pan Am assets (including my vigilantly protected trademarks) went with them.

Meanwhile I was devoting attention to our property in Telluride (what that really means is I was skiing a lot). Chuck would come out to ski, but he gravitated to the business side rather than skiing and became an owner and a board member of Telluride's ski company.

The founder and CEO of Telluride, Ron Allred and his wife, Joyce, became and remain very close friends. With a group of partners, including Ron and Joyce, we then purchased Kirkwood, a ski resort with valuable property near Lake Tahoe ornia, followed by the acquisition of Purgatory, a well-positioned ski resort near Durango, Colorado, which we re-named Durango Mountain Resort. From a business perspective, ski resorts are like golf resorts: there is a central amenity in a beautiful location around which people congregate in hotels or condominiums and many buy homes. Our company's interest and expertise was in master planning and developing the real estate surrounding such resorts. The actual operation of ski resorts is just like farming. As our friend Ron Allred says: "Ski resorts are capital intensive, labor intensive, and weather dependent." Telluride, Kirkwood, and Durango Mountain Resort provided interesting business challenges and great skiing opportunities.

The business of skiing took us to a number of ski resorts around the world. Our intent wasn't the pleasure of skiing but to learn about different approaches to ski management and equipment variations. (Ski lifts cost a lot of money, so it's good to get that part right.) In August 1997 Ron suggested that Chuck and I join him and Joyce with our mutual dear friend Mickey Salloway, on a trip to Australia and New Zealand to investigate resorts where many US ski team members trained during the North American summer months. We visited two well-known resorts in Australia, as well as a friend's huge sheep ranch. At the resorts we met the managers, viewed the processes and skied just an hour or two at each. I had had a bad ski accident late March in Telluride in which I ruptured every ligament in my left knee. Surgery was delayed for a month because my orthopedic surgeon was on vacation in New Zealand, but all were repaired (or replaced) before our trip. I was able to ski in Australia and New Zealand but obviously very cautiously.

When we got to Queensland, New Zealand, Chuck, Ron, and Joyce set aside a day to play golf. I do not play golf, so I decided to drop them off and take a solo drive (Mickey had not been able to join us) around the area. On arrival in Queensland we had happened to drive by the Kawarau Bridge, the world's first bungee jumping site. I was curious about that experience and intended to check it out, but I didn't say anything to our group, because they were going to be busy with their golf. That first night at the hotel I faxed a question to my orthopedic doctor in Miami, whom, by then, I knew had recently done the Kawarau Bridge bungee jump. After he returned from his vacation in New Zealand, he replaced the ACL, MCL, and LCL in my left knee. "Dr. Uribe, what do you think...it's been almost eight weeks since my surgery?" Amazingly he faxed back. "This will not hurt your knee." Unbeknownst to me, at the hotel Chuck had intercepted my doctor's return fax. At breakfast the next morning he said, "You're not going to do that jump, are you?" My secret plot unraveled. Happily, Ron thought it was just a great idea and promptly canceled the golf game. Chuck and Joyce definitely did not want to do a bungee jump but off we went to the Kawarau Bridge. Chuck decided that if Ron insisted on doing it, he had to do it. Joyce would do a video. Chuck and Ron trotted off to buy our tickets. When they came back, they were laughing. We had just celebrated my sixtieth birthday a day or two earlier and the ticket revealed that for bungee jumping I got my first ever senior citizen discount!

Bungee jumping is the biggest adrenaline rush I've ever experienced, before or since. Later, when we showed our bungee video at a party in Telluride, a vote was taken by a group of friends as to who had the best style. When the votes were counted, I barely beat Ron, which really wasn't fair because he had a gorgeous swan dive. However, General Norman Schwarzkopf had swayed some votes in my direction by declaring that I must get additional credit for my "initiative and execution of the plan."

As we moved through the '90s, Chuck returned to the investment and finance world in which he started his business life after graduating from the Stanford Business School.

I, on the other hand, by the mid-'90s had been out of Greenberg Traurig for over ten years. The firm had been a wonderful place for me to practice law, but life had evolved. I will always be grateful for the education and the friendships I gained from my time at the firm. I was proud of the Public Finance Department I helped to build. I made lifelong friends both at UM Law School and at the firm. My life would not be the same without the friendships of Dorothy and David Weaver; Marcia Bailey Dunn; Cristina Morales Moreno and her husband, The Honorable Federico Moreno; Mel Greenberg; Bob Traurig; Larry Hoffman; Cesar Alvarez; Marlene Silverman; Raquel ("Rocky") Rodriguez; their spouses; and their families.

The '90s also offered time to reflect on my life and my family. Chuck and I had been married over thirty years. Our sons had graduated from college and both obtained MBAs. They were gainfully employed and on the verge of getting married. Life continued to evolve, possibly with a little more purposeful reflection.

Other than Chuck, my two boys have been the joy of my life. It was not because of athletic goals that I have purposely stayed fit for most of my life. It is because I wanted to do everything my boys were doing. I wanted to be with them all the time. I was a pretty worthy companion in most pursuits, until they hit about the eighth or ninth grade. Then, as anticipated, they suddenly became more interested in their school friends and much younger female companionship. Darn! But naturally no one would want it any other way.

Many years later, Toby expressed our relationship this way:

> One of the things that was very special for me is I loved to snow ski when I was very young and I was a capable, competitive skier.

Actually, I was a real hot shot at twelve and thirteen and I could really shred it. I loved that. And I had this mother who was thirty-five or forty and still better than me and who would still push me. It was extraordinary. I definitely loved the years we skied together – skiing hard, skiing the bumps, skiing the trees. That was a very special period with my mom. Those were fun years and – wouldn't you know – she can still ski the black diamond runs.

My mother was tough, rather stoic and had extraordinary discipline. However, she has an almost unknown silly side to her. She would give me "wet-willies." That's when you lick your pinky finger and stick it in somebody's ear. But all along, for me, she was just my Mommy. She was always a loving, caring, concerned mother and I never felt as though my mother was any less available than any of the other kids' mothers. So her life and her progression really was kind of a model of a modern woman in the sense that when it was expected of her she would be a house mom – a stay at home mom. Then as the world changed and expectations were for women to work and to become professionals and have their own pursuits, she did. I think she's unique.

She's unique in her time and a lot of people recognized that. I think it was one of the reasons she was so sought after for the positions and boards that she served on and still serves on to this day. To attain the success that my mother attained is impressive, but to have done it and still executed the responsibilities of Mommy, and simultaneously be a successful athlete and professional throughout the years is extraordinary. I know it enhanced strong bonding relationships between mother and sons.

Tobin Templeton Cobb, September 23, 2017

I am not an overtly religious person, but I am of the Christian faith. One of the reasons is because a loving God brought me together with Chuck Cobb at an age when I would not have had the wisdom to make such a choice. He is my partner in life and forever. In February 2019 we enjoyed our sixtieth wedding anniversary. Reading this far you will know that we each have done epic projects independently, but always rushed back together.

Chuck is ambitious, competitive, and assertive, no doubt, but he also is very caring and has an admirable, unyielding moral compass. He is a superb leader and team builder, which manifested itself in corporate affairs, in government positions, and within our family. He is exceedingly direct, which sometimes hurts, but he never intends to harm. Rather he wants everyone to be their best selves. Sometimes that was hard on me, and I am sure, on our sons and grandchildren. Though what I learned was that at his urging, we did become better selves. I admire, respect, and love Chuck Cobb. I am grateful to him and I am grateful God has supported us and provided two sons and seven grandchildren. I am grateful that our boys brought Kolleen Pasternack Cobb, Chris's wife, and Luisa Salazar Cobb, Toby's wife, into our lives. Both came accompanied by their extremely gifted parents and very large, wonderful extended families. No mother could be more proud of her two sons, their spouses, and the nearly perfect seven grandchildren with whom we are blessed.

Toby's wife Luisa's family hails from Cuba, and in the mid-'90s, in short order we gained three half-Cuban grandsons: Luis Eduardo Cobb (1994), Charles Edward Cobb (1996), and Sebastian Griffin Cobb (1999). Our son Chris and his wife Kolleen presented Frederick Todd McCourt Cobb (1995), Nicholas Ruschmeyer Cobb (1997), Cassidy Elizabeth Cobb (2000), and Benjamin Pasternack Cobb (2002). No greater gifts could we have received. We did not know it at the time, but the most satisfying roles for the rest of our lives would be that of grandparents.

Nonetheless, getting re-engaged in politics and government also captivated us during the '90s. In 1993, Jeb Bush and George W. Bush were both in gubernatorial campaigns for the 1994 elections; Jeb in Florida and George in Texas. Barbara and George H. W. Bush chose to be in Florida to watch the '94 election returns, and that night Chuck and I were sitting with them on a hotel sofa in downtown Miami as the returns came in from both state elections. George won his election in Texas. Unfortunately, Jeb lost to the then sitting Florida governor Lawton Chiles by a small margin. It was an emotional night as George and Barbara Bush were elated to have son George elected governor of Texas but depressed to have son Jeb lose such a close race in Florida. That night was special to me though, because it was the catalyst for a long, warm friendship with Barbara Bush.

This is a real digression, but I will tell you the funniest thing that happened to me with Barbara. As a newly minted former ambassador, I was in Washington for a meeting and was invited to a Republican event in Kennebunkport, Maine. There was to be a big lobster dinner, preceded by a reception for a small number of people invited to visit the senior Bushes at their home at Walker's Point. At the reception, Barbara and I were sitting on the patio wall with our backs to the ocean. Another woman was on the other side of Barbara. We were just sitting there chatting, but I had not stopped for lunch, so I was very hungry. I was watching the kitchen door from which hors d'oeuvres were emerging. One server came out but went in the other direction. I was trying to see what was on the tray but couldn't quite make it out. I was thinking to myself that if there is something really, really good, I'm going to take it; otherwise I'm going to wait for the lobster dinner. A second server arrived and offered her tray to Barbara first, then moved the tray in front of me. It contained a pretty unappealing cheese puff thing. I was still thinking through this whole process as I looked at the server and declared my decision, "I can live without that."

Barbara turned to me and stated loudly and emphatically, "Ambassador, a simple 'no thank you' will do." If I hadn't known her, I would have fallen off the seawall in embarrassment. Later, as I was seated to Barbara's right at the big lobster dinner, I knew she was not really upset with me. Not long after that I ran into Jeb and told him the story. His response was not sympathetic. He said: "Well, now you see what I grew up with." I also told my two sons because it was sort of ridiculous for a person trained in protocol to say what I had said to the server. It was hilariously stupid, but I did tell the boys, and still hear it back from them at every opportunity…"a simple no thank you will do."

Despite our active business lives, neither Chuck nor I have ever let our interest in philanthropy and civic activities be diminished, nor our interest in international relations and geopolitical matters wane. The full extent of our philanthropy in the '90s included one or the other of us serving on the boards of the United Way of Greater Miami and the Keys, Goodwill Industries, Metro Zoo, the Orange Bowl Committee, Florida Council of 100, the American Red Cross, the University of Miami, the Miami Heart Institute, and various other health, education, museums, and historical societies. I was honored when the American Red Cross in 2001 gave me their Humanitarian of the Year Award.

Chuck founded the second ever charter school in the Miami area, and the Cobb Family Foundation was heavily involved in supporting all kinds of education – from early childhood education to sports programs for underprivileged youths, to literacy programs, to colleges and universities around the country. We also continued to travel a great deal. As the '90s was coming to an end, Jeb Bush was again in the news as the potential new governor of Florida.

Chapter Ten

Education is the most powerful tool
you can use to change the world.

Nelson Mandela

STATE GOVERNMENT: SECRETARY OF THE LOTTERY, FUNDING EDUCATION IN FLORIDA

We knew Jeb Bush well. He and his wife Columba lived in Miami and Jeb was active in business and civic affairs. He ran for Florida governor in 1994 and lost in a very close race. He decided to run again in 1998. Chuck and I became engaged in this campaign. Florida gubernatorial candidates must pick a lieutenant governor running mate prior to the election. Typically, this is seen as the first view of a candidate's policy orientation, character, and judgment evidencing what his or her future positions might be and what kind of leadership he or she will provide. Thus, the selection of who runs on the ticket as lieutenant governor is a critical decision. Everybody watches closely for that announcement.

I was not yet a part of Jeb's campaign team and had no early involvement. I do not think I had given any money to the campaign, but in late 1997 Jeb called me out of the blue to ask if he could come over to my house to see me. That seemed unusual, so I suggested stopping by his office instead. "No, I want to talk to you privately," he replied. He came to discuss a clandestine assignment that he wished for me to undertake. Nothing sinister, but intriguing work relating to picking his potential lieutenant governor and others he might view for future cabinet appointments. Jeb called me "Secret Squirrel." He was requesting that I help with the final vetting of the small group of candidates whom he was considering for lieutenant governor. This was a short list of high-profile people in our state – businessmen and women, government leaders, and senators – proven leaders whom he felt would be aligned with his policy goals. He planned to use a questionnaire based on that of his father. President George Herbert Walker Bush's questionnaire had eighty-eight specific questions for high-level candidates. It was thorough. I think Jeb also remembered Ronald Reagan's famous words: "Trust but verify."

Those who reached Jeb's top ten faced the onerous questionnaire and also had to provide ten years of tax returns and submit to a final private interview. I knew about half of those selected for the full vetting, but none of them well. The idea being that after all the questionnaire responses are read, after all tax returns are analyzed, one last person sits down with the individuals who have survived scrutiny for a final interview and a final chance to reveal any undisclosed potential problems. Essentially a forum for the interviewer to say: "Tell us what you haven't told us. If you tell us now about bones in the closet that could become public, we can be prepared. We can help you resolve issues if we are aware of them. However, if you don't tell us and a public issue arises, you're on your own. We can't help you. You will be out of the administration the same day."

Almost everybody has something they would rather not discuss with a stranger or have publicized. As Secret Squirrel I pledged not to make such matters public unless it became public from a third-party source. But we explained that if we were already aware of an issue, we would figure out a way to try to help ease the circumstances if it did become public.

I can be extremely serious, and I was definitely serious in the presence of these candidates. Most, not all, admitted something they would rather not have talked about, but they were actions or events that could be expected in the course of a human life. One had an affair with another public figure. One person had cheated on his income tax one year. One had a long ago, but undisclosed, arrest, others had done this or that...all different things that human beings do.

My part of the vetting process was very personal. In the end, I felt that I got a good sense of each candidate to the extent they were candid with me. Jeb initially selected a person who was already serving in state government and appeared to have been candid in our interview. Jeb's chief of staff and his team did a parallel investigation inside that person's agency. Jeb named the person as his likely running mate. Within two weeks, a disclosure arose within the agency concerning a matter in which that person was allegedly involved, that, if found to be true, would be automatically disqualifying. Jeb knew the suspicious matter had not been revealed to me and immediately cut that candidate.

The final selection to run as Jeb's lieutenant governor was Frank Brogan, Florida's secretary of education, who had teaching and government experience and who was deeply committed to improving education in Florida. Frank continued in an education advocacy role as Jeb's lieutenant governor, later becoming president of Florida Atlantic University, then chancellor of the Pennsylvania State System of Higher Education.

I was all over the state in my Secret Squirrel role, then returned home to Miami. I was not in Miami long. Jeb won the election in November 1998. His chief of staff called asking me to return to Tallahassee to be on Jeb's transition team which was very similar to George H. W. Bush's transition team of

1988–89. So I flew back to Tallahassee, rented an apartment for November and December in anticipation of returning home after the inauguration on January 4, 1999.

Presidential or gubernatorial winners often put together a transition team of policy-aligned supporters to delve into each agency or department that the new leader will be overseeing, to learn what they can and to talk with the people in the previous administration who have been managing the departments. State governments, not unlike the federal government, are largely managed by cadres of civil servants who frequently have served in their jobs for several years. They are employed on the basis of their knowledge, capability, and experience; and for the most part they avoid politics. If they become politically active or vocal, they are asked to relocate when a new governor comes to town. As with a newly elected US president, leadership in tone and policy must emit from the top levels.

In the federal government, for example at the State Department, often the top three people in every functional and geographic bureau are presidential appointees. That is so the guidance in all these bureaus that are staffed by career civil servants comes from a leader who is fully briefed on the president's policies and goals. It is similar in state government where the key agency heads are appointed by the governor and become members of the governor's cabinet. The "rank and file," the vast majority of state government employees, are civil servants working in their professional capacities. In Jeb's case, all state employees had been working for former governor Lawton Chiles for eight years and many had forthrightly absorbed, or perhaps by osmosis absorbed, the policies and ways of the Chiles team. Nonetheless, I found that a high percentage of those to whom I spoke tried to be honest brokers in this change of administration as they gave the transition team their views on the strengths and weaknesses within the agency in which they worked.

I was on a three-person team assigned to assess three agencies: the Department of Management Services (administrative and support services for all the government agencies, facilities, vehicles, etc.); the Department of Business Regulations (licensing and regulating Florida businesses and professionals); and the Department of the Lottery (revenues of which go to public education in Florida). My transition teammates were Ana Navarro, a talented young Nicaraguan-born Republican lawyer who became a close friend and later a well-known political commentator on major cable channels and Charlie Christ who, as charming as he was, devoted very little time to our mission. Charlie later was a Republican governor of Florida. After which, he declared himself to be a Democrat and became a member of Congress.

In our team's investigation, we were to determine what, if any, problems existed, where improvements or savings could be made, and material issues to be aware of in each agency. On our transition team, for two months two of us actually worked hard on the job. That was Ana and me.

We learned that over the course of the eight-year period of the prior administration a serious problem had developed in the Department of the Lottery. It was essentially a complicated legal problem and potentially extremely costly to the state. The Lottery at the time in Florida raised several million dollars annually for Florida's educational system. To have a scandal or even distrust in the Florida Lottery could be a huge embarrassment for Governor Bush, who was not crazy at all about the concept of the Lottery. He recognized its impact on public education, but he surely did not want a lottery scandal on his watch. Moreover, the governor recognized that the Lottery was in Florida to stay, so the question was how to manage it well.

In late December 1998, our transition team did its work and I relayed the pertinent information to the governor's incoming staff who would be working in Tallahassee under Jeb's leadership. I reported in detail what we had seen and learned in all three state agencies, including the potentially damaging, complicated, and controversial legal mess at the Lottery.

Then, happily I moved out of my Tallahassee rental apartment and home to Miami for Christmas with my family. Chuck and I returned to Tallahassee on January 4, 1999 solely for Jeb's swearing-in ceremony. I had no interest in working in the administration, but I stopped to say hello to many friends in the governor's office including the chief of staff to whom I commented, "I see you've selected heads for all the state agencies, but I don't see who you've named to be secretary of the Lottery."

"Nope we haven't been able to find anybody to run the Lottery," he said.

Knowing what I knew of the problems, I responded, "You cannot let Jeb Bush put his hand on the Bible and take the oath of office without having someone from his team at the Lottery monitoring the issue we've talked about. You've got to have somebody in charge there."

We had all learned along the way that when government employees, perhaps employees anywhere, are in an administration for a long period of time, things tend to really get lax, good intentions wane, and procedures slip. There just isn't the energy and focus that exists in a new four-year administration, when it goes on to the sixth, seventh, and eighth year. By then even dutiful employees become very "comfortable" in their jobs. They know the job's not going to change, they are happy with the stability, they get a good salary, and they don't necessarily go to work every day. I had learned that one of the key officials at the Lottery was among the worst. He signed in electronically every morning and then went to the beach most every day. He was in charge of a large section at the department but was simply infrequently at work. There were others with similar work habits and there were employees who were, unfortunately, obviously intent on undermining the new administration. Over and beyond the dangerous legal problem, this agency was not going to present a happy situation for the Bush administration. There were just so many things that could go wrong in Florida's Department of Lottery in 1999.

That was the reason I told Jeb's chief of staff that the governor must have a strong manager there. "We just don't have anybody at this point," he insisted and quickly added, "You are the only one that understands the problem. You have to do it."

"I'm not going to do it," I replied adamantly. "No way I'm moving back to Tallahassee. Yes, I know the problems, but I don't know anything about running a lottery. No, I am not going to do it." It's now about ten minutes before the governor's inauguration.

"Would you be willing to do it for six months?"

"No, I would not."

"Ninety days?" he asked.

"No!"

He actually got down on a knee and pleaded, "Would you do it for sixty days?"

On the morning of the governor's inauguration, with the chief of staff on his knees saying, "Sue would you do it for sixty days and I promise you we'll find somebody?" I acquiesced. I felt that the situation was so bad and I'm thinking to myself that's just two months I said, "Okay. I can try, but you must find the right person to be the secretary of the Lottery."

We agreed I would be the interim secretary of the Florida Lottery, the CEO, while the governor's office would find somebody who knew how to run a lottery, which several months later in the year they did. Thus, in early January 1999, I moved back to Tallahassee, got a nicer apartment, and became the CEO of a gambling enterprise. While I was secretary of the Florida Lottery, I sat on the governor's cabinet with all the agency heads who were managing state affairs. It was definitely a very educational experience. I enjoyed every minute of it.

One of the first things I did, at Jeb's suggestion, after learning of my surprising new job, was to call Harriet Miers, a brilliant attorney who at that time was helping Jeb's brother George as secretary of the Texas Lottery. Harriet had lottery experience, a level head and provided sage and welcome advice. We became good friends. As life unfolded George W. Bush was later elected the nation's forty-third president and Harriet became White House staff secretary to the president and later a nominee to the United States Supreme Court. For primarily political reasons, the Miers Supreme Court nomination was not well received by some and Harriet removed her name from consideration.

The White House staff secretary is a powerful position. The incumbent is usually very close to the president, along with the chief of staff, and manages the paper flow and the people who gain access to the president, and when and where that happens. It is a position of influence and total trust. George W. Bush had three staff secretaries during his eight-year tenure. Ironically, the person who succeeded Harriet (2001–2003) was Brett Kavanaugh (2003–2006), who in 2018 ascended to the US Supreme Court taking the just vacated seat of our Stanford classmate and longtime friend Justice Anthony Kennedy.

In my first two weeks at the Florida Lottery, I reviewed all employee records and removed twelve employees. The previous secretary told one of her colleagues, who was still employed at the Lottery, that she was going to do a public records search to find out everything she could about my background, surely there was something amiss, and release it to her PR firm. I called the former secretary's colleague to my office and said quite simply, "Listen, it has been reported to me that the former secretary is going on the attack against me personally. I want you, her dear friend, to tell her that if she wants to take that approach and that attitude, I will be releasing all the notes I've taken from phone conversations with every lottery secretary in the United States before coming into this job. I still have them and I will release to the press what her colleagues said about her." I never heard another word. I was kind of looking forward to that contest, me versus her, but I ended it with that one statement to her friend. Simultaneously, "friend" went job hunting.

Support was what I really needed because I knew nothing about lotteries. Leadership and management (good and bad), I know quite a lot about, but I was thrust into this job with little notice, so I was really scrambling. I assessed some employees as potentially helpful and determined that the chief financial officer, Barbara Goltz, was a good civil servant, a smart woman doing her best to keep all lottery records in order. She would be helpful. She was a careful professional accountant doing her job. I felt I also needed an inspector general who could get down to the nitty-gritty of a lot of things that were going on in the department. Inspectors general have both power and access.

The head of security, Frank Carter, was a professional, a man in whom I had confidence and a pro in the security world. He kept his eyes open and provided useful advice. One day when I was talking to him, I brought up the inspector general position, he said; "I have the perfect person for you." He described a high-ranking officer at the Florida Department of Law Enforcement (FDLE) named Gerald Bailey. We called Jerry who said, "No." He didn't want to leave FDLE. I begged him to come just for an interview, which he finally agreed to do. We met in an undisclosed location after dark because we did not want to be observed. Jerry and I just hit it off immediately. I loved his attitude, his experience, his character, and his potential. I liked his brightness and business judgment. I liked everything about him. I talked him into becoming our inspector general. It was a brilliant move. My instincts were right. Jerry later returned to the FDLE and became head of the entire Florida Department of Law Enforcement and served in that capacity for almost a decade. He was an outstanding public servant.

At the Lottery, I created an executive committee of three whom I was confident I could trust: the chief financial officer, Barb Goltz; the inspector general, Gerald Bailey; and the director of research and policy analysis, the very knowledgeable Dennis Harmon. The executive committee would meet regularly, and I would receive reports on everything. I called them the green team. I told the executive committee to use green pens, so I would immediately know the origin of a note in my inbox. Everybody would know that this was an executive office communication. It was so effective that I have used the green pen for in-house executive communications ever since, including as ambassador.

Governor Bush remembers the lottery situation, thankfully, positively:

She did phenomenally well. The Lottery was a really difficult challenge. It was a scandal that wasn't publicized. That doesn't normally happen. I came in as governor of the state. The Lottery had one big contract through which they operated their business. They outsourced the operations of how you buy tickets and how the whole thing is administered. The marketing was done by the Department, but the guts of the business were done in an outsourced manner. I did not think the contract was done appropriately. So rather than make a big stink of it, which a new guy could easily do, I asked Sue to fix it. And she did. Which is not an easy thing to do in a private sector setting, but it's a lot more complicated in a government setting because of procurement laws, and the Government-in-the-Sunshine Statues 1967, Chapter 286 of the Florida Statutes. She did it with integrity. She did it efficiently. She did an extraordinary job. And I was totally confident that she would, just because of her business background, her legal background and the kind of person she was.

Governor John Ellis "Jeb" Bush Sr., November 16, 2017

Leadership at the top really matters. It's true in business, true in state government, it's true in federal government. The chief executive officer, whether he or she is a corporate officer, an entrepreneur, a governor, or a president, must be a firm and thoughtful team builder. The leader of the organization needs to set the tone at the top, the strategic plan, the policies, and the direction of the organization. The tone at the top is hopefully one of a high level of integrity, transparency, and communication, working with and for the people. Jeb Bush was a superb leader. But each of the state agencies has a head who reports to the governor; and, as with our federal government, their level of ability and knowledge differs from person to person. Some are good leaders, some are good managers, some are good people, but many are not all those things. Working in state government was an opportunity to observe how people managed their strengths and weaknesses, how they managed problems, how they managed the press. Governor Jeb Bush's leadership and his cabinet provided for me a terrific observation post.

The unexpected lottery experience provided many lessons about people, about state government, and about how bureaucracies function and can be manipulated. Government employees are public servants subject to close scrutiny when an administration changes. In the Bush administration, the key new employees at the Lottery melded smoothly with the experienced civil servant cadre, and we collectively got our arms around the major issues, the mechanics, and the karma of the Florida Lottery. The executive committee had an enviable work ethic. All employees knew we worked long hours every single day. They were very aware of the emphasis on ethics and integrity; operations were going smoothly, and a spirited moral had returned. Then after several months, the governor's team identified a person who had lottery experience and was willing to move to Tallahassee, Florida. We all agreed that I could leave. By that time, the leadership team had won over most everybody, and we were well on the way to resolving the dreaded legal problem.

The Lottery personnel decided on a going away party for me. They had a huge cake, the entire Lottery staff attended, and I was asked to give a speech. For the occasion, I wore white slacks, a sleeveless white blouse, and a red jacket. Towards the end of my speech, I said, "Wow, it's really hot in here. Do you mind if I just take off my jacket to finish my remarks?" I was wearing the sleeveless blouse for a purpose. On my bare left arm, I had put two large heart shaped stick-on tattoos. As I slid the jacket down and turned to place it over the chair behind me, I exposed my left arm to the crowd. There was an audible gasp. I was giggling inside. The room went silent. The employees knew me as a stern, all business executive. They couldn't figure out whether the tattoos were real or what their reaction should be until I started to laugh, then the crowd just broke up. I don't know why I did that. It just came to me and I did. Toby would say it was part of my silly streak. My new friends laughed and clapped, and we all devoured the beautiful cake. I appreciated the great party, but what touched me most happened the following day on my final day at the Lottery.

On the day of my departure, Frank, our head security officer was not at the department. I said goodbye to everyone else on the executive floor, went to my car and headed to the Tallahassee airport. Midway en route, I got a call from Frank telling me that he had just returned to the office, gone to the executive floor and found all the women sitting in a circle crying. He quickly asked them, "What is going on here?" One of the employees turned to him and said, "Sue Cobb is gone." That really touched me. After almost a year of firing people, questioning results, beating them up, making them work harder than they ever had…they cried when I left. Yes, I was deeply, deeply touched.

It was absolutely fascinating being in the cabinet of Jeb Bush as secretary of the Lottery. For me, the state government experience was educational and enjoyable. Part of that may have been because I was so favorably disposed to the state's chief executive officer to whom I reported. Part of it was because we worked hard and we solved problems. It was a great experience that I did not expect to replicate.

Presidential candidate George Walker Bush with the Cobbs in Miami, 2000.

Chapter Eleven

Whatever your hand finds to do, do it with all your might.
Ecclesiastes 9:10

BUSH *v.* GORE: FLORIDA LAWYERS FOR BUSH, BUTTERFLY BALLOTS, AND HANGING CHADS

By the fall of '99, I was back in Miami, feet on my desk, a little bored. My office is at our home, my preference. Sometimes I go into Cobb Partners' corporate offices in Coral Gables, but mostly I work at home so that I can wear shorts and T-shirts and go for a run or bike ride when I want. I knew for sure that I was never going back to practice bond law. Reading fine print at three in the morning was no longer very enticing. A thought struck me: Governor Jeb Bush's brother is running for president. A presidential campaign is something to think about. I did not know George W. Bush personally, but the minute that it was announced that he was running for president, Chuck and I were on board. We knew his parents and his brother Jeb well. We knew the Bush family to be dedicated to service, to be dedicated to liberty, and to be dedicated to America. While I had never met W., I was aligned with these concepts and began thinking to myself about how I could help elect George W. Bush to be president of the United States.

I knew some of the candidate's policy priorities. I knew he had already come out strongly for tort reform an issue in which I was interested. I had long felt the legal system was askew with respect to tort reform litigation and related monetary awards. The process tended to be abused, individuals sued for sometimes minor injuries, injuries were not infrequently "staged," and sympathetic juries returned with multi-million-dollar verdicts. It was particularly damaging in the medical arena, forcing many doctors to carry unusually large amounts of insurance, "just in case," and raising healthcare costs. The biggest abuses at the time were claims against anesthesiologists. Many doctors became uninsurable due to the number of suits and the size of awards. I knew that George W. had concentrated on how to solve the problem in a way that was more equitable for everybody. For that one simple reason I convinced myself, I should try to help in this presidential campaign. There had been some chatter among my Republican lawyer friends of putting a group of lawyers together. That's when I decided to put my efforts into organizing a Florida Republican lawyers' group to support the Bush campaign.

The Bush campaign, I felt, had not yet explained a number of George W.'s policy positions well enough to the public, at least in the all-important state of Florida. In my judgment the campaign needed help in articulating why their positions made both humane and economic sense. I decided to seek out lawyers of the Republican persuasion who were trained to explain complicated subjects. Most of my friends in the Florida legal community were Democrats, but I thought there would certainly be a fair number of Republican lawyers throughout the state. I touched base with the Dade County Republican Committee but was told that "Austin" (the Bush campaign headquarters) did not want independent groups being formed around the country. I called my friend Rocky Rodriguez who had been an associate at Greenberg Traurig when I was a partner there. I knew she was brilliant and had a plethora of contacts, including many among the state's Hispanic voters, who, as a group, were continuing to gain influence statewide and nationally. Rocky had dual outreach and was very much aligned with the general philosophy of governance articulated by our candidate, so she enthusiastically agreed to help my small effort.

We discussed our personal philosophies on interpretation of the constitution, the three co-equal branches of government, the rule of law, civilian control of the military, and our fundamental concept of states rights: that what is not specifically delegated to the federal government is reserved to the states. I do not like to use labels, because over time labels change meaning, particularly in the political world. With the exception of national security and foreign affairs, my constitutional interpretation is closer to a states rights type of approach, although the federalists at the inception of our country were what we now call the liberals or progressives. However, if I say I'm a conservative now, it sounds like I'm a right-wing nut. I am personally a conservative individual and naturally rather politically conservative, but I also have a strong social liberal streak, because I believe in equality and in protecting individual rights and liberties. I insist the word conservative does not have the same meaning today as it had in the past. Today I probably would be viewed as a "moderate." I do consider myself a moderate, a realist, a pragmatist, and an internationalist.

My brother and I grew up with a man who was born in 1896 in New Mexico Territory and my mother's father was born just a few years earlier in Texas. They indeed were conservatives and individualists. They were unfailingly polite gentlemen, and internally strong in the values and the traditions of the Old West. My father genuinely felt that a man's word was his bond. You did not need a written contract. You shook hands and that was it. You perform your part. I perform my part. That was the way it was in the Old West. And the Code of the Old West was a big influence on me and my brother in our early years.

Having been tangentially a part of the first Bush presidency as a US ambassador's spouse, I knew well what kind of a man President George Herbert Walker Bush was and how he addressed issues and challenges, largely in a manner with which I was very much in agreement. Also, from my time of working with Governor Jeb Bush, I felt I had insight into a general Bush philosophical approach. With respect to George W., I quickly concluded that "the apple doesn't fall far from the tree." I also had great admiration for Laura Bush. I looked forward to working on GWB's campaign and said to myself, "Like it or not Austin, I'm going to get some ground support together here in Florida."

My impression was that in the state of Florida, while there were a large number of attorneys who were politically active, they were mostly Democrats. I thought maybe there could be a hundred attorneys in the entire state who were active Republicans. They were not known to express themselves collectively in a sustained and vocal manner. So, I decided to try rounding up a dozen or two or however many Republican attorneys I could find who were willing to work at supporting the Republican candidate. We would call ourselves "Lawyers for Bush." The initial idea was to study Bush policy recommendations and write letters to editors across the state. At the time of the election, we would send attorneys to the hot polling spots to make sure that everybody followed all the statutory election laws about polling places, poster displays, time, and distances. I didn't know all the rules and regulations myself, but I counted on finding attorneys who did. Rocky and Veronica Angulo, also a learned attorney, were quickly on board and helped gather together the first small group of Republican attorneys. Ultimately, Rocky brought in many attorneys and was a driving force for Florida Lawyers for Bush. When I had commitments from a couple dozen attorneys from around the state, we began making suggestions, communicating by email. Rocky or I might say to our group, "Next week we'll write op-eds on tax policy and get them placed in local newspapers. Our directions are to explain what the Bush positions are, explain the economics, explain the effects, and why our candidate will help our country grow while providing appropriate safety nets."

When I began my calls and emails in the fall of 1999 and early 2000, George Bush's official campaign headquarters in Austin still did not want any outside groups independently using their own ideas or working without Austin's guidance and control. They were overtly discouraging about our meager little effort to get opinion pieces placed in Florida newspapers. But there were so many Republicans and so many Republican attorneys interested in electing George Bush that I made the simple decision to just carry on. As time went by, we picked up significant backing, including from Jillian Inman, then running the Miami-Dade County Republican Party office.

Chuck meanwhile was working with the campaign fund-raising team. We agreed to have a fund-raising event for George Bush in August 2000 at our home in Coral Gables. That's when I finally met the candidate. As far as I know, at that time he had never been informed about our Florida Lawyers for Bush.

This spur of the moment movement became more than I bargained for with Republican lawyers coming out of the woodwork (some might say the swamp). Before long, we had over 300 Florida attorneys involved. I decided to divide Florida into a dozen logical geographic districts and to pick the person I thought was the strongest attorney advocate in each district, one who had a good reputation and a lot of energy and request that he or she "captain" a geographical district. Soon I had twelve geographic captains covering sixty-seven counties. Periodically, I would send the captains some kind of specific direction, but they were all quickly engaged, enthusiastic, and making their own way spreading the word, fighting for tort reform and other GWB policy positions while I was happily sitting at my home computer building the team, reading the papers, and suggesting, "Let's comment on this or that..." By August we had so many lawyers put together, I told Austin we were really making a difference in Florida and we needed bumper stickers or a way to announce our presence as "Lawyers for Bush" (which became "Lawyers for Bush-Cheney"). Austin politely said, "No." I understood that they were busy doing all the things a national campaign must do. We just kept chugging along right through election night 2000, which led to the infamous thirty-six-day recount in Florida.

Everybody remembers the 2000 Election. Anyone engaged at all in the national political scene remembers the 2000 election, November 7, 2000. Election night I was at home with Chuck watching the returns, which were dragging excruciatingly on and on and on. Finally, Al Gore conceded, then he came back and said that he had changed his mind and he had not conceded. TV analysts were as confused as everyone in America. I called Tallahassee and Matt Schlapp, a young aide in the Bush campaign, answered the phone and said, "It's not over. Hang on."

At about 4:30 a.m. on November 8, I forced myself to go to bed since there was nothing I could do to help. At 5:00 a.m. the phone rang. It was Austin calling. A man's voice said, "We know about your Florida lawyers group. Can you have Republican attorneys in all sixty-seven County Clerk's Offices in the State of Florida by 8:00 a.m.?" It was the campaign national field director. I said, "Yes, that's not a problem at all." I immediately called our twelve captains and told them to man the electoral offices in every county by 8:00 a.m., to read the statutes governing Florida elections, and to be ready for whatever we might need to do.

Off we went to man all sixty-seven counties. There was a lot of confusion about the recount laws due to the manner in which Florida statutes were written. I personally went into the Miami-Dade County Clerk's Office. By 8:00 a.m., we had about fifteen attorneys inside the Clerk's Office. We were the first to have a chance to influence the county clerks on how they were going to interpret the law and manage counting ballots. The absolutely brilliant thing I did that morning had nothing to do with statutes or counting ballots. It had to do with me bringing the power cord for my cellphone, which nobody else had remembered to do. I did a lot of power sharing that morning. By 11:00 a.m., the Austin troops had landed in Miami and Tallahassee. The Austin team must have gotten on a plane by six in the morning because they arrived at the Miami-Dade Clerk's Office shortly after 10:00 a.m., found me, and we discussed our next steps. Later in the day, the Democrats started to arrive.

Jim Baker and his team of attorneys set themselves up at Republican headquarters in Tallahassee. One of our very good friends, Al Cardenas, was chairman of the Republican Party of Florida at the time and he managed the Tallahassee operation. I was at the Miami-Dade County Clerk's Office every day and helped manage the Monroe, Miami-Dade, Broward, and Palm Beach County court cases. Palm Beach County provided the nation a view of the first ever and surely the last butterfly ballots.

The hearing that sent Bush *v.* Gore to the Supreme Court was in Tallahassee. I flew up for that decisive argument and was one of about six Republicans allowed into Judge Sander Saul's courtroom when he made the dramatic ruling that sent to the US Supreme Court, Bush *v.* Gore, 531 U.S. 98 (2000). Suddenly, there was nothing to do but sit back and wait.

I later related the story of Lawyers for Bush to the Association for Diplomatic Studies and Training (ADST) interviewer Charles Stuart Kennedy for publication in ADST's "Moments in

Diplomatic History," October 2016, for which ADST provided this foreword:

> *The presidential election of November 7, 2000 was one of the most memorable and controversial in the history of the United States. It pitted Republican candidate George W. Bush, then-governor of Texas and son of former president George H. W. Bush (1989– 1993), against Democratic candidate Al Gore, then Bill Clinton's vice president. Around 2:15 a.m., numerous news sources and television networks called the State of Florida for Bush and declared him the winner. At 2:30 a.m., Gore called Bush and conceded the election. However, Gore advisors continued to maintain that with a +/- 600 vote margin no clear winner had emerged. At 3:30 a.m., Gore called Bush back and retracted his concession. Ultimately, the 2000 presidential election would hinge on the vote in Florida. The outcome was one of the closest in U.S. presidential history.*

> *By November 10ᵗʰ election officials calculated that Bush led by around 400 votes out of almost 6 million cast. In such a close contest Florida law demands a full machine recount in all its 67 counties. But such laws and implementing mechanisms were open to interpretation. Numerous lawsuits and hearings ensued. Voters became familiar with butterfly ballots and hanging chads. The Florida Supreme Court eventually ordered a manual recount in four counties: Miami-Dade, Broward, Palm Beach, and Volusia. The Bush attorneys filed in federal court to stop the hand recount based, inter alia, on principles of equal protection. In late November, Florida's canvassing board certified Bush the winner by 537 votes, but legal actions by both parties kept the outcome uncertain.*

> *Thirty-six days after the election, on December 12 more than a month later, the U.S. Supreme Court halted the manual recount. By a narrow 5–4 majority, the Justices ruled that the recount in four selected counties violated the principle that "all votes must be treated equally." The 2000 presidential election was the first in 112 years in which a presidential candidate lost the popular vote but captured enough states to win the electoral vote.*

The Supreme Court decision was, of course, controversial and frequently misinterpreted. The outcome is often cited as simply a 5-4 decision by the court in favor of the petitioners,

George Bush and Richard Cheney. The facts paint a much more complicated conclusion involving a 7–2 *per curium* opinion relating to violation of the Equal Protection Clause, a 5–4 vote relating to the state's inability to implement a timely legal alternative method of counting votes under Title 3 U.S. Code, and several distinct concurring and dissenting votes. The net effect produced a win for the Bush-Cheney ticket in Florida's Electoral College sealing the Republican victory.

The election was over. George W. Bush would be the president of the United States. I felt I had done my part.

The remarkable thing to me through the 2000 aftermath was how peaceful George Bush was at home in Texas with his family during the harrowing thirty-six days. He rarely talked and when he did, he made calming statements. History now tells the story of how America went through thirty-six days of counting and recounting and multiple court challenges in several Florida counties. By its decisions, the Supreme Court ruled that George W. Bush would be the forty-third president of the United States. I admit to a deep sense of satisfaction for having launched a group that played a crucial role in the election of an American president. For me, however, that was the end of that particular journey. It was over. I had absolutely no thoughts at all about being in the new Bush administration. It simply never crossed my mind. I was excited to head to Telluride to ski with my family over the Christmas holidays.

In an unusual twist of fate, after I concluded my term as US ambassador to Jamaica (2001–2005), I became Florida's secretary of state which manages the Florida Department of Elections. I was charged with supervising the Florida 2006 mid-term federal elections…by which time I knew quite a lot about election law. In the 2006 election, Republican candidates, in general, were soundly defeated.

GREETINGS

from

THIS YEAR THERE WERE 1,600 APPLICA-tions for the 162 ambassadorships worldwide. Presidents traditionally use at least a third of those as political and personal rewards. George W. Bush is no different. Though most of the following are still awaiting final clearance, these W. FAMILY FRIENDS and BASEBALL CHUMS will probably end up in desirable locations. Those who RAISED or DONATED the most MONEY should get the best spots of all.

RICHARD BLANKENSHIP
Florida investment banker who lent his private jet to Bush family members for campaign hops
• POST Low-profile backwater with little work but lots of sun, sand and surf

BAHAMAS

RICHARD EGAN
Founder of EMC, a data-storage-systems firm with a plant and offices in Ireland
• POST Was a low-profile backwater, now an economic miracle. Rains a lot, but great whiskey

IRELAND

WILLIAM FARISH
Chairman of Churchill Downs, a horse breeder whose family roots are in Texas oil
• POST Plum job. Great digs. No foreign tongues. Downside: must entertain lots of visiting U.S. VIPs

BRITAIN

MERCER REYNOLDS
Investment banker and former partner in Texas Rangers helped bolster W.'s oil company and raised more than $3 mil for Bush campaign
• POST Not much at risk politically, leaving time for fondue and skiing

SWITZERLAND

SUE COBB
Director of Florida investment firm and adviser in Jeb's 1998 race. Her husband was Bush Sr.'s ambassador to Iceland
• POST Great scuba diving, but too many U.S. college kids on vacation get wild and need bailing out

JAMAICA

GEORGE ARGYROS
Head of a West Coast investment company, the former owner of the Seattle Mariners raised millions for Bush
• POST Not as luxurious as other European spots, but embassy has great art collection

SPAIN

MARGARET TUTWILER
Longtime loyalist and State Department spokeswoman for Bush Sr. helped out during Florida recount
• POST Not one of the big-power countries but great deals on rugs

MOROCCO

HOWARD LEACH
Billionaire investment banker and businessman is former finance chair of Republican National Committee
• POST La crème de la crème. Great food and enviable venue with embassy just off the Champs Elysées

FRANCE

JIM NICHOLSON
As Republican National Committee chair last year, Denver real estate developer oversaw record-breaking efforts to raise campaign funds
• POST Job has the benefits of being in Rome without an unruly amount of work

THE VATICAN

Time *magazine's assessment of President George W. Bush's first ambassadorial nominees, Vol. 157, No 17, page 27, April 30, 2001.*

Secretary of State Colin Powell and Sue at one of many diplomatic events at the State Department (2001–2005).

Swearing-in as Ambassador Extraordinary and Plenipotentiary to Jamaica. Back left to right: Toby, Luisa, Peter and Suzanne McCourt, Chuck, Secretary of State Colin Powell, Chris. Front left to right: Charlie, Luis, me, Nicholas, Fred, August 15, 2001.

*Chuck and Sue with the Most Honorable P. J. Patterson,
sixth prime minister of Jamaica (1992–2006).*

*Executing an important cooperative security agreement with Dr. Peter
Phillips, then Jamaican minister of national security.
Courtesy of Jamaica Observer Limited © 2004.*

US Southern Command Headquarters
Miami, FL
 15 Interagency Partner Organizations with 28 representatives
 9 Partner Nation Liaison Officers
 3 Partner Nation Staff Officers

Joint Interagency Task Force – South (JIATF-S)
Key West, FL

Joint Task Force Guantánamo (JTF-GTMO)
Naval Station, Cuba

Joint Task Force Bravo (JTF-B)
Soto Cano, Honduras

US Air Force South (AFSOUTH)
Tucson, AZ

US Army South (ARSOUTH)
San Antonio, TX

US Naval Forces Southern Command (USNAVSO)
Mayport, FL

US Marine Corps Forces South (MARFORSOUTH)
Miami, FL

Special Operations Command South (SOCSOUTH)
Homestead, FL

US Southern Command Headquarters

~6,000 forces deployed

21 Security Cooperation Offices
21 Senior Defense Officials
Based in Embassies throughout the region

 Headquarters
 Components
 Cooperative security locations
 Task Force locations

Team Leader ★ Team Player ★ Team Builder

SOUTHCOM Area of Operation (AOP) 2019. This public map gives a sense of the Command's depth and breadth. CENTCOM, US Central Command is also based in Florida and addresses US security matters in Northeast Africa, the Middle East, Central and South Asia.

Florida Governor Jeb Bush and Deputy Chief of Mission in Jamaica, Richard Smyth, (rt.) at Richard's next post, Bagram Air Base, Afghanistan, 2005.

At work. Ambassador Cobb en route to opening of Jamaican Parliament.
Courtesy of Jamaica Observer Limited © 2004.

United States Ambassador to Jamaica Sue Cobb (centre) and Moira Tamayo-Cole (right), regional vice-president of Western Union International, enjoy the company of students from the Rousseau Primary School in Kingston, following yesterday's launch of the "I PLEDGE" (I Promise to Lend Encouragement to Develop Growth in Education) programme at The Courtleigh Hotel in Kingston. Mathematics textbooks for 350,000 primary school students will be provided under the programme. It is an initiative of Grace, Kennedy Remittance Services, Western Union International, the United States Embassy, the United States Agency for International Development (USAID) and the government, through the Ministry of Education, Youth and Culture. See related story on Pages 4 & 5.   (Photo: Michael Gordon)

I PLEDGE, a Building Bridges program supporting public/private partnerships and corporate responsibility to fund early childhood education in Jamaica. Courtesy of Jamaica Observer Limited © 2004.

First two female American ambassadors to Jamaica, Sue Cobb and successor Brenda LaGrange Johnson with retired secretary of state General Colin Powell at State Department, 2017.

Chuck and Sue with Jamaican business dynamos Michael Lee Chin, Butch Stewart and Tony Hart, Jamaica, 2008.

Three recipients of the Order of Jamaica, the Hon. Maurice Facey (1988), non-citizen the Hon. Sue Cobb (2010) and the Hon. Raymond Chang (2011), National Heroes' Day, October 2012.

President George W. Bush and Ambassador Sue Cobb in the Oval Office.
My exposed shoe is protecting an ankle sprained at Jamaica Inn, Summer 2003.

"Thanks, and Goodbye" from President George W. Bush, February 2005.

Chapter Twelve

Leadership to me means duty, honor, country. It means character and it means listening from time to time.

President George W. Bush

SWEARING-IN BY SECRETARY COLIN POWELL

Sometime before the end of December 2000, our home phone in Telluride rang. It was one of my friends who had gone to work in Washington for President-Elect George Bush's transition team. She said, "What do you want to do in the George W. Bush administration?" I said, "Nothing." I hadn't even thought about it. Organizing Florida Lawyers for Bush was not done to get a position in Washington. I wasn't seeking anything and said, "I'm not interested at all; I'm very glad the president won, but I'm perfectly content to be home in Miami." As I said that I was thinking about how I did get a little bored when I wasn't one hundred percent engaged in some challenge. But I said nothing to my caller. Then the White House Office of Presidential Personnel called Chuck. We began to wonder about what, if anything, we might want to do. Chuck suggested I look at the Plum Book, which lists jobs in every agency open for political appointees, including those at the State Department.

The third call then came to me from a higher-level person in Presidential Personnel who said, "Look we're going to have thousands of applications for jobs in this administration. We'd like you to be involved, so I need to know what you want to do." I still said, "I haven't thought about it." He pressed. And I responded, "Look, if I did anything at all it would have to be something that reported directly to the president." I was not going to go off into the depth of some agency, sit around Washington, and chat with other bureaucrats. He said, "Fine, we would like you to be one of our ambassadors." Wow, what a surprise! I was speechless, but I was thinking – Chuck was an ambassador. I understand that role.

Chuck and I talked. It was not really an easy decision, though it was very flattering. Chuck encouraged me to continue the discussion. I would have to send papers to the White House Office of Presidential Personnel, so they could do background checks. Almost nobody knows what you have to go through to become a United States ambassador. The FBI checks your entire history. Candidates have to list every single place they've ever lived and give references from those places. The FBI checks them all. They sit down with you, the potential nominee; they sit down with your neighbors, they sit down with your doctors, with your family – everybody. You never get feedback. You just answer questions. It's weird. I had people tell me when the FBI had called them and what questions they were asked, but I never got a full picture.

I did send in the required papers, but it still didn't seem real. This was just so unanticipated. How did this happen? Chuck and I might need to decide where we could add value and would be comfortable living, what would work for both of us, how were we going to stay close to our then six grandchildren? We had the little book many will remember called the Official Airline Guide (the OAG). In those days instead of looking on the computer for a flight, you looked in the OAG to find all the flights you were interested in. I had been carrying around my OAG religiously because of going between Miami and Tallahassee frequently, knowledge of flights was critical to me. I was thinking that if

I accepted an administration job, I'd better stay pretty close to home, so I'd better look at the Western Hemisphere flights. The largest English-speaking country in the Western Hemisphere is Jamaica. It's 481 miles from Miami to Tallahassee and 524 miles from Miami to Montego Bay, just about the same distance I'd already been commuting. Importantly, a quick look at the OAG showed that while there was one flight a day between Miami and Tallahassee, there were twelve flights a day between Jamaica and Miami. I had some, but not extensive knowledge of that country. I quickly did some research and concluded that if I could actually ask for a specific country, I would love to go to Jamaica! There were many reasons, but my grandchildren and the close proximity to Miami weighed heavily.

Gaining additional knowledge of Jamaica's history and its challenges was next on my agenda. In 1988, while Chuck was undersecretary of Commerce, Jamaica had a disastrous hurricane. Gilbert struck Jamaica at nearly a category 4 hurricane on September 12, 1988, increasing to a monster category 5, wreaking havoc in the Caribbean and Mexico for almost nine days. In total, it killed 433 people and caused about $7.1 billion (1988 USD) in damages over the course of its ravaging path. Hurricane Gilbert decimated Jamaica. The United States, as always, was looking to see what needed to be done and how we would be able to help the recovery of Jamaica. President Ronald Reagan had a very good relationship with Prime Minister Edward Seaga. The president wanted somebody from the Commerce Department (which is home to NOAA, the National Oceanic and Atmospheric Administration) to go to Jamaica to make an independent assessment of the information the United States was receiving from on the ground sources. Chuck was assigned that role. He and I flew to Kingston and stayed with United States Ambassador Michael Sotirhos (1985–89) in the guest quarters of the United States official residence on Long

Lane in Stony Hill. We were escorted around the island by the Jamaica Defence Force to the most damaged areas. Although we were in this disaster scenario, the Jamaicans whom I met on our tour struck me as very smart, very capable, and very caring. Although the country was a total mess due to the hurricane, I had a genuinely positive feeling about the people. They made a strong impression on me.

Later we had a good friend become the United States ambassador to Jamaica at the same time Chuck and I served in Reykjavik. Ambassador Glen Holden (1989–93) and his wife, Gloria, routinely reported terrific experiences in Jamaica. They could not have been more positive about the country, its people, and its potential. Early in 1989, Chuck and I had been in the same ambassador seminar class as the Holdens, which was the beginning of our lifelong friendship. I discussed with the Holdens at great length their experiences in Jamaica. Ambassador Holden's predecessor, Ambassador Michael Sotirhos, also had many positive things to relate. Both strongly encouraged me to make Jamaica my highest priority. I knew I liked the people. It was a beautiful island close to home, and there were certainly sufficient challenges to keep me deeply interested. I was very much leaning toward Jamaica, but it wasn't for me to decide.

The president usually appoints about thirty to thirty-five non-career designees from among several hundred applicants. Career Foreign Service officers (FSOs) have the remaining approximately 160 to 170 chief of mission posts (chief of mission, or COM, is a State Department term corresponding to ambassador). Most, but not all, ambassadors carry the title of ambassador extraordinary and plenipotentiary (meaning full authority to represent the president and the United States government). Early in a new administration, the White House Office of Presidential Personnel starts juggling candidates who are available. The State Department, generally through a newly appointed secretary of state, weighs in with the president and responsible White House personnel in the selection of ambassadors. As a non-career candidate, one frequently does not have a choice of location, although those involved with White House personnel do their best to accommodate interests and skill sets. Of course, the president makes the final decisions. Our situation was encouraging. My husband had served in the administration of both the president's father and his predecessor, President Ronald Reagan. I had recently served in the cabinet of the president's brother. And I had initiated the plan to bring all Florida Republican lawyers together in preparation for the 2000 election, which preceded the thirty-six-day hotly contested recount in Florida that George W. Bush had won. Because of these circumstances, I was not unknown at the White House.

The Office of Presidential Personnel usually manages all communications with candidates. However, my first direct knowledge that I was going to be selected to be ambassador to Jamaica came in early January 2001 right after George Bush's inauguration, when a close friend of the president whispered in my ear, "The decision has been made, you will get the country you want." It was terribly exciting – I was giggling inside (I am not known for giggling), but I was sworn to silence because my designation hadn't been officially announced. Chuck and I were soon told, but we were the only ones advised of my potential new job. We just waited. The actual formal announcement was made along with a few other ambassador-designates around the end of February. We immediately signed up for the first class of ambassador seminars set for April 2001. As an ambassador-designate's spouse in 1989, my first State Department ambassador seminar was as Chuck's spouse; now he was coming to this one as my spouse. Life has many twists and turns.

Once some Bush administration nominees for ambassador became public, the media began weighing in on the merits, or lack thereof, of each designate and alleging the usual charge that these non-career ambassadors took the place of trained diplomats and only got the job because they had given gobs of money during the president's campaign (the latter being sometimes true and sometimes not true). *Time* magazine proved a good early example of this in an April 30, 2001 article. Of the nine of us highlighted in the article with our photographs, mine appeared with this pithy caption:

Jamaica

Sue Cobb *Director of Florida investment firm and adviser in Jeb's 1998 race. Her husband was Bush Sr.'s Ambassador to Iceland. Post Great scuba diving, but too many United States college kids on vacation get wild and need bailing out.*

Obviously, what some of us gave in monetary support to the president's campaign could hardly have changed the course of history. This dichotomy – some would say argument – about the means and effectiveness of non-career ambassadors, vis-à-vis career ambassadors, arises on a regular basis, often due to journalists who have little or no exposure to the actual work of a United States ambassador. I would be the first to say that an extremely high percentage of the United States Senate-confirmed career ambassadors are extraordinarily good representatives of the United States They are largely non-partisan, smart, knowledgeable, well trained, and dedicated to their jobs. To even start a career in the Foreign Service requires studying for and passing the Foreign Service written and oral examinations, which I have been told is harder than being accepted into the Harvard Business School. Then, if successful, Foreign Service officers (FSOs) face the harsh judgmental grading system of the State Department. The structure of the State Department was originally based on the United States Navy. It is an "up or out" system, with each level culminating in either a promotion or probable stagnation, leading to an honorable early retirement. This is similar to the military services in which captains in the Navy and colonels in the Army, who do not make general or admiral, are frequently headed for retirement. Those who make it to the Senior Foreign Service (the top four grades in the Foreign Service) have been continually tested and have demonstrated the character and skills necessary to reach the highest levels and to help put out fires around the world. How could anyone say that these men and women would not be capable ambassadors?

So why is it that the president, the secretary of state, and some host country officials actively seek out successful private sector individuals to be United States ambassadors? I believe there are several reasons successful people in all fields in America's competitive culture are chosen for diplomatic appointments. They have demonstrated leadership skills, are smart, knowledgeable, dedicated to our country and, importantly, are known to have a high degree of loyalty to the president and policies articulated by the president.

The president naturally wants people he knows and likes on his own team. From the host country's perspective, many leaders prefer to have non-career ambassadors serve in their country because non-career ambassadors are perceived (usually correctly) to have a closer direct relationship with the president and secretary of state and with other influential United States administration officials. Being more closely aligned to the president's policies and having direct access to him may or may not be true, but it's definitely the perception.

What is true for sure is that both career and non-career ambassadors are human beings – and there has been ill behavior, mismanagement, and egregiously bad behavior in both groups. There have also been extraordinarily capable and productive ambassadors in both groups. From my perspective, I can say that while there is a lot of chatter on this subject, I personally never had anything but strong support from and for my career counterparts.

Upon learning that after approval of the Senate, I was going to join the ambassadors' club and have that news disseminated to the world, I began in-depth studying. I looked and listened for all the president's policies that might affect the Western Hemisphere; what United States goals were established; what the National Security Strategy would reveal; and what our posture was in the Western Hemisphere, in the Caribbean, and in Jamaica. Unable to take my training lightly, I moved to Washington, took an apartment, went to the State Department every single day, and read all the unclassified cables and all the background materials I could get my hands on, so that I would understand the history of all the things that could affect me in my new post. I learned which of the agencies of the United States government touched Jamaica and the Western Hemisphere so that I could understand their roles and meet their Washington personnel with whom I would be working. Trying to unravel the inter-agency processes was fascinating. I delved into how the relationship between the White House, the National Security Council, and the State Department might work. I dug deeply into what my chief of mission job would really be.

Serving the president and the people of our country is an honor and a privilege. I knew of course that a United States ambassador represents the president and the United States government in a host country (or to an international organization, such as the United Nations). In a bilateral context, the ambassador leads a team that is responsible for the safety and welfare of all United States citizens living in or visiting the host country. An ambassador is a policy advocate, conveys American values, is a strategic planner, and a crisis manager. An ambassador is a fiduciary for American taxpayers. The job description includes integrity, dedication, discipline, and patience. It is a challenge that will require the full use of a designee's leadership and management skills and requires sacrifice (time commitment, lost opportunity costs, financial disclosure, and upheaval of accustomed family life). Being an ambassador offers the opportunity to serve, to educate, and to be educated – in effect, to make a difference. Almost all non-career ambassadors report that the experience is one of the best of their lives. How could I best prepare for such an experience? For starters, I had a respected and admired personal instructor at the dinner table every night – Chuck Cobb. That was a great bonus.

Every country with which the United States has diplomatic relations has within the State Department what is called a country desk officer. He or she is the person who coordinates the flow of information between an embassy abroad and the State Department, making sure the information from an embassy gets to the right place within the State Department, to the right people, and that necessary communications from the State Department are sent to the relevant ambassadors. The desk officer is within a larger geographic bureau, in our case in the Office of Caribbean Affairs within the Bureau of Western Hemisphere Affairs (WHA). My first desk officer was terrific – very helpful in introducing me to State Department processes and to information flow. There were several people in the Caribbean office and many more in WHA due to the number of countries in our region. They kindly found a little desk for me, brought me relevant materials, and were as accommodating as they could be. I interacted with other WHA officers, all of whom I found to be extremely capable. I think they were surprised that this ambassador-designate wanted so much information, and those in the Office of Caribbean Affairs at that time, such as Marcia Barnes, Meg Gilroy, and Carl Cockburn, might be surprised that to this day I remember with appreciation their kind tutoring of this neophyte chief of mission.

Among other things, they taught me how to make appointments with people in Washington who were going to affect my job. With the Desk's help, my DC calendar was soon set up to cover a broad range of potential contacts. Privately, I set up a number of appointments with other United States government agencies and actors beyond those the Desk had in mind for me. Those meetings turned out to be beneficial. The new head of the FAA (Federal Aviation Administration) was not on the Desk's list, but after all, Jamaica has two international airports, and something might go wrong (and it did). Many were obvious fits. The Drug Enforcement Administration (DEA) had a big presence in Jamaica, as did the United States Agency for International Development (USAID), the Peace Corps, the Department of Defense, and others. Awaiting Senate confirmation, I had plenty of time to get on the calendar of each DC-based agency head and I didn't need to settle for number two. I waited until I could meet with the top person and would initiate our conversation by offering to help their programs at my post in any way I could during my tenure in Jamaica. Establishing face-to-face relationships while awaiting Senate confirmation was a very worthwhile endeavor.

Ambassador seminars had initially been inspired by Shirley Temple Black who stated on her return from serving in Ghana (prior to her tour in Czechoslovakia) that she would have liked to have had more preparation. She recommended training for both political appointees and career appointees. The two-week seminars were uniformly imposed on all designees and were valuable to everyone. (The seminars are currently three weeks, with the career diplomats attending only the last two weeks.) Originally, the State Department contracted with two former Foreign Service officers who had been ambassadors to manage the seminars, including Chuck's seminar in 1989. Their stewardship continued for a number of years.

By the time I was in the seminar in early 2001, the State Department was changing that structure but not the substance. I had a real advantage over the other non-career designees because I'd lived in an embassy for three years in Iceland and understood quite a lot about practices and procedures. For the brand new non-career people, the State Department introduction can be daunting. The acronyms alone are bewildering when you come from the private sector. Non-career appointees initially can't understand a word the leaders and the career officers are saying. But soon everyone is on board together, building comradery, and learning a broad range of administrative responsibilities and diplomatic requirements. There was little discussion of policy. We studied ethics, the official residence requirements, medical issues, security issues, reporting by officers to the State Department, managing a country team, locally employed staff, what an inspector general would expect from an ambassador, what the different officers and different agencies did, and how a new ambassador might meld the country team together so all were working as one.

The Ambassadorial Authorities are thoroughly covered as well as communications with the State Department and communications with a foreign ministry and others in your host country. There is discussion of protocol, intelligence, military authorities, and in our case, quite a bit about "drugs and thugs." There are two very worthwhile days of media training. Spouses are included in everything not classified. A ton of reading material is provided – designees are force fed with a hose during the day for eight hours and then have homework as well.

Most everybody is new to the ambassadorial role and excited about what they are doing. The contacts made among other ambassadors, both career and non-career, were enjoyable, useful, and lasting. The seminars abound in an atmosphere of excitement and anticipation. Everyone knows they are leaping into the unknown. During the seminars, several different scenarios are shared with designates demonstrating things that could possibly happen at an embassy abroad that one might not even think about. These ranged from real physical dangers, to domestic issues like internal fights between a married or tandem couple at your post. You might get a call late one evening that a wife has stabbed her husband, they are both on your payroll; what guidance do you provide, to whom? Or a call about somebody taking photographs of your embassy doors and windows from adjacent roofs. Was the chancery (the building housing the Executive Offices) in danger? What actions can we take? I remember reading five scenarios given to us one day at the seminar and thinking: these are simply not going to happen. Guess what? Every one of them happened at my embassy during my tour. Every single unlikely scenario they gave me actually happened: the lady knife wielder; the rooftop photographer, the employee who went completely berserk and issued death threats to another embassy officer – which in our case was a sad, long, and dangerous, situation. More than one employee got drunk and disorderly in the public eye. Turns out, real human beings occupy embassies.

Now to the extent possible, the deputy chief of mission (DCM), a well-trained and experienced career officer, would manage such incidents, but for some incidents or at some level the ambassador has to know and has to weigh in. These are challenging parts of the job.

The State Department training is indispensable, particularly in the areas that you are not normally exposed to – like understanding the function of the OPS Center (Operations Center, the nerve center and "Situation Room" of the State

Department) and knowledge of their processes. How and when do you contact OPS? When and how quickly do you need help? The consular section was important. How does the visa section work? In what manner do some of our intelligence units operate? In my case the DEA, DIA, and the United States Marshal's Service were important. We were one of three posts in the world that had a United States Marshal's presence. It is important for the ambassador to know who the United States-based leaders of agencies are at their post, where they are, who should you call if you really need them, and who should you leave alone unless you really have to reach them. All those things come out to some degree in the ambassador seminars. One valuable book the Foreign Service Institute uses is called *This Worked for Me*. It's a collection taken from interviews of many ambassadors explaining incidents that happened to them and how they dealt with the problems. That was quite helpful, because as I learned, it is more probable than not that you will end up facing a lot of the problems you had never thought about.

Many lessons I imported from Colin Powell's *My American Journey* in which he articulated leadership lessons from his career in the military and in public service. It was important not just because he was my secretary of state (2001–2005), but because I was concerned about pulling the country team together and gaining my team's confidence. Here I was, at that time a sixty-four-year-old woman with government experience at the state level but not the federal level, coming in to tell all these well trained, professional career officers how they were going to be responsible to me and how we were all going to work together and why. I spent quite a bit of time thinking about the subject because I very much wanted the tone to be right from the beginning. I wanted to be informed but humble, to ask logical and knowledgeable questions, to look to the leadership of my country team in their areas of expertise, and to learn from them.

In addition to going to the Desk at the State Department for three months and participating in the ambassador seminar, I wanted lessons in what the United States' goals were around the world, in the hemisphere, and in my host country. To do that, I read other important materials like the National Security Strategy, the State Department strategic plan, and cables put out by other countries in our area and by the Western Hemisphere Bureau. I wanted to know everything I could about the circumstances that I was getting into.

The three months of preparation in Washington was also time well spent in managing my appearance at my Senate Foreign Relations committee hearing in July 2001. Everybody gets very nervous when going before the "murder board" conducted at the State Department prior to a Senate confirmation hearing. A group of experts in the area, in this case from the Western Hemisphere Bureau, grill the candidate on current questions he or she could get from the Senate. It's anxiety-ridden because you don't know what the murder board or senators are going to ask. The senators are well primed by their staffs and have prepared questions, usually on a difficult or controversial subject or incident. It's just innately scary to sit down with eight people who are going to try their best to test your knowledge and character. But I told myself that at one point in my career I was a trial and appellate attorney, so I had stood before a lot of knowledgeable judges.

Again, I had luck on my side. Two of us approval-seeking designees went to our senate hearing together. I was paired with Roger Noriega, nominated by the president to be the assistant secretary for the Bureau of Western Hemisphere Affairs, the top job in WHA. Roger had worked in the Senate for Jesse Helms and Roger was known to be a hawk on the subject of Cuba. He helped to draft the 1996 legislation, the Helms-Burton Act, that clamped down on Cuba and established the embargo. By 2001 Roger had become somewhat controversial. All the senators knew Roger because of the Helms-Burton Act and his previous service on the Hill. My home state Florida senators – Bob Graham and Bill Nelson – both Democrats, walked me down the aisle and introduced me to the senators on the Foreign Relations Committee. In other words, I was introduced (very kindly) by the opposition. The senators focused on Roger. All the senators' questions were directed to Roger. I got two questions that were total softballs. And that was it, over and out of the hot seat. My Senate confirmation hearing had gone well, and I was unanimously approved by the full Senate on August 1, 2001.

On August 15, 2001 in the historic and very beautiful Benjamin Franklin Room at the Department of State, I, Sue McCourt Cobb, was sworn in to be the next United States ambassador extraordinaire and plenipotentiary to Jamaica. Accompanying me were my husband Chuck; our son Toby and his wife Luisa, their children Luis, Charlie, and Sebastian; and our son Christian, his wife Kolleen and their children at the time, Fred, Nick, and Cassidy; my brother Peter McCourt and his wife Suzanne; Chuck's sister Patricia and her husband Jack Veatch, along with Ambassador Richard Bernal of Jamaica, his wife Margaret Bernal; and many friends from all over the United States. To my great delight, the person swearing me in was none other than the secretary of state, General Colin Powell, whose remarks I remember well and of course saved. He said:

> It's a great pleasure to welcome all the friends of the Cobbs and those who are friends of Jamaica. This is a bittersweet occasion for me. This is the job I wanted. The president calls me and says, 'Colin, we want you to be secretary of state.' I said, 'No, mon. I want to be ambassador to Jamaica!' But that was not to be the case. He said, 'I have a better selection than you to be the ambassador to Jamaica' and here she is.

He was wonderfully entertaining as he continued in a nostalgic mode:

As you might guess, I am a little envious of Sue in reality because in the Powell family, going home to Jamaica for a visit was everyone's idea of heaven. Going back to listen to the poetry of Louise Bennett, to drink a touch of Appleton Estate rum, to enjoy the beauty of the island, and the friendship of the people. And so, it's an important post for us. It's a nation that means a great deal to America, not only in terms of geo-politics but in terms of friendship, in terms of family. And in choosing Sue Cobb to be his personal envoy in Kingston, President Bush continues a fine tradition of sending distinguished Americans abroad to represent the United States and especially in Kingston.

Not only does Sue know the business of resort development and management, she also brings three decades of experience as a teacher, an attorney, a CEO, and a financial executive. Above and beyond all that, Sue's passion for life, her independent, enterprising nature, her warmth, and her love of family as you can see so vividly illustrated here today will find many kindred spirits among the Jamaican people.

His words were leavened with the acknowledgment of the work that lay ahead of me:

The Peace Corps has been sharing American know-how with Jamaica since its independence in 1962. Today almost 100 volunteers are working in Jamaica in the Peace Corps in the field of education, environmental protection, and public health. The United States Agency for International Development has a wide range of programs in Jamaica as well as working with Jamaican organizations to promote sustainable growth, sustainable development, and to strengthen democratic institutions. Our two governments are working closely to ensure the safety of our citizens through international law enforcement programs. So we've got a lot going on with Jamaica and a lot more that we want to do in the future. It's an important account, as one might say in business; but as I like to say, it is part of my family, it is part of my home in the broadest sense. And so Sue, I'm sending you home!

President Bush and I look to you to deepen and expand our partnership with Jamaica in the years ahead, a partnership that will reap benefits in democracy, prosperity, and security for both of our countries and for the Caribbean region as a whole.

General Colin Powell, August 15, 2001

After placing my hand on the Bible and being sworn in, I responded with a few words of my own, saying:

This is an exciting and challenging time for the United States, for Jamaica, and for the Western Hemisphere. We are now preparing to enter a new era of progress and cooperation. One of the challenges is to set a course for sustained growth that leads to prosperity for all citizens and ensures stability in our region. We may have a few bumps in the road, but I am very confident the future is bright and exciting. I very much look forward to working with our friends in Jamaica to maintain a steady course that allows open markets to expand our economies and to improve the lives of people in both of our countries. We in the United States greatly value our traditional ties with Jamaica, and I go to Kingston committed to strengthening those deep and enduring bonds and building on our cooperation in important areas that affect the safety, welfare, security, and prosperity of both of our countries.

I concluded my remarks:

On the last page of My American Journey *I came across these words written by Colin Powell but equally applicable to me: "Jefferson once wrote, 'There is a debt of service due from every man to his country, proportioned to the bounties which nature and fortune have measured to him.' As one who has received so much from his country, I feel that debt heavily, and I can never be entirely free of it. My responsibility, our responsibility as lucky Americans, is to try to give back to this country as much as it has given to us, as we continue our American journey together."*

Imagine how I felt in December of that year when I received an essay written by the granddaughter of one of my closest friends, Joyce Allred, which captured the feeling of hope and inspiration at my swearing-in ceremony. Ron and Joyce

Allred had attended my swearing-in and brought along their granddaughter Samantha, who returned to Colorado and wrote the following for a school assignment.

Essay on Sue Cobb

Could it be that I was standing in the towering presence of Colin Powell, spending my birthday in a room so magnificent it made me proud to be an American? In spite of the warmth of the day, chills ran up my spine. I tried to steady my breathing as I stood up as straight as my 5' 4" frame would allow. Aunt Sue approached the podium. Sue Cobb, the most inspirational woman in my life, is not my real aunt; she's more than a blood relation. She's one of those close family friends whose loyalty and friendship is so strong that the bond is unbreakable. Momentarily she would be given the opportunity to achieve her goal of serving her country. As Secretary of State Powell prepared to swear her in as Ambassador to Jamaica, I envisioned someday standing in the rose garden as Ambassador Sue was inaugurated as the first woman president. Sue has no limits and has inspired me to set my standards high as well.

As if the reality of seeing Colin Powell outside of the 24" TV screen wasn't enough, my opinion of this woman who exemplifies strength and tenacity to me was validated by her national recognition. So, it wasn't just me who saw her greatness. Dressed quite appropriately in a bright pink suit, she began to take her oath. As she raised her right hand high, I thought of the advice she had given me as a child. 'You are special,' she would often say, 'a leader among your peers. It is your responsibility to reach for the stars, to strive and stretch to become the best that you can be.' All of my life I have embraced her ideals as my own.

Her voice steady, she did not allow her breath to quicken. No nervousness, no need to be nervous, she had worked for this. Determined from day one to work her way up, she achieved her goals one step at a time. Sue is a woman and a fighter, but she is also just a person, like me. I remember her rosy cheeks as we raced down the ski hill and the impatient tapping of her foot as she made an effort to sit through the ballet. She has consistently encouraged me by telling me she wished she had my potential. While watching Sue take this next step in her life, I realized that my highest aspirations were within my reach as long as I recognized that there will be obstacles to cross, but no limitations as to what I can achieve. She has proven that ambition coupled with hard work leads to success. I know that it will take determination, motivation and energy to make my life fulfilling, but something in my personality has enabled me to seek the opportunities others have cast off as impossible or too risky. I am aware that without risk there is no reward.

This most significant and important event in my life was coming to a close. With the swearing in ceremony over, I couldn't help but nod in agreement as Colin Powell proceeded to inform the impressive array of guests of the list of Sue's accomplishments, the steps she had taken to fulfill her dream. Through hard work and realistic goals, she has taken a step-by-step road to success. She has created a path that I am eager to follow.

Heart racing, I joined the receiving line to congratulate Ambassador Cobb. Her smile deepened when she saw me. She winked and whispered, 'Happy Birthday.' In that moment, in the Benjamin Franklin Room that has historically recognized the accomplishments of great Americans, I held the hand of the woman I've admired for years, and in that touch took away with me the potential for greatness.

Samantha Hilbert Thomas, 17 years old,
Fountain Valley School, December 7, 2001

To say that Samantha's comments were heart-warming to me is beyond necessity. Whatever challenges lay ahead in my term in office, it was reassuring to know that over the course of my life I had been able to influence some people, some events, for the better. I would make every effort to do that in my new job.

Chapter Thirteen

Demand excellence and empower people to achieve it.
General Colin Powell

UNITED STATES AMBASSADOR EXTRAORDINARY AND PLENIPOTENTIARY TO JAMAICA

September 11, 2001: A plane hit the World Trade Center. I watched my television in disbelief, in shock, as a second passenger plane hit the World Trade Center. I knew immediately that it was an act of terrorism. I also knew immediately that there would not be one single person in Washington during the next four years who would care one bit about what happened in Jamaica. And I was the new ambassador of the United States to Jamaica. Yes, on September 11, 2001 I would arrive at the embassy for my first day of work as the United States ambassador to Jamaica. I had prepared for my first day in the embassy to introduce myself to my country team. I would seek to gain their confidence in me, which I knew was critical. But on 9/11 the whole world changed. I was now on duty in Jamaica, and we were on our own. Was I prepared to take command of a near offshore mid-size United States embassy? Could I represent the United States government and its 330 million frightened citizens?

The first order of business at the country team meeting was the immediate tragedy. I discussed with the team how they could get in touch with family members and friends, what our next steps would be, what kind of information we expected to receive, and what my expectations were. And I asked them to support me and to give me their best advice. I announced that my husband, former United States Ambassador Chuck Cobb, would be meeting later in the day with all embassy spouses to share information and offer what comfort he could. It definitely was far from a normal introduction to embassy life.

Our military and law enforcement staff, of whom we had quite a few, immediately began addressing our embassy on personnel security procedures. We were in offices on the fifth, sixth, and seventh floors of a commercial building with all glass windows, on the busiest intersection in New Kingston. There were adjacent sidewalks, but no setbacks whatsoever. We were extremely exposed. Our country team immediately began working on the logistics of how we could protect this embassy and our people – the Americans and the Jamaicans who work in our embassy. We determined that the ambassador must make statements and have a public presence. It was a tough start. The Jamaican prime minister at the time remembers:

> I had to go to the American Embassy to sign the condolence book even before she [Ambassador Cobb] had presented her credentials. That was very unusual, unique, and the circumstances which brought me there tragic, not only for the United States but for the entire world – one which included the loss of lives for many people from Jamaica and the Caribbean.
>
> The trauma was unprecedented, so we had to cut through the formalities of her not formally presenting her credentials to the governor-general and not formally calling upon me, a prime minister, to respond to the situation. I think it's true to say we struck up a very, very good relationship.
>
> The Most Honorable P. J. Patterson, March 10, 2018

My mental challenge in that first country team meeting included assessing the strength of my team and who I might really rely on. Who in that room were thoughtful, knowledgeable, stable people whom I could depend on? I'd had the advantage of spending a day in Miami with my deputy chief of mission (DCM) when he came to meet me while he was still chargé d'affaires in Kingston. A new ambassador is completely free to choose a new deputy, so the change is automatically an unsettling experience for the incumbent DCM serving as chargé d'affaires. Chargé Richard Smyth struck me as an extremely capable person. I remember saying in Miami, "Look, I know this is always difficult because frequently an ambassador wants to make a change, bring in his or her own DCM, and that may not fit with your plans as a career officer." I continued, "I assume capability, but I think a lot of this is chemistry. I know you know your job and you don't know if I know my job, but we're going to figure that out within six months, so consider yourself fully employed for a minimum of six months. We'll talk."

Was I ever lucky! I loved my DCM, Richard Henry Smyth. Richard was a minister-counselor in the State Department who had served in Afghanistan, India, Iraq, Indonesia, Denmark, Pakistan, and Sri Lanka. I knew Richard really didn't want to be in Jamaica, he wanted to be back in Afghanistan, but he was assigned to serve with me in Jamaica for at least another year and a half. He had already been at Embassy Kingston for several months as the chargé d'affaires (the head of an embassy without a Senate-confirmed ambassador), so I knew he understood all the issues. He obviously had very good contacts in the Jamaican government; I had none. He turned out to be a brilliant individual of enormous integrity and unusual vision. Rich was totally dedicated to doing the right thing for the embassy, for the State Department, and for his country. Fortunately, he also had the capacity to step away from his command position due to the fact that there was a new ambassador in town. He did everything he could to help me and to steer me in the right direction. This was a very good relationship. I learned a great deal from Rich and was proud of our work results. I still feel that any successes I had as United States ambassador in Jamaica are attributable to Richard Smyth.

I was the United States ambassador in Jamaica for three and a half years, a post that suited both my high-powered spouse and me. I did not seek it. I had never once given a thought to being a United States ambassador until the White House Office of Presidential Personnel called me, then I did. I gave a lot of thought to choosing Jamaica as a post I would consider. I knew that almost all-important meetings relating to the Western Hemisphere, which includes South America, Central America, and the Caribbean were convened either in Washington or Miami. If they were in Washington, I would have to transit through Miami. So I would be assured that every few weeks I would be in Miami, or in Washington via Miami, on State Department business.

This also meant that Chuck wouldn't have to go through a full-scale move to Kingston. He could be in Miami and carry on our businesses. I could call him any day and say, "Okay, you've got to be here Friday night." Or, "Come for the weekend." In total, he was with me in Jamaica close to half the time. And he was happy to be there. He met a lot of people, played golf, and turned out to be a great host and an extremely popular figure on the diplomatic circuit. But Chuck is an action-oriented person. He cannot sit around. He has got to be working at something. Sitting idly by was not his forte. We could also both see in the first few days we were in Kingston together, that it would not work to have two decision-makers for issues that arose, with only one of them authorized to call the shots. Chuck and I have completely different management styles. We generally get to the same end result, but in quite a different manner. In our case, it worked out well that he could easily come to Kingston in less than two hours, but also keep his own businesses and interests on track.

The Country Team: Each of our embassies around the world has a group of State Department representatives and representatives of other relevant government agencies stationed at the post. From State, in addition to the DCM, we had a consul general, a political officer, an economic officer (or combined political/economic officer), a public affairs officer, a management officer, and a couple of specialized personnel. The ambassador either brought or retained a personal high-level administrative assistant, known as an office management specialist (OMS). We were considered a mid-size embassy. Depending on the bilateral circumstances, there are representatives of other agencies in all embassies either temporarily or permanently. In Kingston, we had the DEA, Agriculture, USAID, and the Peace Corps, two military representatives with support staff, the Marshal's Service, and other representatives of United States agencies sent to help manage instant circumstances.

In the early days of my tour, I delegated DCM Smyth much of the "law and order" portfolio such as meeting with the Jamaican commissioner of police whom he already knew well and staying in close touch with the military side, ours and theirs, because he had a great deal of experience in the area and knew all of the embassy's law enforcement interlocutors. Unseasoned as I was, I needed to study that arena before jumping into it. Richard forewarned me about how all the different people he had come to know would react to me and to our issues and how we might manage various temperaments and egos. Every single morning, we met in my office, went over everything from the day before, and everything that was coming up. Every day. I don't think we ever missed a day unless he or I were off the island. I was also a voracious reader of cable traffic and met with country team members frequently. I was not hesitant to provide advice. Nor was Richard. We did everything together. We simply worked well together and in all the time we worked together he never violated my one hard and fast rule: "no surprises." When Richard left at the end of his tour, I talked to personnel advisors at State and became the beneficiary of another very fine senior FSO, Cliff Tighe. By the time Cliff arrived, I was a pretty well-established ambassador (at least in my own mind), so Cliff and I had a different kind of relationship. Cliff was a pro and an extremely knowledgeable administrative officer. I greatly appreciated his use of those skills and his guidance over the remaining months of my tenure.

Jamaicans were extraordinarily sympathetic over 9/11. Prior to presenting my credentials in the proper manner, both the prime minister and the foreign minister called me and offered sincere sympathy and condolences, asking how they could be helpful. The church community, supported by the government, held a massive candlelight memorial at the Stella Maris Roman Catholic Church for those lost in the Twin Towers tragedy, Jamaicans among them. Almost everyone was deeply sympathetic. The hard core progressive socialists and many non-aligned thinkers didn't necessarily want to align with the United States in any way but they, too, were touched and, as were all of us, scared about terrorism. Everyone was scared. Jamaicans were largely sympathetic and appreciative of the fact that the United States would go all out to take care of this new turn in world affairs. In truth, Jamaicans reacted like most human beings – shocked and appalled, sorry about the losses, scared for themselves, for their own country, and scared for humanity. That's what most people felt. As time passed, attitudes changed and many hardened. Of course, in 2002 and 2003 we had to contend with questions about why the United

States should go into Iraq. I supported the decision for the same reasons that George Bush and other senior level US officials did. Jamaicans were of mixed feelings.

Strategic Planning: One of the first projects in which I became totally immersed initially arose from the State Department's Office of the Inspector General's (OIG) 2000 report. The Inspector General and staff had been in Jamaica about a year before I arrived on their normal five-year rounds of embassy inspections, so I had the benefit of a very current OIG report and knew from the OIG's perspective where problems existed within Embassy Kingston.

Shortly after my tour commenced, we had to prepare and submit the annual Mission Performance Plan (MPP), essentially the embassy's strategic plan. It is now called the Mission Strategic Plan (MSP). The embassy's current budget had already been set two years earlier. In 2001 Embassy Kingston's budget had been set based on the 1999 MPP. Going into 2001–2002 we were planning the 2004 budget. Trying to project ahead two years is tricky enough, and suddenly we were heading into a war and had new security concerns. Some of the professionals in the State Department and in my embassy kind of brushed off this strategic planning process. They said, "Look, Ambassador, you don't have to spend any time on this. It's a form. We'll get last year's and check the boxes like we did the year before. Nothing's going to change because it is what it is." To them this was just a routine pro forma long document to fill out for the Department, but to me it wasn't. There was a new administration in Washington, facing different circumstances. I was not going to just check off on boxes of the previous administration. I felt that we should really go through every single line item in every section, whether it was public affairs, consular services, USAID, DEA, or other area. My goal was to align our resource requests with Washington policy prescriptions and to set out priorities for what our team wanted to accomplish during their assignment in Jamaica. Moreover, I wanted to give my input for the upcoming three to four years that I was actually going to be in place providing leadership.

I arrived in September. The MPP was due in February. It was an inch thick in the special language all State Department people know by heart, but I didn't. DCM Smyth had said, "Usually we just have the section heads do their part, we put it together, and we send it in." And I said, "This time we're going to talk with the section heads. We're going to interview them, you and I, and we're going to go over this document and our requests are going to be really thoughtful."

I did not know that the Bush administration was so focused on fiscal accountability that State Department management had actually budgeted to give a large cash award for the best 2002 embassy strategic plan. I just wanted to make sure that our priorities were aligned with the president's National Security Strategy and that we were putting the right resources into the right areas. When I got everybody at the embassy together to really focus on a strategic plan for the ensuing four or five years (including the 2004 budget), the whole team did a superb job and leaders in the State Department in Washington realized that.

I felt that by 2004 Kingston definitely had to have a new embassy. If big trouble erupted, our people might as well have been standing nude on Old Hope Road. I knew it would cost a ton of money. Really a lot of money. Typically, a new ambassador does not go to a country and ask for a new embassy. However, from a security perspective, we could not have been more vulnerable in the chancery or in the consular and USAID buildings a few blocks away. The Peace Corps leadership headquarters was also in an exposed building. All the buildings would have been very easy to take out. At the chancery, where my office was located, we entered through a basement that originally was open for public parking with no guard at the entry. Even with our new guard on duty anybody could easily drive into the basement and blow up the whole building simple as that. It was beyond unsecure. My immediate thoughts after 9/11 were since it is possible to smuggle drugs anywhere in the Caribbean and certainly through Jamaica it was also possible to smuggle people, arms, and explosives. How might terrorists or collaborators damage America from or in Jamaica? The United States ambassador is responsible for the lives of every single American in the host country. This was an old, inconvenient, inefficient, vulnerable, mid-size embassy. I decided a new embassy complex was going to be my highest priority for my first Mission Performance Plan.

When our MPP hit the State Department, five men from Washington wanted to talk to me on Skype about my request. A couple of the senior management officers at the State Department, Chris Burnham and Grant Green, the heads of what we called "M" (for Management), were seriously high-level financial types and clearly understood the costs. But they were also knowledgeable and practical men. For starters, all of us were very much aware of the 1998 bombings at our embassies in Nairobi and Dar es Salaam, and I knew that the then United States ambassador in Nairobi, Prudence Bushnell, prior to the bombings, had repeatedly explained to State Department personnel how exposed her United States Embassy was. Everyone in Washington knew that story.

So when Chris Burnham said, "Ambassador Cobb, why in the world would you put a new embassy as your highest priority?" I replied, "It's pretty obvious to me that we have a very high degree of exposure here in Kingston for our American citizens who we ask to work here and serve our country. Obviously, our Jamaican employees are exposed, too. If the ambassador doesn't make it a high priority, certainly nobody else will. Just to be clear, that's my highest priority, to keep our people safe." So, they approved it.

There is a division of the State Department called Overseas Building Operations (OBO), which has a list of the year in which an embassy or an American official residence has been redecorated, reconstructed, reinforced, or changed in some manner. My asking for a new embassy in Kingston was out of order and highly unusual; giving it to us was even more unusual. The head of OBO in George W. Bush's administration, General Chuck Williams, had been the head of the United States Army Corps of Engineers. He was imminently qualified to build an embassy and build it quickly. I gained General Williams's support to move the United States Embassy in Jamaica up the chain, and Secretary Powell signed off on it. OBO went on to build several more, new embassy structures as part of Secretary Powell's Diplomatic Readiness Initiative.

Prior to my arrival, my predecessor had convinced the State Department to purchase the 130-room Crowne Plaza hotel property, which was in bankruptcy. The State Department bought this tower hotel with a swimming pool and tennis court, located in a nice area of town. The decision had been taken that the tower could be successfully used as a new embassy. However, my team and subsequently my government felt that there wasn't enough space for all embassy functions and due to certain topographical features, the building would require not only considerable renovating, but unusually high security costs. We advocated use of the tower for other embassy needs and constructing a larger structure for the new embassy on a ten-acre property called Bamboo Pen, which the United States had owned for many years. That location had the ground space, was in a less congested traffic area, and could be properly secured for significantly less money. Building the new embassy and reconstruction of the tower took my entire tenure, requiring very significant oversight as well as considerable hand-holding and public relations work. The new embassy was completed in late 2005 and dedicated by my successor, Ambassador Brenda LaGrange Johnson a few months after I left Kingston.

When I arrived, the official residence for the United States ambassador was another beautiful ten-acre property owned by the United States for many years, located on Long Lane in Stony Hill. The residence was a comfortable Caribbean style house with large lawns, many gorgeous mature trees, a swimming pool, and a detached two-bedroom guest house. As chief of mission residences go, it was a modest sized house in a lovely area where well-to-do city dwellers in days past built country homes as a welcome retreat on weekends. The bad part was that if you drove to work from this beautiful property during normal working hours, leaving the house at 7:00 a.m., the traffic on the two-lane road into town would already be so heavy it would take an hour and a half to go the nine miles. So I always left no later than 6:30 a.m. when it would only take a half an hour. Returning, I would never go home at a normal hour because it was the same thing in reverse. Usually, I would leave the embassy around 6:30 p.m. or 7:00 p.m. Many evenings, I would go directly to that evening's diplomatic function and reach my Stony Hill home much later. These were routinely pretty long working days, and the staff noticed.

When I retired, members of the staff would stop by my office to say goodbye, usually including something about me being "a hard-working ambassador." I'm glad they noticed, because it sets a standard. One day our top IT officer came in and said, "Ambassador Cobb, I just want to tell you that I really admire you." And I asked, "Well now, my friend, why would you say that?" And he said, "Because I am required to come to work at

5:00 every morning and because of my work I could see when you came in every single morning. It was always between 6:00 and 7:00 a.m. You were frequently the first person here. I also saw or had records of when you left at night. I knew you were really paying attention to your job." While I appreciated his comments, I thought to myself, "Oh my, what else have I done that I didn't know they've seen?"

Of course I do not expect others to work as I do in time or intensity. But I would expect them to understand that in doing so I probably have a pretty good idea of their circumstances and of the kind of job they are doing. One friend asked me if I'd ever heard of 'work-life balance'? I really laughed (only to myself) when I thought of all the time I spent over the years on that exact subject on my own behalf and that of others.

Ambassador Brenda Johnson (2005–2009) was the last United States ambassador to live in the lovely old residence on Long Lane. We were and still are very close friends and I was in Jamaica fairly frequently during her tenure. Ambassador Johnson and her husband Howard always invited me to stay with them, so to me it felt like I lived on Long Lane for eight years. After Ambassador Johnson departed, the department sold the old residence and purchased a new residence closer to the new embassy, eliminating an hour or more of driving. Ambassador Pamela Bridgewater (2010–13) was the beneficiary of the shortened drive. Ambassador Luis Moreno (2014–17) lived in yet another official residence, which Ambassador Don Tapia inherited. All were very adequate. All had their pros and cons.

Through the hard work done in preparing the MPP and advocating our priorities, we received approval for the new complex, and we were soon to learn that we got a bonus. Embassy Kingston's MPP won the State Department's worldwide competition for the best Mission Performance Plan in the world. Embassy Kingston won! Secretary Powell had our plan put on the State Department opening page as an example for all United States embassies worldwide to use as a model. We were elated. I admit it – I was ecstatic. I was told that a monetary award was originally set at $300,000 for the winning post. However, Ecuador had also written an outstanding MPP and State decided to split the money between these two mid-size Western Hemisphere embassies. I said, "Fine just send me a check." I think Kristi Kenny, then ambassador to Ecuador, whom I greatly admired and respected, felt exactly the same way. Had the winner been London or Paris, the money would have been a drop in the bucket; but for a post like Jamaica, it was big money and one of the few times in my experience when money was allotted to a post that wasn't pre-designated as to specifically how it could be spent.

Ambassador Seminars: Another extremely fortuitous event happening early in my tenure was a call from Ambassador Prudence Bushnell. I did not know her personally, but I knew she was a highly respected Foreign Service officer (FSO) and was the United States ambassador in Kenya in 1998 when the terrible Nairobi and Dar es Salaam embassy bombings occurred.

Ambassador Bushnell gave a sober account of that traumatic time in her book, *Terrorism, Betrayal, and Resilience: My Story of the 1998 U.S. Embassy Bombings.* She explained that the explosion left over 200 dead and 5,000 injured. The State Department made a training video of the steps Ambassador Bushnell and her team took managing that crisis after the ambassador realized she wasn't dead, simply bleeding. She is a real leader and a terrific human being.

In 2002, as the new dean of the Leadership and Management School at the Foreign Service Institute (FSI), part of the George P. Schultz National Foreign Affairs Training Center in

Arlington, Virginia, Ambassador Bushnell had a lot of ideas about how to structure the FSI leadership seminars, particularly the ambassador seminars. I think Ambassador Bushnell must have known, and it's still true, that I am the only woman in the United States who has been both a non-career ambassador and the spouse of a living non-career ambassador. There are a few career FSO ambassador couples, but my husband and I are the only non-career ambassadors in the history of the country to be married and to serve as chiefs of missions while both of us are alive. Pru recognized the significance. She said, "Because we at FSI have non-career spouses included in our two- or three-week ambassador seminars, you would be a perfect person to provide both views." She invited me to visit with her the next time I was in Washington to discuss how to address both husbands, wives, and later partners, during the leadership and management classes of the ambassador seminars.

The Leadership and Management School sought feedback through an interesting subject specific survey sent to about 600 or 700 senior level State Department persons who were either ambassadors or top-level FSOs. They structured two questions asking: "What are the strengths and weaknesses of good ambassadors, and what are the most important characteristics of an effective ambassador?" They also did a similar survey relating to DCMs.

Personally, I thought the most important characteristic was to demonstrate invincible integrity. That was my number one. The poll responses received had, in order, decisive, empowering, and integrity at the top of their list. Team building, charismatic, and visionary were among the other desirable traits chosen by the responding diplomats. Pru put together the demanding new course that became the ambassador seminar as of 2002 and invited me to co-chair the seminars with her. The State Department gave me permission to periodically leave post for two weeks. I continued as co-chair of three or four seminars a year for the entire eight years of the George W. Bush administration. When Pru moved on to be ambassador to Guatemala and later ambassador to Mali, I served with the next appointed deans of the Leadership and Management School, all of whom were former ambassadors. It was truly a great pleasure for me to serve with Michael Guest, and later with Tom Robertson and the other outstanding ambassadors who became deans. Chris Powers was an experienced and able consultant throughout my years at FSI and Gail Neelon, now associate dean at the Leadership and Management School, was an invaluable resource on all things relating to the State Department.

I would leave Kingston about once a quarter for a couple weeks to co-chair the FSI ambassador seminars. When I could not do so, another non-career ambassador would step in; but through those years, I probably co-chaired about fifteen ambassador seminars. I really enjoyed that unique opportunity to meet both career and non-career ambassadors-designate who would serve all over the world. It was also a great opportunity to learn about the State Department in further depth and to make and solidify friendships with many Foreign Service officers. I was and am proud of the State Department and the incredible, frequently unrecognized, work our FSOs do for our country.

Chuck felt the same way and when he left Iceland, he worked with the State Department to create and support an award to encourage trade development, called the *Charles E. Cobb Award for Initiative and Success in Trade Development*. The winner could be an ambassador or a Foreign Service officer (now it is solely for a career ambassador) in any embassy in the world. Through a nomination and review process, the individual selected receives recognition at the State Department annual awards ceremony and $10,000. The award became very popular. Due to Chuck's award, I frequently went to the annual awards ceremonies during the years I was co-chairing the ambassador seminars. I noticed that there were about thirty prestigious awards presented by the secretary of state to State Department personnel and foreign employees, but there were no awards for even a truly outstanding non-career ambassador. We non-career ambassadors were fully a part of the State Department, and I thought it would be fair if there were at least one award for the non-career ambassador deemed to exemplify the ideals of the State Department in representing our country.

I worked with the department leadership to get the approvals for a non-career ambassador award. They named it the *Sue M. Cobb Award for Exemplary Diplomatic Service*. The $10,000 that accompanies this award does not go to the individual, but rather half goes to the Leadership and Management School for leadership training and half goes to the winning ambassador's post as program funds for use at the chief of mission's direction.

The State Department maintains specific criteria for these two Cobb annual awards and nominations can come from any embassy in the world. Often nominations are submitted by a deputy chief of mission who has worked most closely with the ambassador. Nominations must be approved by several officials at the State Department. Once approved, the nominees' achievements go to a selection committee composed of ranking department officials and selected non-career former ambassadors. It is fascinating to read the nominations and satisfying to see the great work and brilliant diplomacy of many of our non-career ambassadors.

The Consular Section: In the Inspector General's 2000 report on Embassy Kingston there were two areas that concerned me. One was in what we then called Admin, pertaining to administrative matters and management of financial resources. In my judgment, people just weren't being as careful as they needed to be, merely getting through the paperwork perfunctorily without any questioning of the underlying work and little oversight of work performed. The second was with respect to specific criticisms of management in the consular section, which I felt might derive from leadership issues. Fortunately, Kingston was just receiving a new experienced consul general, Donald Wells, with his wife, Natalie. Don's reputation preceded him. He was an absolutely superb officer in whom I quickly gained complete confidence, and management problems were soon put to rest.

Natalie Wells and Rich Smyth's wife, Janice, were both Foreign Service veterans and played significant roles in staff morale and other areas of embassy life like the American Women's Club and the American International School of Kingston. As far as I was concerned, Natalie and Janice were both superstars and critical players on the embassy team.

Don Wells faced significant challenges since Jamaica is one of the largest visa-issuing posts in the world. We had new officers, in the consular section, mostly young, all on their first tour of duty. Several were inclined to be extraordinarily strict because they didn't have a history of judging applications and people. And we were always shorthanded. The work hours were long and lonely, compounded by the fact that our consular section was about four blocks from the executive offices in the embassy chancery.

In addition to the inspector general's report, I heard by the fairly reliable grapevine about the simmering discontent in our consular section, so I made a habit of visiting the consular section. However, I carefully stayed out of any adjudication discussions. In my early days, some Jamaicans would direct impassioned pleas to me (all with good stories) asking for help in getting a visa to the United States. I learned not to get caught in such discussions and I never advanced anybody to the consul general. I knew that was a path to certain turmoil for me, because if one Jamaican knew that the ambassador interceded or tried to intercede, I would see a deluge of requests. I quickly earned a reputation for just saying "No." Nonetheless, to this day, Jamaicans or their United States-based relatives call to ask if I can help with a visa. The answer is still "No."

I've always had a little bit of the teacher in me and wanted our mostly young consular officers to have the best access to the ambassador that we could arrange, so Consul General Wells agreed to have programs for the junior officers, JOs as we called them at the time, in which I or another senior member of the embassy team would discuss policies or processes. I often talked to the JOs about economics and would pick one or two who showed an interest and give them special educational projects. We rotated a junior officer through the ambassador's office on eight-week assignments, which they loved because they could then see how embassies really function, what kind of internal policies we had, and exactly why we were there. It was not possible to see the broad picture when sitting at a consular window all day adjudicating visas. I like to think that we did a really good job of educating the junior officers during my tenure, not because of me, but because we had such an excellent consul general. After Don Wells left Kingston, he became consul general in Paris. Our very strong pol/econ officer Mike Koplovsky also took an interest in JO training. I was truly blessed with terrific key senior officers during my tenure.

Terrorism and Guantanamo: Terrorism obviously had become a very big concern after the Twin Tower bombings, and I continued to worry about the known and unknown drug routes being used for nefarious purposes against the United States. We remained on high alert. I spoke frequently with our military and law enforcement personnel. One group of Jamaicans who had adopted the Islamic faith came to our attention. Some, we knew, had converted while in prison in the United States and had been returned to Jamaica. The law enforcement view was that many had gotten into the States illegally, gotten involved with illegal activities, got caught, and were tossed into the slammer. There, it was thought, they were radicalized and later came home to create a small group of activists in Jamaica. This really concerned me. However, there was another small group of the Islamic faith whom we knew were unhappy with the activists, and we were discreetly kept abreast of all serious threats, a couple of which I found credible and scary. Fortunately, all potential enforcement issues that came to light were manageable. Of course, criminal activity continued, corruption was abundant, and drugs continued to flow, but we had no unmanageable incidents. In later years, the drug traffic diminished in the Caribbean and a great amount shifted to Central America and Mexico. The Jamaicans remained creative though with schemes and scams that challenged their authorities and ours.

I visited Guantanamo three times during my years in Jamaica. The first time was in July 2003. Career Foreign Service officer Ambassador Vicki Huddleston (who in 2018 published a fascinating book, *Our Woman in Havana*), was head of the United States Interest Section in Havana, the equivalent of our ambassador. Vicki invited Chuck and me and the then United States Ambassador to the Dominican Republic, Hans Hertell, and his wife Maria to visit Guantanamo and Havana. Chuck and I had offered our small Cessna and Mike Lee, our pilot, went through all the rigmarole of getting everyone cleared into Guantanamo and from there into Havana.

The Guantanamo experience was a strong shot of reality. The day we landed at Guantanamo, July 11, 2003, we were still standing by our plane on the tarmac as another larger plane arrived. Off came men in orange jumpsuits, fully hooded and shackled at both wrists and ankles – one of the very first deliveries of battlefield combatants. In those early days, Guantanamo facilities had only the miserable chain-link fence enclosures seen in many newspapers, which looked like dog kennels. Other facilities for the early arriving prisoners were under construction but had not been completed. Photos of the lodging were embarrassing to the administration and generated a tremendous push to get a proper prison built quickly. I couldn't help but think about what an odd moment in life it was to be standing on the tarmac in the Caribbean – close to home – as these shackled prisoners were dropped in from a war zone some 7,000 miles away. It was stunning. I'd never seen anything like that. The closest memory I had was when the United States interred our own citizens of Japanese descent during World War II. I remember vividly from childhood a Japanese internment camp about two miles from our ranch in California. It was fully fenced, but I was afraid to even go by the facility in a car. Now these orange clad prisoners were within feet of me. They couldn't see me because they were fully hooded, but I could see them. Suddenly the war was very close.

As the head of the United States Interest Section in Havana, Ambassador Huddleston went to Guantanamo periodically. During that July visit, because we were United States ambassadors serving in nearby countries, we got a full tour of the prison as it was at the time. We also toured the Naval base, which is a separate facility, though in close proximity. We spoke at some length with the Naval attorneys about the interrogation of prisoners and what the plans might be for future judicial procedures and for humanitarian protections. Early in 2003 there were not many good answers. There was a totally unexpected, confusing experience being played out on a world stage with yet to be resolved ramifications. This was a long way from the ranch in Chino. After concluding our visit, we were off to visit the capitol of a State Sponsor of Terrorism.

When Ambassador Huddleston greeted us at the Havana airport she warned us, "There is total surveillance of all Americans in Cuba. Every word you say will be heard. You can count on that. You will be photographed. You might not know you're being photographed, but you will be. Be careful what you say and how you say it. Even in my car, you cannot talk to me about anything of importance."

Vicki held a reception that night at her official residence in Havana. Constructed before WWII, it was one of the most beautiful residences built for United States ambassadors, located in an exclusive part of Havana where Fidel Castro also had a home. Ambassador Huddleston hosted the embassy team and a number of dissidents who gamely explained their stories and experiences to us. The Foreign Service officers described what it was like living in Cuba. They would come home after a day at the office in our old United States Embassy on the Malecon, and Cuban agents would have been inside their homes. They could tell by something the Cubans had purposely done. Sometimes agents would leave a window open, or if a window had been open, they'd close it. Odiously, they sometimes left excrement in the houses. The Americans would try clever schemes to keep Cuban agents out or at least determine if they'd come in without leaving a trace. Think about a spider web stuck on one wall and wrapped around a door handle. It was clear the Cubans regularly intruded.

Vicki was heroic in her efforts on behalf of the dissidents. At dinner in the gorgeous tropical home of the United States Head of Interest Section, we met the well-known dissidents Osvaldo Paya, Elizardo Sanchez, Vladimir Rocha, and Oscar Espinoza, among others. Joining us were ambassadors to Cuba from Belgium, the Netherlands, Switzerland, Canada, as well as the UK chargé d'affaires. Peter Corsell, Lou Nigro, and Ryan Dooley of the Interest Section watched over us. To this day, Ryan Dooley, one of the officers whom I met that night in Havana, still serves our country. He now lives in Miami operating our United States Passport Office and remains a close friend. From every perspective this was a fascinating trip. Ambassador Huddleston's book sheds much light on the historical circumstance of this clash and on lives of Americans and dissidents living and working in Havana.

The following day we had lunch at a restaurant at Havana's gorgeous harbor. We were three sitting United States ambassadors, two important spouses, and three or four Americans from the Interest Section – maybe eight or nine of us seated at an outdoor rectangular table overlooking the harbor. It seemed idyllic, but reality quickly encroached. We weren't seated for more than three minutes when workmen walked alongside with ladders, put them up against pillars just two feet away from our table, and attached what were obviously listening devices. They went around our table making sure that every single person could be heard. We clearly saw what they were doing. You couldn't miss it. We laughed and carried on, but we definitely could not talk shop!

One night we went to dinner, not at the residence, but at one of the few private spots that Castro allowed to operate as a family restaurant. Il Guardia was situated on the top of five floors inside a large mansion that had been privately owned before 1959. The grand marble staircase remained in the center and as we made our way up each floor level to the restaurant, which seated seventeen people, we could not avoid looking into the rooms on each floor that opened onto the grand central staircase. In every one of those rooms a family lived with children, dogs, cats, noisy chatter, and considerable litter. Dinner was excellent.

Another memorable excursion on the same trip was when Vicki took us around Old Havana, which was beautiful on the exterior, but we learned was like a stage set. The United Nations supported restoration of colonial frontages for some buildings in Old Havana, which were gorgeous, but if you walked through the front doors, there was complete desolation behind each facade. There were no interior improvements, just trash. Each building was a carefully restored facade on an empty shell.

Of course, we went to Hemingway's old hangouts, La Bodeguita del Medio and La Florida. Though mid-afternoon, Vicki said, "Let's just go in and have a beer or something." We went into La Florida. Musicians were playing Cuba's enchanting music. Ambassador Hans Hertel demanded, "We can't have a beer, we have to have a mojito." With my preference for Pinot Noir wine, I had not had a hard alcoholic drink for forty years, but that day I had a mojito. Hans had one, and despite the guards' incessant gawking, we decided to dance. It was really quite something – maybe a little like a scene from a vintage movie. That's a long time ago now, 2003, but a warm memory. I still feel pride in Vicki's helping United States efforts to bring democracy back to Cuba, a story that continues to unfold.

I returned to Guantanamo in August 2003, transported by the United States military from Kingston to the United States Navy base. The purpose was to give a Jamaica Independence Day speech for the Jamaicans who work at the base performing grounds keeping and maintenance at the base hotel and Naval billets and serving in the post exchange. Almost all of the service providers at the base (not at the prison) are from Jamaica. A group would come from Jamaica every Monday, stay all week through Saturday, go home, and another group would arrive. The workers constantly rotated back and forth. In 2004, I was again invited to speak at Guantanamo on Jamaica's Independence Day. The prison facilities and a hospital had been built quickly and were impressive in quality and scope. Each visit provided opportunities to learn with only one minor misstep. A junior officer I took along on one trip almost landed in the brig for taking forbidden photos. I rescued him as he was being escorted away by a United States security officer for his interrogation.

Another vivid memory I have of my time in Jamaica was captured by *The Daily Observer,* one of Jamaica's two leading newspapers. They printed a supplement entitled *The World Remembers 9/11* with the headline "Jamaica shows solidarity with US." There on the cover of *Pure Class* magazine September 15, 2002, was a photograph of Portia Simpson Miller beside Chuck and me, hands on our hearts, an American flag in the background. Portia Simpson Miller, future Jamaican prime minister and minister of tourism at the time, joined Chuck and me in lighting a unity candle at Webster Memorial United Church in Kingston. The commemorative service on that first anniversary of the tragedy reinforced the goodwill that the Jamaican people felt towards America.

What stays with me in a profound way from my tour in Jamaica is the hundreds and hundreds of times that I stood beside the American flag representing my country and 330 million Americans. The *Star-Spangled Banner* would start to play. To me it was always a moving experience and, in those days, weeks, and months following 9/11 a chill would run through my body as our National Anthem commenced.

Jamaican Elections and Economy: Both President George Bush and Secretary of State Powell told me they would visit Jamaica during my term as ambassador, but due to world events, they were not able to do so. Other officials and celebrities travelled in and out of the country but almost always to the north and west coast resorts. In Kingston we dealt with the government and business leaders. Congressman Charlie Rangel came once early in my tour and told me that elected officials in the States couldn't politically afford to come to Jamaica because many taxpayers saw trips to the Caribbean as boondoggles. They don't see it as an elected official trying to understand and work through whatever issues may exist between two countries. As a result, those elected officials who did come for R&R wanted to stay under the radar and away from probing media. Few called on the United States ambassador to avoid generating a front-page photo in *The Gleaner* or *Observer*.

I did welcome former president and Noble Peace Prize-winner Jimmy Carter to the island and held a reception in his honor at our residence. He came to Jamaica with a team from the Carter Center to observe the Jamaican elections of October 16, 2002. The People's National Party (PNP), founded by Norman Washington Manley, won thirty-four of the sixty seats, and Percival Noel James Patterson, was returned as prime minister, becoming the first political leader to win three successive elections. He served from 1992 to 2006 and was prime minister throughout my four-year term. Portia Simpson Miller replaced P. J., as he was called, on February 26, 2006, becoming Jamaica's first female prime minister. The Jamaica Labour Party (JLP) was founded by Alexander Bustamante. The JLP took power in 1962 and Bustamante became prime minister from 1962 to 1967. He was followed by JLP prime ministers Hugh Shearer (1967–72), Edward Seaga (1980–89), and Bruce Golding (2007–11). Andrew Holness was elected for a brief stint October 2011 to January 2012, and re-elected in 2016 and again in 2020.

I leaned to the view that Norman Manley's son, Prime Minister Michael Manley (1972–1980 and 1989–92), who declared in 1974 that the PNP would follow a socialist platform, was an extremely charismatic man who led Jamaica in the wrong direction for long enough that many lost the incentive or interest in working to produce and create goods and capital. The turbulent elections in the '70s led Edward Seaga to a landslide Jamaica Labour Party (JLP) victory in 1980, promising to end the socialist practices and the violent crime which had become a way of life for some. Prime Minister Seaga was the first national leader to be invited by President Ronald Reagan to visit the White House after Reagan's election in November of 1980. When Edward Seaga died on May 28, 2019, he was saluted by opposition former prime minister P. J. Patterson for his "monumental contribution" to the nation. He was honored with three days of mourning, a state funeral, and laid to rest in National Heroes Park in Kingston.

The PNP came back into power in 1989 with Manley offering a more moderate platform, but due to ill health, Manley handed over leadership to P. J. Patterson, who then served for fourteen consecutive years. During Prime Minister Patterson's time in office, Jamaica's politics were relatively stable, but the economy was not growing. Throughout history we've seen that management and execution often deteriorate when administrations last a long time. It's just human nature. In Jamaica when I was there, the PNP was in its second decade of governing, and I admit that I felt their *modus operandi* wasn't as crisp and disciplined as their acolytes proclaimed. It was not my job, however, to judge. My job was to work with the elected leadership of the country to advance bilateral relations in ways agreeable to both countries.

When I arrived in Jamaica in 2001, it was generally conceded that Jamaica's large debt was a major problem. The effects of globalization on small island economies was becoming obvious. Technology was growing by leaps and bounds enhancing trade around the world. In those early years of the twenty-first century, Jamaica was having a hard time keeping up. Without a growing GDP, it is exceedingly hard to meet debt service and domestic obligations. A country deeply in debt cannot build schools, hospitals, road systems, ports, railroads, or other infrastructure.

Though Prime Minister Patterson created a promising road network and port plan, the country remained in large part an agrarian society without the infrastructure that would allow it to benefit from the increasingly global trading environment. This economic condition attracted the interest of China and the first of many Chinese loans came to Jamaica and other countries of the Western Hemisphere. With respect to Jamaica, evidence suggests that loans obtained from China were cautiously approached as they remain a small percent of the country's debt.

Having served several years on the Federal Reserve Board in Miami, I was fairly well educated in macroeconomics. I had benefited from Chuck's experiences as undersecretary of Commerce in the United States and through working with our company, Cobb Partners, which managed many large developments. I was keenly aware of both monetary and fiscal constraints and how difficult the existing situation was for the government and people of Jamaica. Early Chinese investments in the Western Hemisphere did not seem to cause much concern in Washington, and in fact were frequently brushed off as China simply filling its commodity needs. But as China's investments grew and loans were spread to strategic sites around the hemisphere, the subject captured Washington's attention and finally has become a high priority concern.

The Gleaner, the oldest newspaper in the Caribbean, invited me to their Editor's forum which traditionally focused on matters of significant importance in the bilateral relationship. I focused on the manner in which the Free Trade Area of the Americas (FTAA) and the World Trading Organization (WTO) measures might impact negatively on the Jamaican domestic market, particularly farming. I discussed some intricacies of the negotiations, pointing out among other things:

> *The United States has proposed to eliminate export subsidies with reductions phased in over a five-year period in equal annual*

increments; to reduce all agricultural tariffs and expand all tariff rate quotas (TRQs in the trade language) and eliminate the special agricultural safeguards.

I assumed *The Gleaner* editors were intensely interested in these trade matters. In an article the following weekend entitled "Cobb Speaks Green" in *The Gleaner Farmers Weekly* (November 16, 2002), no such critically important topics surfaced. I was somewhat taken aback that the article skipped over trade and ended with this question:

"When your tour of duty comes to an end, what's next for Ambassador Sue Cobb? Will she be seeking political office elsewhere?"

Seeking to avoid a serious answer, I had responded: "I will probably retire in Port Antonio!"

It was widely known that I was very keen on scuba diving, so Port Antonio, on Jamaica's northeast coast was a great escape – no media, no interviews, no questions under water! I may have been one of the few United States ambassadors in Jamaican history who did not spend weekends at Round Hill, Tryall, or other north and west coast villas and resorts. I just wasn't very interested in social activities. I focused on my job, which was all I really wanted to do. Rarely did I leave Kingston on the weekend unless there was an important event that I had to attend in another town. Usually I stayed at the residence and read cables or articles about United States policies and government actions or about the Western Hemisphere.

Other than evening social events, I'd leave the house on weekends only to scuba dive in Port Antonio or to run at the Mona Reservoir in Kingston. Running was something of an inner need. I've always been a runner which was a surprise to my drivers and guards (of whom I became very fond). They had to figure out how to deal with that unexpected new guard duty. Sometimes we'd go out in the country and I would just run down a country lane and they would drive behind me in the car, or we'd find a beach that was accessible for them. The best place I could run in Kingston was at Mona Reservoir, which had a fenced oval with a path about a mile and a half around. Located on a hillside adjacent to the University of the West Indies, it is very suitable for walking or running. The first time I suggested we go there, my guards arranged to have a golf cart so that one of them could follow while I ran around the oval. I think they got embarrassed, so one of them started jogging behind me, but he would only go halfway around, and the other guard would drive the golf cart halfway around in the opposite direction so that they could meet in the middle. The first one could then stop running and drive the cart back to the car while the arriving guard had to run with me. Gradually they got into running shape. One, whom I will not name but dearly loved, probably fifteen years younger than I, told me on the way to the airport my last day as ambassador that prior to my arrival he had put on weight and that while I was there, he lost fifteen pounds. He whispered to me, "You were the best thing that could have happened to me." I hope he has kept up the exercise. I was and still am very proud of my drivers and guards – hardworking, polite, skilled Jamaicans.

Over the years, I had learned the importance of public-private partnerships, philanthropic organizations, and how voluntary efforts help support any society. This prompted Chuck and me to take a personal interest in promoting volunteerism and contributing personal funds when possible. Our efforts on improving voluntary efforts by Jamaican businesses received considerable media coverage. My speech, and that of Chuck, at the American Chamber of Commerce (AMCHAM) were reported in *Pure Class* November 3rd, 2002.

In her brief, but earnest speech, Ambassador Cobb reflected on her many years as a United Way volunteer in Miami, Florida – first volunteering in a legal capacity and then working as a fund-raiser. It was therefore very natural for her to be interested in United Way of Jamaica, and the work being done to improve the lives of the less fortunate.

Charles Cobb spoke of their passion for voluntary work, and his years as an employee of Kaiser Alumina (sic), where contributing to United Way was actively encouraged by Kaiser's management.

He applauded the management and employees of the Jamaican bauxite sector for their pledge to raise $15 million and encouraged representatives of the business sector to encourage their employees to give through salary deduction.

'The voluntary sector desperately needs help from the business community in Jamaica,' he said, adding that it was more important to contribute something than to worry about how much to contribute.

I spoke on many occasions – probably no less than once a week – on many topics and in a wide variety of venues, from the inner city of Majestic Gardens to King's House. I like to prepare my own speeches but, of course, rarely had time for that luxury. Our Public Affairs Office, headed by Orna Blum, did a fine job of supporting the ambassador and Embassy Kingston.

Security and the War on Drugs: Not many American visitors get into serious trouble in Jamaica. Those who do have problems are usually involved in some manner with illegal substances. The business of drugs was of great concern to both the United States and the Jamaican governments, and it was an area on which we worked together closely. Because of my particular concerns about United States border security after the terrorist attacks of 2001, I felt that I needed to know the decision-makers in the arena of law enforcement. I needed to know the leaders who strongly influenced decision-making in both Jamaica's Defence Force (JDF) and in the Constabulary Force (JCF). Dr. Peter Phillips, minister of national security at that time, impressed me as having a good grasp of what the circumstances were, what the United States would be looking at throughout the Caribbean, and what was possible within Jamaica. Every minister ardently protects their own country and country's positions, but he was amenable to hearing arguments about why we wanted to do this or that. We got along well. I found that I liked him as a person. He and his wife Sandra were good, solid citizens, deeply engaged in and trying to contribute to their country, which is what I thought I was doing, too. Speaking with Minister Phillips was also convenient as I could walk right across the courtyard from my office to his and talk to him in his office. We established a good working relationship.

The primary interlocutor of a United States ambassador is the minister of foreign affairs, in this case, Minister K.D. Knight. He was an astute, knowledgeable lawyer and a well-versed minister who, in my judgment, was a fine minister of foreign affairs of Jamaica. On other than a few discreet law enforcement matters, on which I personally reached out directly to Minister Phillips, I was always in touch with Minister Knight. Jamaica was very serious about protocol, and I am pretty sure Prime Minister Patterson got annoyed with me, because at times I would avoid protocol and would call directly to K.D. or Peter or even the governor-general Sir Howard Cooke, whom I admittedly adored. I definitely agree that diplomatic procedures are important and necessary, but my practical nature would sometimes propel me into quick action.

The Drug Enforcement Agency was a big player in our embassy because of a tremendous amount of hard drug and marijuana trafficking, much of which came from Colombia. Jamaica grew its own marijuana, but we made it as hard as possible for them to do so. We had a big eradication program and we had been pretty successful in shutting down the dirt runways that dotted the island. However, more weed was coming in bulk out of Colombia for processing in Jamaica and onward shipment. Locals would break up larger loads arriving into the country, place them into smaller containers and onto go-fast boats, or find other ways to send the cargo into the labyrinth of the Bahamian archipelago, Haiti, or the United States. Many creative methods were used and fighting the trafficking was difficult. Jamaica is mountainous and unlike some other Caribbean islands, rich with lush forest and foliage. It's not that hard to hide a 1,000-foot runway, load drugs onto small planes, or slither into small ports to load boats and make a quick profit. As in Colombia and other places, the United States tried to provide crop substitution programs and other incentives, but the quick profits from drugs were intoxicating. It's a tough problem and, as a matter of fact, the drugs got harder. We were fighting coke, meth, and other synthetics that are generally worse than marijuana and eagerly sought by many Americans. At that time, we were not far removed from Miami's era of the Cocaine Cowboys.

Beyond the use of national waters for transiting, Minister Phillips was also very worried about the negative influence within Jamaica of the drug activities. George W. Bush and President Uribe of Colombia were putting together Plan Colombia (which by 2008 cost the United States $1.3 billion) to help Colombia fight the drug trade. At the same time, Colombians were entering Jamaica and setting up their own operations in much higher numbers than government officials could tolerate. The concern was such that the United States and Jamaica coordinated programs useful to both countries.

Jamaica and the United States signed a Memorandum of Understanding on November 29, 2002 with the United States providing US$2.2 million to assist the Government of Jamaica in funding and training on equipment to strengthen border controls, including a state-of-the-art immigration system. Everyone agreed that the island's ports could and should be monitored more closely, especially in relation to illegal immigration and human trafficking. Minister Phillips and I worked together on a number of projects until my departure in 2005. Of that partnership Minister Phillips remembers:

I think it's fair to say that for us in Jamaica, and for me personally in the Ministry of National Security, it was a period of the closest cooperation imaginable. At the level of country to country cooperation, at the level of the institutional linkages between our security services, the Jamaica Defence Force, and SOUTHCOM, for example, in relation to the United States Army and Air Force, and naval cooperation, in relation to DEA activities and our own counter-narcotics agencies, it was seamless.

A lot of that, I think, was attributable to the qualities of Sue Cobb's own leadership. She was very sensitive to the particular needs of Jamaica. At the time, she was very well connected to the United States administration. And we developed what I would call a good friendship over the period.

She certainly used all her connections to advance Jamaica's interest in deepening collaboration. For example, I had the opportunity to meet with then governor Jeb Bush, who was a personal friend and associate of hers. We were able to arrive at an agreement to station Jamaican police personnel in Florida, in association with the Florida Department of Law Enforcement, which helped develop some of the intelligence regarding criminal groupings operating out of Florida who were targeting Jamaica.

In this and other areas in Washington as well, when George W. Bush was the president, she was able to leverage that influence to secure deep cooperation with the various United States agencies there. For context, one should recognize that at that time Jamaica was a main transit point for cocaine, originating in South America, mainly in Colombia, but transiting to the United States of America.

According to UN estimates at the time, about twenty-plus percent of the cocaine originating in Colombia was making it through Jamaica's territorial space. We had Colombian militia who had taken root in parts of our North Coast, in Montego Bay and other areas. And the country was being deluged by this drug trade, which generated billions of dollars in resources, which financed a lot of other criminal activity, was central to the importation of high-powered small arms into Jamaica. And the creation of a number of criminal militias, you could call them, in the country.

Interestingly, that's not a problem now. And it's largely not a problem now because of the successes garnered in that period where we were able to basically lock up a large number of those criminal operators on the basis of cooperation, which was widespread within the Caribbean, including Colombia, other members of CARICOM, including Bahamas, United States, United Kingdom authorities, Canadian authorities, and Central American authorities.

I would say that the pivot of much of that cooperation was Sue Cobb, her influence, her determination to be helpful to Jamaica and the kind of partnership she was able to facilitate....I think that her own personal affection and attachment to the country went a far way in allowing her to not only represent her country well, but to do it in a way that was not overbearing to the Jamaican people.

Dr. Peter Phillips, February 24, 2018

My goal was to secure United States borders and reduce drugs reaching the United States, so it was an area in which our two countries could definitely cooperate. I worked quite closely with SOUTHCOM, the United States military's Combatant Command for the entire Western Hemisphere. The Command covers a huge area of operation over the southern part of our globe covering thirty-four countries and several dependencies, with fifteen interagency partner organizations, accounting for approximately one-sixth of the landmass of the world. Each year, the State Department's Western Hemisphere Affairs (WHA) ambassadors would meet at SOUTHCOM headquarters in Miami to brief the combatant commander, to hear the military priorities, and to collaborate on relevant matters.

The United States had a Status of Forces Agreement with Jamaica. The men and women of SOUTHCOM came to Jamaica periodically to offer humanitarian support – perhaps renovating a modest school, building a dental clinic, or focusing on another useful program. SOUTHCOM was prepared to help with a variety of humanitarian operations – earthquakes, floods, hurricanes – as well as emergency operations. Importantly they held "mil-to-mil" training missions in Central America and the Caribbean.

SOUTHCOM as a military element wasn't in charge of combating drug trafficking operations, but tangentially they could be of help. Providing air observation capabilities out of the Florida Keys was important because Jamaica did not have that capacity. Though SOUTHCOM was and is a powerful presence in many ways it is not a law enforcement agency per se and needs United States Coast Guard support for the law enforcement portion of counter narcotics interdictions, including arrests and seizures. The United States Coast Guard District 7 is headquartered in Miami. It has a very substantial impact in and around our ocean borders. Coast Guard D7 is a strong force multiplier for SOUTHCOM.

The current commander of SOUTHCOM (2019), Admiral Craig Faller, USN, former deputy to secretary of Defense James Mattis, recently gave me an outline of his Area of Operation. As can be seen from that document (see photo section two) SOUTHCOM's reach is impressionably deep and broad.

The leaders of SOUTHCOM knew that I had a particularly high regard for Rear Admiral Hardley Lewin, who was head of the JDF during my tenure. The JDF was considered by our officers to be stable, extremely disciplined, with high quality officers. When possible the JDF joined in training missions with SOUTHCOM to the benefit of both.

We have learned that establishing positive mil-to-mil relationships around the world and nurturing them pays huge dividends when necessities demand actions. The brightest of the JDF would join exercises with SOUTHCOM and other countries of the Caribbean and/or Central America. I was invited to go on training missions to El Salvador and to Honduras. The missions consisted of ideas and knowledge sharing with military officers of selected neighboring countries, and simulations designed for potential future collaboration as circumstances might warrant.

I recall also going out with a JDF helicopter crew to the Pedro Cays, a group of small, relatively isolated islands about sixty miles off Jamaica's southwest coast. The Pedro Cays are administered by the Port Authority of Jamaica and defended by the JDF. The primary inhabited cay is basically a fishing village and a prime location for harvesting Caribbean Queen Conch. Poaching by Hondurans, Venezuelans, and others in these Jamaican fishing grounds is detrimental to Jamaican interests, so the JDF Coast Guard is charged with protecting the cays. Additionally, though I had no proof, it was hard to believe these cays were not facilitators in trafficking illegal substances.

The village itself I can hardly describe. The JDF crew was worried about my being there – about my security and any trouble that might bubble up. The men and women who live in this fishing village are rugged types with little discipline, living in a very unclean environment. Since the Pedro Cays are islands in the middle of a large sea, almost everything deteriorates quickly, corroding from the salt air. Dirty little shacks (many were shipping containers converted into living quarters) pushed together, intersected by tiny alleys, created an atmosphere of almost apocalyptic confinement and fear. With little in the way of hygiene opportunities, I imagined the inhabitants might have the appearance of pirates in the 1600s and 1700s, always on edge in an environment from which there was no escape. I was warned that there is an attitude that goes with that environment, and it did not encourage socializing. To me the visit to the Pedro Cays was akin to voyeurism – going to look at people who do not want to be looked at. Obviously, if you are the United States ambassador and you are there, you are looking at people and their living conditions. I was not happy and neither were they. Since this visit was almost twenty years ago, I hope that conditions have improved.

I was there to determine what the JDF had done with funds previously provided by the United States government to help build a pier, and whether or not I could recommend to my government to put any more money into helping protect this Jamaican outpost. The original pier was apparently constructed in a place of fierce tides and was thought to have washed away. My government was refusing to give any more money to this project. Ambassadors need to weigh in with his/her approval and back projects deemed worthwhile, or they are unlikely to happen, just as it was with the new embassy in Kingston. Washington usually listens to the ambassador on the ground, though ultimately may or may not agree.

A new lieutenant general had arrived at SOUTHCOM whom I convinced that a pier in Pedro Cays was a good investment for the United States to help control the drug trade threatening our own border. The JDF very much needed to have a presence there and I thought it was a reasonable use of a million dollars, despite the previous experience. At the very end of my tenure, the project was approved.

Reflecting on our working relationship during these years, Admiral Lewin wryly noted:

> *Sue Cobb was a most energetic, focused, and determined person. She has an engaging personality with an impish, disarming sense of humor and has been a tremendous diplomat for her country and a great friend of Jamaica.*
>
> *Rear Admiral Hardley Lewin, March 9, 2018*

I must admit it was comforting to have SOUTHCOM nearby. I stayed in close touch with each SOUTHCOM combatant commander, two of whom became great personal friends of

Chuck and mine. We also had a Defense Intelligence Agency (DIA) representative stationed in Kingston. I was very impressed with our DIA officers. All in all, with a Marine detachment (which many people don't know is only charged with protecting United States property, not United States personnel), our United States Army military attaché, the DEA, the DIA, the United States Marshal Service, and others coming and going, I was comfortable that we had a solid security presence in Jamaica.

Our consular district included the Cayman Islands (a British Overseas Territory), which everyone knew thrived on a large offshore banking culture. We covered the Caymans from a United States consular perspective only and didn't have any responsibility with other United States interests, though United States Treasury officials paid attention to sometimes questionable financial activities in the Caymans. I became tangentially involved with our Treasury Department, when Jamaica sought US$18 million of debt relief for a Jamaican Nature Conservancy project. A decision had been made to forgive Jamaican debt in a "debt for nature swap" whereby Jamaica agreed to create and manage a large reforestation project on the island with funds that were originally destined to pay down United States debt. I was very much in favor of that action and helped to guide it through its many levels of approval. Several countries in Central America, South America, and the Caribbean thought it was a pretty big deal for the United States to forgive close to $20 million. To me, it felt like a "win-win."

In addition to United States Marshals on site in Kingston, I was told we and only one other United States embassy in the world at that time had a dedicated visa fraud agent. The visa fraud agent was assigned one goal: identifying fraud within the consular section's area of operation. These aren't exactly things to brag about, but they were, indeed, a part of our job.

Jamaicans so desired to get into the United States, they created numerous schemes to obtain visas. In addition, convicted United States felons who abscond to their native countries are located by United States Marshals in the home country and brought back to the United States to face justice. I'm not sure who did a cost benefit analysis on this, but it was our law at the time. One of the really big issues in Jamaica and other nearby offshore countries is deportees – those who are returned by the United States to their country of origin who either received a United States visa and overstayed it, or came to the United States illegally, or committed an illegal act in the United States, all of whom are subject to deportation. Such deportees are sent back by the thousands to El Salvador, Honduras, Guatemala, Jamaica, and other countries. Immigration policies and procedures were contentious then and remain contentious now.

Jamaica's police force, the Jamaica Constabulary Force (JCF), was modeled on the British constabulary. At the time of my tenure, the JCF was generally deemed to be a corrupt entity (with exceptions at the highest levels) and did not come close to meeting the best policing standards known to man. The leading Jamaican authorities were extremely cooperative for the most part, particularly on drug trafficking and any potential terrorism threat. However, it was difficult to find the best routes to work effectively with the JCF. Not everybody in the force could be called scrupulously honest which made it difficult for our law enforcement personnel to rely on JCF information and cooperation.

In some areas, the Government of Jamaica (GOJ) was definitely not cooperative with us. Jamaica is member/leader of CARICOM, the Caribbean Community and Common Market, consisting of fifteen full member nations and five associates from the Caribbean region. CARICOM always seeks unanimity among their members on international matters. Jamaica was also an adherent of the non-aligned movement of independent countries, a 120-member organization of developing countries at different stages on their economic paths. Started during the cold war, the shared goal was to remain independent of the two major power blocks, the United States and the Soviet Union. Anytime a vote came up in the United Nations that the non-aligned movement had decided to vote against, Jamaica routinely voted with them, not with us. Rarely would they break and vote with us, or even just abstain. Many objectives were complicated for us by CARICOM because they formed a block of fifteen votes in international bodies. I talked to Jamaican leaders endlessly about United States frustration on this subject. They responded politely with their rationale on each subject. I felt United States trade goals were adversely affected, one example being the eventual failure of the Free Trade Area of the Americas. "How can you accept monetary support and aid or assistance in other ways from the United States, then come to the United Nations and vote against us every single time? How can you do that?" The response included sharing certain principles with other CARICOM member states and with the non-aligned countries. Former prime minister P. J. Patterson was chairman of CARICOM during my tenure, and he explained his government's position on their voting at the United Nations, speaking specifically of the United States:

> They take umbrage that we don't vote with them. We take umbrage that they don't vote with us. Let's understand something simple. We belong to a group of developing countries. The United States and other countries belong to the developed world. In terms of trying to create a just and equitable global order, there are going to be profound differences on issues which pertain to – Let me give a good example.
>
> We did not support the invasion of Iraq. When the Americans went to Afghanistan, not only was there no demur from us, but Jamaica was a member of the Security Council, and in fact, Jamaica presided

over the Security Council when most of the decisions were taken by the Security Council and all the resolutions that were passed creating a new regime in the fight against terror. We thought that there was a legitimate right in respect of Afghanistan. We were not so persuaded in respect of Iraq, and history has proven us right.

I speak as a former foreign minister of this country under Michael Manley, and I speak as a former prime minister. Jamaica believes in sovereign equality. Jamaica will never, I hope, exercise that right of sovereign equality by voting in accordance with what a donor country is providing. That line leads to some serious problems. As of now, the European Union is a larger donor than the United States, and Venezuela triples, at least, the assistance that has been available. It's immoral.

So, when there are issues on which our interests coincide, we're happy. In things like democracy, human rights, the fight against terrorism, yes. But I repeat, not only were we on the Security Council, we chaired the October meeting. 9/11 was in September. In November, by the time all the resolutions had to be passed, we were in the chair. We led the Security Council in all the decisions about terrorism. All the new laws that have been implemented by countries which were as a result of Security Council decisions, Jamaica's Ambassador Pat Durrant was in the chair for most of it. On one occasion K.D. Knight as foreign minister was in the chair, and on one occasion, I was actually in the chair myself....

What I'm saying is Jamaica takes a principled position. We judge each thing on our merits. We cannot be expected to vote on whether we get some assistance or not.

The Most Honorable P. J. Patterson, March 10, 2018

The world of diplomacy is delicate. Only a couple of times did I need to express distinctly opposite views from the Government of Jamaica that brought real confrontations. Most of our demarches were directing the ambassador to tell the foreign minister what our government would like for his government to do on a particular issue, indicating the reasons why. What I wished I could say directly was: "We think it's important, and because we think it's important, you should think it's important." My Jamaican interlocutor would sit in the chair across from me and say, "We understand your arguments and we're always willing to listen. We love the United States, but we just can't assure you that we're going to be able to vote with you on this issue. As you know, our close colleagues in the non-aligned movement have a different view." It was always so cordial, so friendly, and so thoughtfully stated on both sides. Strangely, on most things I didn't find that frustrating; it just was what it was.

Building Bridges: Due to 9/11, I knew I was in a job where Washington wasn't going to be watching us like hawks and because of the money awarded for our embassy's Mission Performance Plan, I had a little money to be creative. That led to one of the projects that I was later told was one of the primary achievements of my tenure. In October 2003, I decided that we would create a year-long program of events for calendar year 2004 that actually could make things happen. These events would act as a catalyst, fostering economic development opportunities, knowledge sharing, and strengthening of links between the public and private sectors of Jamaica and the United States, particularly Florida. I was sure we could enhance and coordinate innovative programs in areas of mutual interest to our countries. I knew many Jamaicans who had settled in Dade, Broward, and Palm Beach counties who were successful businesspeople, although they usually kept a low profile. I wanted to engage Jamaica's large diaspora and raise the profile of their leaders for the benefit of both the United States and Jamaica. I called the program "Building Bridges: The Florida Jamaica Connection." Of course, states don't have foreign policies, but health, education, and building economies are desirable everywhere.

Building Bridges was run from the front office (me) with a rotational junior officer. His name was Les Thompson, a consular officer who prior to joining the Foreign Service was a stockbroker. I threw him headfirst into all kinds of projects and he did beautifully. Some of our MPP money went to hiring Building Bridges staff, including a junior officer's wife and a superb Jamaican administrative aide.

All our projects were within the scope of President Bush's National Security Strategy, focused on the "three ds:" democracy, development, and defense. In those broad categories we could fit in programs on health, education, economic development, trade, defense, environment, women's leadership, most anything we conceived of we just took the initiative to do. We brought in as partners several important Florida and Jamaican organizations, and their leaders – including Jamaica's Investment and Trade Promotion Agency (JAMPRO), the Private Sector Organization of Jamaica (PSOJ), and the American Chamber of Commerce of Jamaica (AMCHAM) ably run for years by Becky Stockhausen. The key Florida-based partners were: the Office of the Governor of Florida; Miami-Dade, Broward, and Palm Beach County Mayors and Commissioners; the Broward County Economic Development Office; the Beacon Council of Miami-Dade County; the World Trade Centers of Miami and of Palm Beach; and the Jamaican Consul General's Office in Miami.

In a report prepared for the embassy in November 2004, Caroline E. Mahfood, Building Bridges' star Jamaican administrator, noted:

> *November 2003's Building Bridges Women's Leadership Exchange marked the first event of the Building Bridges program. Held in Kingston, the successful exchange united influential women from Jamaica and South Florida in a forum to share ideas, information, and best practices on education, health, volunteerism, and philanthropy. A reciprocal Building Bridges exchange was held in Miami in January 2004. The events were the result of more than eight months of intense planning between the United Way of Jamaica (UWJ), the United Way of Miami-Dade (UWMD), and the United States Embassy in Kingston.*

The creation of the Women's Leadership Initiative (WLI) proved to be one of the three or four most important outcomes of Building Bridges. Twenty-five Florida women leaders journeyed to Kingston to observe projects, needs, and administrative practices of UWJ, followed by twenty-five UWJ women flying to Miami for planning and collaboration. We arranged a bus to meet the Miami women at Norman Manley International Airport in Kingston to drive us up to the beautiful Island Outpost hotel at Strawberry Hill. I was a little concerned that these Florida women would be worried about security and made sure our plans were mentioned casually to Police Commissioner Forbes before the women arrived. "We'll keep our eyes open," he said.

When I arrived to meet the Miami flight, I encountered our small rented bus surrounded by four JCF motorcycle policemen in black clothes, black boots, black helmets and mirrored glasses, on very large black motorcycles. You get the picture. I was surprised. Commissioner Forbes was really taking care of us. Zipping through Kingston, the police turned on their sirens and escorted us up the winding mountain road into the Blue Mountains all the way to Strawberry Hill Hotel. The entire ride, these four police motorcycles, lights flashing, were on the four corners of our bus. The Miami ladies could not miss this kind of attention and my friends were beyond themselves, just thrilled. It was hilarious – the bus, the policemen, and the ladies. Frankly, we were all totally impressed! I was appreciative of this gesture by the JCF.

Sue Miller, leader of the United Way women in Miami, and her husband Leonard were among my family's closest friends. He founded Lennar Corporation, one of the largest home building companies in the United States, and LNR, a NYSE financial entity, for which our son Christian had worked just out of college. I later served on the LNR board but had to resign when I went into government. Chuck took my place on the board. And in a totally unrelated twist of fate, our son Toby later became the co-chief executive officer of LNR, along with his business associate Justin Kennedy, the son of our long time Stanford friend, United States Supreme Court Justice Anthony Kennedy.

When the Jamaican women came to the United States on their reciprocal mission, the Miami United Way had just started a new program devoted to early childhood education. It was of significant relevance to the Jamaicans who were intent on observing how to develop a similar program. Observances and lessons followed. For their final evening in Miami, we went to Sue Miller's beautiful home on Star Island where their next door neighbors, Emilio and Gloria Estefan, dropped in for the reception. Heads were spinning. It was great fun. Jamaican women and American women bonded as though they'd always known each other. Back in Kingston, these women immediately formed, as part of United Way, the Women's Leadership Initiative (WLI).

In subsequent months, Building Bridges brought the medical director for the North Miami-Dade Health Center to Kingston to speak on HIV testing and health services for women living with HIV/AIDS; and in May 2004, the United States actress Tyne Daly came to speak at a luncheon attended by 300 people, which raised money for a model basic school for early childhood education and for HIV rapid test kits for pregnant women. As a result of these initial programs, the WLI has been an animated force ever since in early childhood education, the fight against HIV/AIDS and other teen sexually transmitted diseases, as well as mentorship for girls and women in business. Pat Ramsay, a dynamic leader, was president for the first six years, and got the organization off to a splendid start.

I was invited back to Kingston on October 14, 2014 by then president Sharon Lake to give the keynote address at the dinner celebrating the tenth anniversary of the founding of the Women's Leadership Initiative. Unfortunately, the morning of the dinner I fell and broke my arm. I simply got a cast put on it during the day so it wouldn't hurt and was able to attend the dinner and give my congratulatory speech at the WLI celebration that night. The next morning, I flew to Miami and had surgery to repair the damage. Today WLI is still going strong. I am very proud of that organization and all the women leaders who give time and treasure to support education and to help women and children in need.

Our small Building Bridges team was equally proud of establishing Youth Crime Watch Jamaica (YCWJ), initially a chapter of Youth Crime Watch America (YCWA), headquartered in Miami. The goal was to strive to create a crime-, drug-, and violence-free environment in schools and neighborhoods. Launched in March 2004 in the inner city area of Seaview Gardens, Kingston, three Miami YCWA staff came to Kingston for a four-day training program, working with community leaders, police, youth, and civic leaders preparing a core group of seventy-five teachers who that same year trained 400 high school students in Kingston and Montego Bay.

Youth Crime Watch Jamaica became a formally registered non-governmental organization and gradually increased its involvement in crime prevention. It inspired and continues work in a wide variety of youth programs: "Grade Nine Achievement Test High Achievers Programme" in 2010, "Change Through Art" in 2011, and "Be the Change Summer Camp" in 2011 and 2012. With a three-year grant from USAID, YCWJ implemented a National Integrity Action Project, "Combatting Corruption and Strengthening Integrity in Jamaica" (2016 to 2019). I spoke recently at their "Integrity Ambassadors Programme" graduation ceremony and was thrilled to see the quality of the teenage graduates. The YCWJ model proved to be a great success.

Economic development was also part of our Building Bridges vision. From June 7 to 9, 2004, the Jamaica-Florida Trade Mission and Partnering Fair took place in Ft. Lauderdale. Basically, we did a trade mission between Jamaica and Broward County. I convinced Ft. Lauderdale city and county officials to give us the use of their beautiful convention center for free; and Dade, Broward, and Palm Beach businesspeople helped to underwrite expenses. Under Les Thompson's leadership, the trade mission was a major success. We had about 200 Jamaican company representatives descend on Ft. Lauderdale, making sales and contacts with Florida businesses.

My favorite memory was that of a Jamaican artist who wanted to take his entire body of work to the trade show. At first I said, "I don't know that we would sell art." I was thinking of normal trade show business promotion: advertising your wares, putting together this manufacturer and that distributor, or these service providers. But we decided the artist should try sales in this environment. His paintings were small, six by eight or eight by ten inches, mostly tropical landscapes with bright Caribbean colors in simple wood frames. He brought 500 paintings to our trade show and sold all on the opening day. He also met a businessman from Florida who owned a chain of restaurants opening and operating throughout the United States. That man ordered 10,000 paintings. So, the Jamaican artist went back to Kingston, hired additional artists, putting more people to work. Later it was reported to me that these paintings are now in restaurants across the United States. The artist, a paraplegic, lived at Sir John Golding Rehabilitation Centre in Mona. This was an exceedingly satisfying success story.

Our attempt to stimulate discussion of all levels of education in Jamaica couldn't have started with a bigger bang than that provided when His Excellency Sir Howard Cooke, governor-general of Jamaica, co-hosted with me a high-powered Building Bridges Educational Forum. Held at prestigious King's House in February 2004, leading educators and business leaders from the United States and Jamaica addressed critical education issues. Dr. Phillip Frost, MD, chairman and CEO of several pharmaceutical companies and at that time chairman of the board of trustees of the University of Miami was there. Patricia Frost, chair of the Smithsonian Institution and a trustee on the board of the State of Florida College System contributed her expertise. (Incidentally, their Philip and Patricia Frost Museum of Science opened to great acclaim in Miami in 2017.) Thaddeus Foote, then the president of the University of Miami discussed the role of research universities. Bosey Fulbright Foote, daughter of Senator J. William Fulbright whose 1946 legislation created the Fulbright Program, spoke on the impact of that worldwide program. You get the idea of what impressive talent came for the forum. An equally illustrious group of Jamaica's educational leaders provided a Caribbean perspective. The discussion included progress on the University of West Indies (UWI) Center for Excellence in Teacher Training (CETT), a US$20 million program, which had been announced by President Bush at the Summit of the Americas in 2001.

My husband also spoke at the Building Bridges Education Forum because education has been his lifelong passion. The Honorable Charles E. Cobb Jr. has served for over forty years on every conceivable committee at the University of Miami, including serving as chairman of the board of trustees. In 1998 he co-founded the Barry University Charter School, and in the nineties was education advisor to Governor Jeb Bush. I can confirm that his presence was much appreciated. He also took the opportunity in the education forum to announce that he and I were endowing two scholarship funds, one for Jamaican students at UWI and one at the University of Miami reserved for a Jamaican student. My husband named each the "Ambassador Sue M. Cobb Scholarship."

Another substantive Building Bridges program was the Law Enforcement Pilot Project. In January 2004 Dr. Peter Phillips, minister of national security, and I met with Governor Jeb Bush; an agreement was reached to assign a trained Jamaican law enforcement officer to a multi-agency task force in the Miami office of the Florida Department of Law Enforcement. I also got Governor Bush and federal authorities to agree to let a Jamaican intelligence officer become a member of our Joint Interagency Task Force South (JIADA South), based at Naval Air Station, Key West, Florida. This joint operation of our military and intelligence groups watches over the Caribbean for illicit goods and illegal immigrants. An agreement was signed for a well-vetted Jamaican intelligence officer to join JIADA South with our officers and officers of other countries from the Central and South American region on that important task force.

Building Bridges conducted an innovative and fruitful remittance program to capitalize on the surge in remittance from Florida. The remittance program was a collaboration with the United States Embassy, Western Union, and the Grace Kennedy Trust. It was called I PLEDGE (I Promise to Lend Encouragement to the Development and Growth of Education). Florida residents who transmitted remittances to Jamaica had the opportunity to give one dollar of their transfer to education in Jamaica. From this program proceeds of US$250,000 were donated to the Ministry of Education to purchase math textbooks for all 300,000 students in grades one through five throughout the country. This program complemented USAID'S numeracy and literacy program then underway in Jamaica.

Building Bridges also tackled the high profile and very serious topic of deportees. Jamaicans had long claimed that immigrants to the United States were young children, who learned their criminal behavior in the United States. The Building Bridges team arranged a study by Professor Bernard Headley of the University of the West Indies who worked with two UWI graduate research assistants to create an academic report entitled, "Deported: Entry and Exit Findings On Jamaicans Returned From the United States." Their independent analysis of United States Homeland Security data from 1997 to 2003, focusing on the age and reasons for deportation of Jamaicans from the United States, disabused that Jamaican claim. The UWI team reported that twenty-three was the average age of Jamaican deportees when they came to the United States. This was not a popular study, but, hopefully the study assisted United States and Jamaican authorities to better understand the thorny deportee issue.

The Building Bridges program attracted a great deal of media attention in Jamaica. I surmise that was because we were attempting to create opportunities to improve lives. We were not just talking about problems, we were bringing people together in a manner that encouraged them to help each other to improve lives, both in Jamaica and the United States. While starting with only a germ of an idea, the creative and mostly low-cost Building Bridges programs succeeded beyond our expectations. They turned out to be impactful and gratifying.

There are close to a million Jamaicans living in the United States, over half a million in the New York area and some 300,000 in Florida and other states. They love their lives in the United States, in part because they enjoy the better salaries they are able to earn and can see the benefits of educating their children in America, but they miss "home." Jamaicans are very family oriented and retain close ties to the island, traveling there as frequently as they can. Jamaica is less than 600 miles from Miami and 1,500 miles from New York, so Jamaicans go back and forth when possible. Tapping into the opportunities which Jamaicans in the diaspora might offer to those at home was indeed one of the reasons for the creation of the Building Bridges program.

Sadly, though declining, Jamaica still has a high crime rate and a very high murder rate. Crime is not directed at tourists or expatriates working in the country. Like the countries of the Northern Triangle (Honduras, El Salvador, and Guatemala), violence is usually gang related and centers around the drug trade, protecting turf, or retaliation for perceived threats and insults. Additionally, quarrels arise over the division of spoils from schemes to scam foreigners via telephone and banking frauds. Within the country, Jamaicans take extra care to be sure that tourists are protected due to that industry's powerful impact on the GDP. Tourists may get hassled to buy homemade goods, souvenirs, or drugs – all strongly discouraged by authorities and easily avoided by tourists. As ambassador I didn't experience the hassling. I liked to walk on the city streets, although my guards did not like it. I would often be recognized because of the media coverage I received. People knew me. I never felt endangered. Random people would call out, "Ambassador Sue, Ambassador Sue!" They would giggle and laugh, wave their hands, or point their fingers. They were extremely friendly to me. It was actually a joyful part of my experience in the country.

In fact, one of my favorite letters came from a retired Jamaican teacher who wrote to me in June 2002, just nine months after my arrival. I don't know exactly what motivated her, but you have to love the fact that she took the time to write a personal letter to the United States ambassador with such enthusiasm:

Your Excellency
Lady Sue Cobb
Ambassador USA

Distinguished Lady

God bless your coming to Jamaica at a time like this. Truly, you are Godsend. You are sympathetic, merciful, honest and God-fearing. Thanks for overlooking our foolish utterances and ingratitude to your God-Blessed country. We the old Jamaicans are more sober and think before we talk. Believe you me, "Lady C", that our PRAYERS are with you, and long live AMERICA. Please forgive our foolish ways. May you stay here until you become the 1st LADY (first Lady) PRESIDENT of our best neighbour, the God-blessed USA.

God bless you, again. Your obedient Servant

PS Do, your Ladyship, do not remember our ingratitude. The thousands of JAM. In your country are praying for you all. God bless AMERICA.

(Signed, but not for publication)

Aristide's Departure From Haiti: I did have a real run-in with the prime minister and the foreign minister on circumstances originating in 2004 when Haiti's former president Jean-Bertrand Aristide was being chased down by gangs in Haiti, literally moving on the Presidential Palace intent on killing him. He retreated to the United States Embassy in Port-au-Prince for protection. He begged us to protect him. Our people got a plane into Port-au-Prince at Aristide's request and took him out of harm's way the night of February 28, 2004. In the morning news, the Jamaican prime minister and foreign minister adamantly denied that Aristide had asked for protection and claimed instead that the Americans kidnapped him and that Secretary Powell and the United States president were lying. I had never heard any foreign official call my president and my secretary of state "liars." I went on Jamaican radio and TV and ardently defended President Bush and Secretary Powell. In the process, I blasted both the prime minister and foreign minister. Being in Kingston there was no reason to believe they had personal knowledge or instant facts; and, in my judgment, it was extremely inappropriate to call the president and secretary of state of a neighboring friend and ally "liars." That was just not acceptable. I accused them of an "unsophisticated" response to the entire incident. Later in an appropriate setting, I actually apologized for that particular word, unsophisticated. In fact, they are sophisticated men and had a very different view of the circumstances. I did not apologize for my defense of President Bush and Secretary of State Powell.

The contention in the local press was that this was a CIA plan and Aristide really did not ask us for help. I remember telling one of the reporters on a popular evening radio program, "You could equate Aristide with Humpty Dumpty. He's fallen from the wall and all the king's horses and all the king's men can't put Humpty back together again." He was smashed and never coming back. They really did not like that analogy. Of course, I did not have all the facts either, but that was not going to stop me from defending my president and my secretary of state. Diplomacy is a serious job. Countries have serious disputes and diplomats do their best to represent their countries' interests and to resolve our differences diplomatically. Sometimes it doesn't work out that way.

On this issue, the press had a field day. *The Sunday Observer*, March 7, 2004 headline screamed, "Swimming with Sharks" with Claude Robinson writing:

> *The row between Caribbean leaders and the George W. Bush administration over the ditching of CARICOM's plan for power sharing in Haiti and the forced exile of President Jean-Bertrand Aristide, underscores the perilous paths that small nations have to tread in a world where practical politics trumps principle.*

In the same paper, I wrote an article "What Happened in Haiti" in which I made clear the United States government's position:

> For the record, Aristide resigned, doing, in the view of many, his only real service to the people of Haiti in a dozen years. We know that Aristide was considered the constitutional president. But we know other things about Aristide, learned over the course of the last decade of his leadership, that influenced my Government's decision making.
>
> His use of mob violence and hit squads as a policy for several years, and his endorsement of assassinations of journalists who dared to criticize his actions, sowed the seeds of his downfall;
>
> The very same group that rose up in Gonaives – the so-called Cannibal army – was a central part of his own network of thugs until six months ago;
>
> He politicized and corrupted the Haitian National Police, systematically driving out honest people and putting his thugs in charge....
>
> His regime distributed arms to his political supporters while the police were left defenseless – and those armed mobs were responsible for most of the violence in Port-au-Prince during the last few weeks.
>
> Based on that spectacular track record, and after any hope of a 'shared government' was quashed, we made a conscious decision not to put American lives at risk for the sole purpose of buying Aristide more time to perpetuate such policies. In other words, we agreed to get him out of the country.

The next day, on March 8, 2004, the prime minister summoned me for a meeting. Our political officer thought they were going to eject me, that I was going to be declared *persona non grata*, i.e., not welcome in Jamaica. I went into this meeting at the PM's office with our political officer in tow. He sat back in a corner to take notes and looked so uncomfortable that I thought at any minute he might throw up. The prime minister was seated on one side of a long table with twelve men from his cabinet lined up to his right and left. I was seated by myself, alone, on the opposite side of the table, directly facing Prime Minister Patterson. The prime minister started talking, turning the pages of a prepared folder. It was clear to me that he was angry, though calm and composed. He was trying to demonstrate to me what evidence Jamaica had that Aristide did not request protection and that the United States had kidnapped him to put him on a plane to leave the country. The prime minister read several pages, which did appear to have accounts that could lead one to believe that we orchestrated Aristide's departure. The prime minister read from the folder indicating that they had intercepted (I assumed Cuban intelligence had intercepted) communications between people in Haiti and the Western Hemisphere Bureau in Washington and from the United States Embassy in Port-au-Prince. I, of course, could not read or even see the papers. The prime minister spent about thirty minutes reading to me, showing me that they had considerable information, and some I thought was probably true, but I had no way of knowing.

I noted to myself that three ministers whom I shall not name, sat with their heads in their hands looking at the table the whole time the prime minister read. I was sure they were embarrassed. I did not know if it was for themselves, for the PM, or for me. At the end of the meeting I had determined in my mind that there was no way I could win a debate in the orchestrated circumstances so when we stood up, I said, "Prime Minister Patterson, I appreciate you taking the time to inform me of your views and to provide potentially new information. Thank you for meeting with me today to explain your country's position. It doesn't change my mind but thank you for the opportunity to be here." That was the end of the meeting. There were no handshakes. I left the room.

I did not say much when we got back in the car; my political officer said, "God, you're going to be out of here." I responded,

"No, I'm not. The PM did what he had to do. It was also a way of trying to intimidate me. We'll see...." The next few times the prime minister and I saw each other at social events, we exchanged polite, but slightly distant, greetings. I had apologized in another news article for the inappropriate word I had used – calling his government's response "unsophisticated." We each had expressed our views. From my perspective, there was nothing more I could do. The incident was out of my hands.

Former prime minister P. J. Patterson remembers the incident from a different perspective:

> *I gave her the moniker 'The Lady of Silk and Steel' because she's both, and I saw both sides of her in evidence during her stay....*

> *The steel of which I spoke, and we'd better deal with it right up front, throughout her entire tenure we had an extremely good working relationship except for one episode which is best described as tempestuous. That had to do with the removal of President Aristide from Haiti at a time when I was also chairman of the Caribbean Community and taking on the lead responsibility for the entire community in addressing: one, the attempts to remove Aristide during his democratic tenure and then: the physical step of taking him out of Haiti and flying him to the Central African Republic. To put it mildly, there was a serious clash between the Government of the United States and the Government of Jamaica, and indeed, the entire Community, about the circumstances of his removal. Upset as one was by the very fact of the removal by force, there is no doubt whatsoever that it was. I had spoken to President Aristide the night before, the Saturday, and there was some support he had asked for, which was on its way to him through Jamaica, support from South Africa.*

> *Let's tell the entire story. We had come into this matter not simply because Haiti was a member of the Community and Haiti is a country which deserves our special respect and admiration as the first country to have fought the imperial masters and to have declared the country a free democratic country for slaves and others of like ancestry. In going in, the Americans, led by the President, had indicated this was a matter on which they expected CARICOM to take the lead, and we kept the US fully in the loop. In fact, most of*

the meetings had a presence from Washington and when we finally agreed on a plan, that was discussed with Secretary of State Powell, who said it was not just a CARICOM plan, it was the only plan, and the Americans would take it to the Security Council.

I spoke to Aristide on the Saturday night, and when I heard on Sunday morning that he had been taken out very early that Sunday morning, there was no question in my mind that the man that I had spoken to hadn't asked to be removed for his own safety. Let me put this out. He had disbanded the army. He was being attacked by rebels. The security which had been provided by a United States American firm had been withdrawn previously. He was out of arms and ammunition for the defense of the Haitian Government. He sought support from South Africa for that, and the Americans were told that he had sought it and was about to obtain it. In fact, the plane had come in from South Africa, landed in Kingston, and was awaiting after my call with President Aristide for orders when to go in. That is the conversation I had with him.

It came in the night before and we wanted to make sure that the Haitian police force and security forces were in a position to receive and deal with it. He disbanded the military before. All he had was the police. His private security had gone. The arms had come. The arrangement was they should land in Kingston overnight and instructions obtained from Aristide as to how to proceed to Haiti. So it was an overnight mission here. And the Americans knew not by intelligence, we informed them.

There's no doubt in my mind that we regard it as a forcible removal, and what irked me personally most of all is that when the plane landed in Antigua to refuel to take him to the Central African Republic, the manifest said 'No passengers. Cargo alone. Cargo only,' and I took the greatest personal umbrage to that. If he was on the plane and they scoop everybody that was in his house when they went, including a goddaughter of his who happened to be visiting, and they put them on the plane, they didn't know where they were going. They landed in Antigua to refuel. The manifest says 'No passengers. Cargo alone.' There's only one inference. No passengers. Anything that is on the plane is cargo. To have people crossing the Atlantic from West to Africa and to describe them as cargo is…Oh, they were hiding it. They were hiding that there were any passengers aboard.

Was it the fact that they called them 'cargo' with the reference back to the Middle Passage something that especially upset me?

Yes. Yes. Yes. Yes. To this day, I'm hurt. She of course was defending the position of the American government, and I was vehemently opposed to the arguments they were putting forward which I knew had no basis. In that situation, she and I were definitely not seeing the story unfold in the same way. There were some sharp exchanges that represented the steel of which I spoke. She was presenting what had been given to her by the US Department.

Once time passed, we eventually brought Aristide back from the Central African Republic to Jamaica to provide him shelter and to allow him to be reacquainted with his family, who had been in Miami when he was taken away. We brought his wife here, his daughters, they spent time until they were ready to go to their preferred destination, which was in South Africa.

The moment that happened and that episode was over, she no longer as far as I was concerned had to reflect the 'steel.' She reverted to being as smooth as silk, as I have described her. She stands out in my mind as an ambassador who not only served her country well, but save and apart from this incident, was always helpful whenever the situation arose in promoting the cause and interests of Jamaica in Washington. I would single out two areas in particular.

As we all know, when it comes to matters pertaining to security, small arms, illegal weapons, trafficking in drugs, the laundering of money, Jamaica and the United States have problems that can only at our best be tackled with cooperation and support. In all of these efforts, she not only understood what the Jamaican position was, what are the limitations in terms of resources, human, technological, which we face in dealing with these problems, and she was always one to enlist the cooperation, the support, and the understanding in Washington and in all the many agencies which relate to that.

The other area that I would also single out where I know she was of particular help is we had the national airline, and the question of the rating whether Jamaica was Category 1 or Category 2 was of very, very vast importance to us, because it affected how the airlines could operate into the United States. As you realize, there's an overfly of Jamaica by so many planes going from South America to North

America, and the rating affects what airline services we supply. It's the whole aviation system. It includes the airports, it includes the overfly facilities, and it includes the national airline itself and the people in it. There's a big difference between Category 1 and Category 2. At times when the needle could move either way, she couldn't determine it, but the guidance, the assistance, the support which she provided was always very welcome, always very timely.

Let me say how I saw her tenure. She has had vast exposure to diplomacy, some of which has come from her husband, who was an American Ambassador to Iceland. She came to Jamaica and I think my reading is that she fell in love with Jamaica, and while accepting that her primary function was the promotion and protection of American interests in the country to which she was assigned, she was always mindful of what she could contribute to making that relationship friendly, positive, and mutually beneficial. I think in that regard she was an outstanding ambassador.

On a personal level, we started on a very high note and we ended on a very high note, to the extent that on one occasion, visiting the United States for a conference in Miami, she indicated that there were facilities in her own residence that would be made available. I'd made other arrangements; I didn't avail myself of that. I was going to a conference and she simply said if I wanted to stay, I would have been very welcome. But I'd made other conference arrangements.

There is something else. She fell in love with Jamaica, but a particular area of Jamaica. The southern plains of Westmoreland and St. Elizabeth were particularly attractive to her and bearing in mind my own representation of that constituency in places like Bluefields and Whitehouse, there was always a special awareness of her visiting in that area and how pleasant it was and the extent to which it made her feel at home.

Now, we have to remember that this is a person who in her own way has overcome some formidable challenges. Indeed, it was during her tenure, not at the start of it, that I realized she was one of those persons who had climbed Mt. Everest. There are not many bigger challenges than that. Simply put, she's a person who knows what her mission is, pursues that mission – sometimes in doing that there'll be conflicts, as I have mentioned in the case of Haiti – but if we agree to differ on that, has never prevented us from having a very, very good, cordial working relationship, and I think her tenure is certainly one of the most successful and productive in the history of American representatives in Jamaica.

The Most Honorable P. J. Patterson, March 10, 2018

Yes, the prime minister and I were destined to disagree on the subject of Aristide's departure from Haiti, but I am in total agreement with Prime Minister Patterson, as he said that we developed a very, very good cordial relationship. I understood that the prime minister was seeking the best results possible for his country from his administration's perspective. I respected the prime minister. He was a statesman and a skilled diplomat.

I was often invited to give speeches, so on April 21, 2004, six weeks after the confrontation about Aristide, I gave a speech on the topic of "Vital Interests and Balancing Equities" at the Hilton Hotel in Kingston. The room was packed, including, as usual, a number of media people. Some of my comments included:

Let me assure you up front that the US-Jamaica bilateral relationship is a strong and resilient one. Let me also assure you that if you came here today in hopes of hearing provocative remarks by the United States Ambassador on the "hot topic of the day," whether it be Haiti, Iraq, terrorism, or the debate about who should captain the West Indies Cricket Team, you will be disappointed.

US Sec. of State Gen. Colin Powell, Amb. Sue Cobb, National Security Advisor Condi Rice discussing US/CARICOM areas of common interest Courtesy of the Gleaner Company Ltd., 2004.

I proceeded to say:

I've learned a lot about Jamaica in more than two and a half years as United States Ambassador....one of Jamaica's wonderful national blessings is the enduring democratic tradition so deeply rooted here and elsewhere in the West Indies. Upon that firm ground is planted my steadfast conviction that Jamaica is a country destined for prosperity.

The Caribbean is the largest concentration of democracies in any part of the developing world....Today economic challenges in the region persist. This is where the leaders of small states face a series of difficult dilemmas. Since a dilemma is by definition a set of options, none of which are optimal, any and all choices necessarily involve tradeoffs and cost/benefit calculations – or – a balancing of the equities.

One such dilemma recently presented to CARICOM is when and on what terms to join the various multi-lateral trading regimes, such as the US-backed Free Trade Area of the Americas (FTAA). In this hemisphere, small nations must ponder whether they can or should commit themselves to full support of open markets as posed by the US and its partners, or to take the less ambitious position backed by countries such as Brazil and Argentina....

What are the opportunity costs of such a decision, politically and economically...Would the Caribbean – would Jamaica – gain substantial benefits from deeper alliances with countries at a similar development stage, but further away in distance? Or would greater benefits accrue from a closer association with a large nearby market partner that also happens to be a major donor nation? Clearly the marginal benefits of either decision require a careful balancing of the equities.

To help in the analysis (taking democracy and sovereignty as givens), it is important to look at what really are the vital interests of the decision-making country. The current 'issue of the day' to which people respond vigorously and about which they almost always 'takes sides,' just may not – in a few months' time – be on the country's top ten list of vital interests. So what may be most preferable is not to make a choice between two instant alternatives, instead seeking the best of both, while focusing with great energy

*on areas that have proven over time to be of value to the well-being
of the nation. In this case, because of size and proximity, most such
issues of importance to Jamaica are more often than not closely
linked to the United States which shares a long and integrated
history with the region, and which has been immeasurably benefited
by Caribbean thought and Caribbean citizens. Such special relations
are built up year over year, layer over layer and are not generally
susceptible to the vagaries of the 'topic of the day.'*

I continued to speak on areas of vital interest: migration, remittances, tourism, transnational criminal activity, and global health. Whether I was being a lady of steel or silk, I was definitely promoting what I was confident was in the best interests of both the United States and Jamaica. Press coverage was favorable.

Leaving Jamaica: Former prime minister Patterson certainly had my number when it came to identifying my love for the southern plains of Westmoreland and St. Elizabeth. Chuck and I, through our Cobb Family Foundation, of which I am president, mobilized our family and friends both in the United States and Jamaica, to donate money and equipment to construct and expand classrooms at the Sandy Bank Primary School in Treasure Beach. It officially opened on April 3, 2004 with four classrooms and a forty-station computer lab and was named by contributors as The Sue Cobb Educational Centre. BREDS Treasure Beach Foundation, under the leadership of Jason Henzell and with the strong support of Tony Hart, whose passion for education knows no bounds, assisted the project including with their time and their own assets and independent fundraising. This project brought together a number of foreign visitors and locals working for the betterment of the community. It was pleasing to see it come together.

Additionally, from the very beginning of my tour of duty, I helped with modest support of First Step Basic School in Top Hill, St. Elizabeth, founded by its American principal, Pastor

William Perkins, who started the school in 1999. USAID was able to provide funding to construct classrooms and sanitary facilities as well as a computer lab. I was greatly honored when on January 12, 2005 First Step Basic School held a lovely farewell function prior to my departure as United States ambassador. There's just nothing like four- and five-year-olds cheering you on!

Finally, on my last day physically in my embassy office – January 31, 2005 – I was able to sign the agreement whereby SOUTHCOM allocated over US$1 million for infrastructure development at Pedro Cays. I also had the great pleasure to recommend to our Congress that the Crowne Plaza tower in Manor Park, which had become home to embassy staff members, should be named Powell Plaza to honor former Secretary of State Colin Powell. Congress agreed.

I left the island in early February 2005, but my commitment to Jamaica has continued to a great extent through the American Friends of Jamaica (AFJ), the New York based charitable entity that includes six former United States ambassadors to Jamaica on its board of directors. This is something unique. No other country can claim that kind of organized dedication to its well-being by United States ambassadors who served in its capitol. Board members of AFJ include former Ambassadors Glen Holden, Gary Cooper, Sue Cobb, Brenda Johnson, Pamela Bridgewater and Luis Moreno. The current Honorary Chair of the Board is United States Ambassador Don Tapia.

Ambassador Glen Holden and his wife, Gloria, were instrumental in promoting this charitable organization that continues to assist Jamaican charities in the areas of education, healthcare, and economic development. Ambassador Holden was president for fifteen years from 1992 to 2007. Following Glen's term, I was elected president and served until 2012, when my successor in Kingston, Ambassador Brenda Johnson, became president. Wendy Hart Schrager, the talented daughter of Tony and Sheila Hart, is now the president of the AFJ. The dynamic Caron Chung remains AFJ's very able executive director. I remain on the board of directors which continues to be a rewarding endeavor.

In 2007 after Hurricane Dean hit the island, I was in my office in Coral Gables when Father Ho Lung of the Missionaries of the Poor (M.O.P.) called. He said, "Sue, we have a disaster here. We must immediately raise US$250,000 to purchase plywood to fix 1,000 roofs in inner city Kingston." I said "Okay." I got on the phone and with five strategic phone calls raised the money. Among the large donors were the families of three former United States ambassadors: the Cobbs, the Holdens, and the Johnsons, as well as Canadian-based Jamaicans Raymond and Donette Chang. Roofs of Love, as it became known, became a reality because the previously mentioned donors were able to work with the AFJ, with Food for the Poor, and with Father Ho Lung and the Brothers of M.O.P., to provide rapid and important humanitarian relief in desperate communities.

While in Jamaica I came to know Chris Blackwell whose company Island Records helped to spread Bob Marley's uniquely Jamaican music around the world. Chris grew up on Jamaica's north coast and acquired a property known as GoldenEye, where Ian Fleming wrote the James Bond series. While I was living in Kingston, Chris was in the process of transforming GoldenEye, then a small luxury boutique resort, into a larger, but still unique luxury resort. I love GoldenEye. It is one of my favorite places in the hemisphere and the resort of choice for the celebration in 2017 of my eightieth birthday. In all the years Chris Blackwell owned and managed GoldenEye he was, in thought, word and deed, supporting the local communities in the region. Because of Chris's dedication relating to sustainable development, Chuck and I found ways to support Chris's Oracabessa Foundation.

Captured by some of the needs in Jamaica, our family foundation made pledges to MoBay Hope Clinic, founded by fellow AFJ director, the indefatigable Sydney Engel. Other hospitals and educational entities around Ocho Rios and Montego Bay drew our support under guidance of our remarkable friend Michele Rollins, who has never ceased to give back to Jamaica. The Rollins family and Cobb family also supported Ambassador Brenda Johnson's inspirational work with the Prince of Wales Foundation's Rose Town Project.

The Order of Jamaica: In 2010, I received a call from Prime Minister Bruce Golding's office advising me that the Order of Jamaica (OJ), the country's highest honor for a non-Jamaican citizen, would be bestowed upon me. That was a complete surprise as this honor typically goes to really famous people or to long-serving, highly-regarded Jamaicans. I knew of only two very famous and deserving Americans who preceded me: Harry Belafonte and General Colin Powell.

The National Honors and Awards has several levels and recognizes those Jamaicans or foreign nationals who by their service have made a meaningful and significant contribution to national development. The governor-general, on the advice of the prime minister, makes the announcements with effect from August 6th each year in celebration of Jamaica's independence from the United Kingdom in 1962. The awards are presented on National Heroes' Day in October so those named have time to invite family members and a select few friends to attend the grand ceremony on the lawns of King's House, the beautiful residence of the governor-general. With the JDF military band in full uniform, the diplomatic corps, government ministers, and everyone dressed in their finest, each person awarded is called upon by name, walks across the expansive lawn to the stage where His Excellency personally bestows the appropriate level of badge, medal, and ribbons (in diplomatic terms "decorations") upon each honoree while the entire ceremony is televised to the nation. It truly is quite special.

I had to ponder again, how did this happen to me? I ultimately believed that the people of Jamaica saw and appreciated the series of activities created under the Building Bridges program, as well as the years of voluntary efforts both during my tenure and after. Prime Minister Bruce Golding confirmed those thoughts in 2018 this way:

> Sue Cobb arrived as ambassador to Jamaica at the time of the 9/11 tragedy. By that time, US engagement in the Caribbean had receded as a result of the end of the Cold War and the fact that the Caribbean was no longer a theatre of conflict between Washington and Moscow over communist expansionism. As a consequence of 9/11, much of America's focus and allocation of resources was directed to countering terrorism. The Caribbean became even more marginalized.
>
> Sue understood this and pursued creative ways of stimulating cooperation between US and Jamaica, particularly in terms of private sector linkages.
>
> Even after she demitted office, unlike career appointees who tend to simply move on to their next posting, Sue retained a continuing interest in Jamaica through the American Friends of Jamaica. She continued to present Jamaica in a favorable light, especially among potential investors. Among the US ambassadors who have served in Jamaica, I rank Loren Lawrence (1979–82) as the No. 1. Sue Cobb is not far behind.
>
> The Honorable Bruce Golding, May 13, 2018

Looking at my tenure as United States ambassador from the United States' perspective, General Colin Powell in 2017 said:

> I had not met Sue before I swore her in as ambassador and she was one of the best of the ambassadors that served while I was secretary of state. What made her one of the best is not just what she did in the

country, but what she has done afterwards as a former ambassador. She never left Jamaica even after her term was over.

She committed herself to the American Friends of Jamaica. She committed herself to scholarships. She and her husband had the means to do wonderful things, and they did! Just one thing after another. If you read her bio, and if you read her story of Jamaica, it's a place she fell in love with. When she moved back to Florida, and became an official in the Florida government, that didn't end it. She raised money for Jamaica when they had hurricanes and other national disasters and they needed relief. She fought for Jamaica. She is as Jamaican as any Jamaican you'd ever want to meet.

I wish that every ambassador who goes out – particularly the non-career or political ambassadors as we call them – many of them are people of means. I think it would be wonderful if every one of them would try to keep that kind of connection after they have left. Many of them do. But very few ever reach the level of continuing interest, continuing commitment, and continuing philanthropy to the country that they've served in and that's why when she left, over the years she's received much acclamation from Jamaica.

When she left The Gleaner *wrote a piece about her. They said: 'We may have disagreed with the government, but they [the United States government] sure did well by sending down Sue Cobb as a perfect representative of the American people.' She continues to be a wonderful diplomat and representative of the American people, through her philanthropy, her charities, her love of the island. And so one couldn't ask for better.*

She is special because she has always, throughout her life, taken on the hard task, done incredible things – climbing mountains and all kinds of other interesting things. But that's who she is. She puts her total passion and energy and love into whatever she's doing at the moment.

General Colin Powell, November 17, 2017

Oh my, it's hard to have a response to such comments. It is humbling – I guess it's not very humble to include the comments in these pages. But I just love Colin Powell, so I have to!

Another person with whom I had the great privilege of working was the man who at the time was special assistant to the president and senior director for Western Hemisphere Affairs at the National Security Council, Ambassador Thomas Shannon Jr. whose experience in diplomacy included, inter alia, service in Venezuela, South Africa, Guatemala, and as ambassador in Brazil. Tom became the highest ranked career official in the State Department and served as assistant secretary of state for the Western Hemisphere, deputy secretary, and ultimately for a short period of time as the United States secretary of state. Tom was very experienced and a "doer." He had this to say about my tenure in Jamaica:

> *First of all, she was in Jamaica and people tend to think that the Caribbean is a vacation spot. It might be for some people if you're going to Montego Bay, or some of the islands in the Caribbean, but the reality is, the Caribbean has been our third border since our birth. Caring for the Caribbean and protecting ourselves from what's happening in the Caribbean has defined a large part of our national security history. Many of the countries in the Caribbean lived through the radicalization that happened after the Cuban Revolution. An enormous amount of effort was put into the political work, and economic, and social development work in these countries. A lot of that work was put into Jamaica.*
>
> *When Sue was there Hugo Chávez was ascendant in Venezuela. She had to work very hard to counter those influences, counter a kind of Cuban presence, and build an understanding between Jamaica and the United States and a friendship between our societies and people that required her to be in motion all the time. Not just in her engagements with the government, but also in her public diplomacy, how she was dealing with Jamaican society, and how she was engaging with the Jamaican diaspora in the United States. I found her to be really energetic, really determined to do a good job, and prepared to put in the really long hours, and sometimes grueling hours, in order to get the job done.*
>
> *Ambassador Thomas Shannon Jr., January 18, 2018*

Jamaica does maintain relatively close relationships with Cuba and Venezuela, because they have strong social and economic reasons for doing so. While there are also political reasons, they are not, in my opinion, truly compelling and are not risks to the United States in terms of Jamaica falling under the control of a communist or socialist autocracy. Jamaicans are extremely independent people, with a unique cultural strength, an active, vocal press, largely democratic institutions, and frequent social intercourse with the United States.

In terms of Venezuela, Jamaica saw opportunity as Hugo Chávez ascended in power. Chávez launched an initiative in 2005 to supply crude oil at discounted prices to selected countries in the Caribbean region through a program called PetroCaribe. Islands have energy needs that are costly and difficult to sustain. Through the prosperity provided by Venezuela's vast oil reserves Chávez provided a partial solution at providential cost. In exchange, Chávez garnered support from a number of Western Hemisphere countries, including Jamaica, for his so-called Bolivarian revolution. Predictably as Venezuela's circumstances deteriorated under the leadership of Hugo Chávez and Nicolás Maduro and Venezuela's oil industry died, PetroCaribe became unsustainable.

Venezuela and Cuba, as close, offshore neighbors have always posed challenges for the United States in one way or another. Now on our horizon is a growing, imposing China, given to "predatory loans" around the globe, funding numerous ports, roads, and other infrastructure projects in the Western Hemisphere. There are vital reasons for this to be of significant concern to the United States. I find it fascinating to study the subtle maneuvers that leaders make that are later unveiled as components of long-term strategic plans affecting the world's geopolitical balance of power. I'm watchful for disguised ploys, whether fake news, dis-information, or predatory loans that expose recipient countries to dependency or expropriation of critical infrastructure when debts become unpayable. When this gamesmanship occurs in key geographical areas in close proximity to the United States, it is imperative that the United States be vigilant.

Ambassador Shannon, now retired from the Foreign Service, was definitely a long-term strategic thinker. In discussing the reduction of drug trafficking, he remarked in his comments on the work our embassy did to counter the drug trade emanating from South America and flowing across the Caribbean:

> It was a combination of the State Department working through our Bureau of International Narcotics and Law Enforcement and United States Southern Command, and then the local police and military, in Sue's case, the Jamaican security forces. Jamaica, because of its location, was often times a first stop for stuff moving out of Colombia or moving out of western Venezuela. Because of what was happening our cooperation with the Jamaicans became very important. The islands were very vulnerable and what we were able to do was shut down most of the major trafficking going through the islands, which of course, rerouted a lot of the cocaine. It's one of the reasons Central America is facing so many problems right now, because the traffickers began moving cocaine by land, or by sea, but instead of moving it in the Caribbean, they moved it to the Pacific. In this regard, you can say that Sue was very successful in how she marshaled United States power and resources and then connected them to the capabilities of the Jamaican's security services.

> She's a marvelous person and a great American, as is her husband. They have had a deep interest in the Caribbean and broadly in Latin America. It was a wonderful combination during the Bush administration because of the president's own commitment to the region, and so there was a wonderful chemistry that developed that allowed us to take advantage of the President's interest, the secretary of state's interest, the very high-profile interests of key ambassadors, like Sue Cobb, and then Chuck Cobb's interest in trading through the Free Trade Area of the Americas, and his really aggressive promotion of Florida and Miami as a centerpiece for trading activity. It connected in many ways the career service and political appointees in a way that we're often not connected. They helped create an esprit de corps within our ambassadorial corps, where it didn't matter if you were a professional diplomat, or you

had come in through a political appointee process, there was great respect showed all around, and I think Sue had a lot to do with that.

Both she and her husband have been remarkable proponents of diplomacy and remarkable proponents of engagements between government and society. I think most interestingly they have a real interest in the people who do the work of diplomacy. This is evident in the awards that they have founded, but also in Sue's case, and also in the case of her husband, the care with which they treated people when they were ambassadors.

Ambassador Thomas Shannon Jr., January 18, 2018

Colin Powell and Tom Shannon are absolutely revered for their leadership. I could not be more honored than by the words of these amazingly accomplished diplomats uttered in their reminiscence of Chuck's and my service to our country.

In Retrospect: During my tenure I had opportunities to visit the White House and to thank President Bush for the honor of serving and for the work he and Laura were doing for our country. I always felt energized when I saw the president. He was kind and thoughtful and never failed to offer encouraging words. Today he and Laura continue to serve through their work with the George W. Bush Library and Institute in Dallas, Texas.

It was an incredible honor for me to serve the president and the American people. In that role, I tried my hardest in every way to emulate the best of my role models, to stay focused on the job, and to take care of my team members. In our Mission we sought every opportunity to protect America's interests and promote America's values. We sought to advance freedom, democracy, and free enterprise – squarely addressing the paramount issues of our day: the global war on terrorism; the fight to sustain human dignity in the face of poverty and disease; the struggle against transnational crime and drugs; and the imperative of pursuing sustainable development in a democratic hemisphere.

As ambassador, I paid special attention to our Mission's strategic planning processes and to developing superior leadership and management skills as well as economic acumen among our young Foreign Service officers. I was extremely pleased that two of three Embassy Kingston strategic plans submitted (our annual MPP) were judged by the Department of State to be the best in the world. An additional part of our work while I was posted in Jamaica was to secure approval from the Department of State and the Government of Jamaica and local authorities in Kingston to plan and launch construction of a new embassy compound, as well as to improve housing at the large hotel property we owned to create a safe, secure, and functional environment in which many of our embassy staff now live and work.

Our embassy worked hard to increase cooperation between Jamaica and the United States in areas of mutual interest, while always focusing on the highest standards of management and our fiduciary responsibility to the American people. Our attention never wavered from supporting American citizens, both those in Jamaica and those in the United States. Our most critical programs focused on defending our homeland through identifying and eliminating threats before they could reach United States shores. I would like to think that my country team and I successfully advanced United States policy objectives and mutual understanding in a forceful, yet generous manner.

I acknowledge again my appreciation of the rare and gracious honor of the Order of Jamaica bestowed upon me by the Government of Jamaica.

My tenure ended in early February 2005. It was time to go home and see my grandchildren.

Chapter Fourteen

Start where you are. Use what you have. Do what you can.
Arthur Ashe

FLORIDA SECRETARY OF STATE
2005–2007

At home in Coral Gables I was decompressing and getting back pieces of my life in Miami. I was really just in a state of "chilling out" after years of high intensity work. I had been missing my grandchildren and was glad to see them again. Somebody always tells this story on me (and not with admiration). When I came back from Jamaica in 2005, I wanted to make up time that I had lost with my grandchildren, so I organized a summer camp at our Coral Gables home for the four children of my son Christian, who lived nearby. I hired Andrew Stevens a young man from our tennis club to help me. We called him Coach and he was the swimming and tennis instructor. I kept an eye on everything, supervised proper climbing techniques on a rock wall about four feet high and managed games and arts and crafts for indoor creative activities. I demanded my four campers wear tennis whites, arrive exactly at 9:00 a.m. and stand with Coach and me to say the pledge of allegiance, hands over their hearts, facing our seaside American flag. Then we would start their tennis and swimming lessons, later letting them play in the pool for fun.

I had two primary rules: (i) shoes were mandatory because it was easy to step on something outdoors and get hurt, and (ii) you could not cry, unless you were really hurt. If you were hurt, and really had something worth crying about, that would be okay, but just to cry because something did not suit you was just not going to work. I explained that I was going to use the soccer penalty system. If the referee (me) determines that you were purposely not following a rule, or you were crying as a "tool" just because you did not get your turn or something similar, you would get a yellow card. If you got two yellow cards, on the next penalty, you would get a red card. If you got a red card, you were going home.

Well, Ben was only three at the time. At the tennis courts one day he started crying and would not stop. He had not been well behaved earlier that morning and had gotten two yellow cards. At tennis, he got the feared red card. I said, "You're going home." I told Coach to take care of the others, got my car, put Ben in it, and did not talk to him. I sternly drove to his house, looked to be sure someone was there, and said, "I hope you can come back to camp tomorrow, but you're going to have to behave yourself." I was really, really tough, and the kids have never forgotten it. They never let me forget giving a red card to a three-year-old! Well, maybe that was a little harsh.

Despite that, the kids (including Ben), loved the summer camp. I got Big Guy and Big Girl award stickers they could wear on their shirts and a whole bunch of prizes and small trophies for them at the end of the month. They really loved it and I did too. Ben did not hold it against me and for a class assignment when he was in third grade, he wrote this:

Ami Sue is the rainbow in the sky. Red is the color of her smile. Orange is the sunset at Cat Cay. Yellow is the hot sun on the cold mountains in Colorado. Green is all the time we went out into her backyard and played. Dark blue is the water in the ocean in the Bahamas. Violet is the color of the blanket I use when she tells me stories. Indigo is all the memories I have with my grandma. Ami Sue is my rainbow.

I read that now and it totally fills my heart. Who could ever have given that boy a red card?

But if you think I was tough on a three-year-old, Chuck remembers another incident, arguably worse, when we were traveling in Greece with our two sons:

> *Designing the Boca Beach Club in Boca Raton, Florida across from its famed tower was going to dramatically expand Arvida's Boca Raton Hotel and Club and set the tone for the total Boca Raton Resort. It was one of my highest priorities in 1976 as the forty-year-old Arvida CEO. Harvard Business School professors John McArthur and Colyer Crum, along with senior executives of Penn Central Victor Palmieri and Frank Loy, suggested I needed to broaden my knowledge of luxury resort hotels and urged me to take a tour of specified Mediterranean resorts.*

> *Our sons Chris and Toby were with us for much of the trip. Everyone remembers the Corfu incident. Sue reserved a car for a driving tour around the island one afternoon, while I was in a meeting. On the drive she got so upset with Chris for bullying Toby and refusing to let him sit in the front seat that she kicked our thirteen-year-old out of the car ten miles from the Corfu Harbor just six hours before our cruise ship was to depart for Italy. She told him to find his way to the pier and to be at the dock by 6:00 p.m. Since he made it to the ship on time, we think that was a good learning lesson and worth the risk but, in truth, it was very scary for both of us.*

Not all our travels were so dramatic for our sons or grandchildren. One, in fact, was more dramatic for me. In my very active life, I have probably had several near-death experiences that I did not even realize I just missed, most relating to high altitude climbing. Ironically, the incident that really frightened me, and almost did me in, came on a family holiday with all seven grandchildren, the youngest at the time about four. We went to the Galápagos Islands. Of course, the children were very excited about snorkeling and about the booby birds and all the things they were going to see. But the adults, (my husband, our two sons and their wives, and I) looked forward to going scuba diving. We prearranged a dive master to take the six of us for a dive. We had been warned that not only is the water extremely cold, but the islands are surrounded by some of the strongest currents in the world.

We wore 7mm cold-water wet suits, full headgear, gloves, masks, and safety regalia. The dive master told us to stay close to him because if not, there was a good chance that one of the currents would get us, and if that happened there was not much chance of recovery. We were certified advanced open ocean divers and I was excited, but failed to check my rented equipment carefully. After we were in the water and underway, I could see that my depth finder was not working. Now this can be very critical, but I was with the dive master and other divers and my plan was to just stay right with them, which my diving buddy was also doing. What I didn't count on was that everybody was younger and stronger than me and I could not keep up with them. And I did get caught in a current.

When we made a turn to return to our boat, I could not tell from my depth finder at what depth we were, but we were not near the surface. I couldn't tell if I was sinking or rising except by watching the divers ahead of me. But I was continually losing ground to those divers, until suddenly I could not see them anymore. I couldn't see anyone. I was fighting the current and I couldn't tell how low or how high I was in the water. I thought I had enough oxygen if I wasn't descending, but I simply couldn't tell. I knew I was in very serious trouble. I was desperately looking for any hint of light that would give me a clue as to depth. I literally did not know which way was up. I had to make a decision. I thought it was very slightly lighter above me rather than below me and I started ascending.

I began to see more light. Of course, it's important to ascend slowly. By the time I reached the surface the divers and our boat were nowhere in sight; I was just being carried along swiftly in the current. That was one of the rare times in my life that I was genuinely scared because I just didn't know how to help myself. I might not have been so uncomfortable if I were in the mountains in a dangerous situation, but I was definitely scared when caught in strong ocean currents 850 miles off the coast of Ecuador. I was really scared. Thankfully, when only five divers got onto the boat, they recognized that I had fallen behind, revved up the engine and came back to find me. All onboard were wrapped cozily in blankets, sipping hot tea. Yes, I reported the malfunction of the depth finder to the dive master, but I have never told the other divers how close I came to ruining their Galápagos vacation. Travels like this not only helped build our family bonds, but were welcome breaks from the challenging and high-pressure jobs which Chuck and I undertook.

I was still chilling out at home after leaving my post as ambassador to Jamaica and Jeb Bush was still governor of Florida with six years under his belt. One day in 2005 Jeb called Chuck and told him, "Glenda Hood is leaving and I have to get a new Secretary of State for my last year and a half as governor." Glenda Hood had been in the post for two and a half years. She was the former Mayor of Orlando and was simply ready to leave Tallahassee. "Do you think Sue would do it?" Chuck said, "No. She won't. Don't bother asking her."

Chuck told me about that call, but we didn't seriously discuss it. Then Jeb's chief of staff, Mark Kaplan, called me. I knew Mark well and have always held him in high regard. Typically, a first call on a business matter from a CEO or governor would always be made by someone else. Jeb would not call me personally and make a request. I might say no, especially since Chuck had told him that would be my response. So either Jeb's chief of staff had not heard I presumably had already said no, or Jeb told him to call me anyway. Mark said, "Would you consider coming up and serving as secretary of state for the rest of Jeb's term

as governor?" I was surprised but by then I had le..
I really was not very good at decompressing. It was an eas,
decision. I said "Sure."

Being secretary of state for Jeb was an honor. It is a multi-
faceted job, but in all honesty, I felt it would be an easier job
than the one I had just left. I was fortunate in that the person
who had preceded me, Glenda Hood, was a smart, capable
woman who had the agency in good shape. Being secretary of
state has lots of moving parts and many things that I did not
know much about, but the department was blessed with good
people who ran their diverse sections with competence. It ran
the way such an organization should run. The leader delegates
duties to people trained for their specific jobs. That's true in
an embassy as well. A leader must encourage people to be the
best they can be, to reach for excellence at every opportunity,
but must also empower them and let them do the jobs they're
trained to do. No micro-managing their operations. If you see
problems, discuss them. Praise competent leaders in public
and criticize, if necessary, in private. It is not very difficult to
identify the "doers" and observe the jobs they get done. The
CEO always gets reports when things are not going quite
right and can straighten them out. I have found that most any
problem can be fixed.

Within the Florida secretary of state's broad portfolio, most
publicly, the secretary of state is in charge of Florida's wild card:
the Florida Division of Elections. In 2005 when I arrived, Florida
was preparing for the 2006 mid-term elections. The goal is to
count all votes properly cast, not to misplace votes, and to try
not to have any shenanigans going on in any of the states' sixty-
seven counties where independent elected supervisors ruled
the roost. The Department of State had a large well-schooled
elections division, which understood manual and electronic
requirements and reporting requirements. The head of the

elections division reports to the secretary of state. The secretary of state reports to the governor and to federal election officials. Florida learned a great deal from the controversial 2000 election when Katherine Harris was secretary of state and the infamous butterfly ballots appeared and recounts occurred. I really was not uncomfortable being in charge of a federal election as I knew Florida's laws had been updated and I knew our election division had very capable and experienced people.

I was sworn in December 2005 as Florida secretary of state. The only way in which I was uncomfortable in my new job in Tallahassee was in the month after I returned to work on January 3, 2006 with three broken vertebrae from a ski accident in Telluride. In late December a large male boarder lost control and slammed into my lower legs with full force causing my feet and skis to fly ten feet (Chuck says) straight up into the air. I landed on the back of my head, neck, and upper shoulders, the kind of fall in which skiers break their necks and become paralyzed. Though stunned, the first thing I did as I lay in the snow was wiggle my fingers and toes to be sure I hadn't damaged my spinal cord. They moved. The young man who hit me sat next to me and cried while we waited for help. I was immobilized by the Ski Patrol, carted off the mountain on a sled, and taken to the local clinic. X-rays revealed no fractures, so I was sent to our nearby home where I hobbled rigidly around for two days to finish packing for my move back to Tallahassee. It was painful and I had to proceed very gingerly. Once I started working in Tallahassee though, I had no time for a medical check-up. I just continued to move slowly and carefully. Finally, at the end of January I went to the head orthopedic surgeon for Florida State University's athletic department. He did an MRI and informed me that I had three fractured vertebrae, two lower cervical and one thoracic, all of which seemed to be healing fine. He said, "try to avoid any impact to your body for six weeks." I did.

Meanwhile back at the department where elections were such a big and important element, I was still trying to master all my other roles as secretary, including head of the Division of Corporations for the state (signing off on all corporation registrations, retaining records, and so forth). It is a big division, with several hundred employees. The head of the Division of Corporations reports to the secretary. A lot of people have told me since that time that my name is on the framed corporate state registration certificate hanging in their offices around the state. That seemed rather odd, but every week I did have to sign numerous registrations and deal with whatever issues may have come up in that division.

The secretary of state also oversees the entire State Library system. Libraries throughout the state report to the head of the Library Division, who reported to me. My job definition also included oversight of historical resources, all the state's cultural affairs, and state protocol. Of course, we had a public relations office, a legal office, and a legislative affairs office all of which were critical to the secretary's effectiveness. I enjoyed working with our legislators, who dealt with constituent interests in all our departments and promulgated laws relevant to the execution of my job. I dealt frequently with the press, sometimes achieving our goals more successfully than others. Only one time did the press actually physically invade my personal office in a very unmannerly way. It was on the matter of paper vs. electronic ballots, which was of passionate interest at the time. Other than that, I generally had quite good relations with the media. One quarrying reporter asked me, "How does it feel to be the bookends of the Bush administration?" (referring to secretary of the Lottery and secretary of state). It felt fine.

Once a week, all state agency heads met with the governor to give reports on the status of their agency. Of course, the governor would already know a great deal because he paid attention and had staff support for such purposes. It was also true that the media in Tallahassee covered every single step any agency head made. As a former US ambassador, I probably had a bit more press experience than most agency heads, so this aspect of the job was not a problem for me. After facing the challenges of being a US ambassador, you have a pretty good sense of what direction to take on just about any question, because most everything has already happened on your watch. All embassies have human resource issues, financial issues, security issues, media issues, and big and little mistakes for the press to cover. The same was true at Florida's Department of State. It is manageable because ultimately you have capable professional staff dealing with the respective issues. Nonetheless, inevitably, something happens that has to go to the ambassador or to the secretary. Serious matters end up on the CEO's desk. Fortunately for me, there were no big surprises while I was serving as secretary of state. My assessment of the division heads within the Department was that they were uniformly capable career people with significant experience.

My job was paying attention where things were a little off kilter. I had to let division heads know I was paying attention to finances and to human resources, which meant the financial aspects of human resources, because people were our most expensive components. My goal was to help manage taxpayer dollars as prudently as possible. My previous exposure in state government as CEO of the Lottery was helpful when I was secretary of state and I was definitely happy to work again with Jeb Bush.

But in the end the reason I said I would contemplate the job as secretary of state was that I did not think there would be anything more difficult to manage after my first morning on the job as a brand new ambassador in Embassy Kingston, September 11, 2001. The world changed that day and everything we had done or planned to do at US embassies around the world changed dramatically. The only thing we knew for sure at that time was that we were in uncharted waters. That was not the case in Tallahassee under Governor Bush's leadership.

Jeb spent some time reminiscing on the days we worked together:

> Sue was secretary of state 2005–2007. The election issues were a big deal in Florida, which we resolved early on, created a single standard and became kind of a model for other states. Having gone through the 2000 election was important. So, the job had a big portfolio. It had all the issues related to the historical assets the state owns, the cultural funding, the election laws, the election issues related to running local elections. Ultimately, the secretary of state is important. Sue did very well. She's a great leader, great manager and very collegial with our team.
>
> Generally, maybe not in Washington where the pay's a little more and it's theoretically more prestigious – doesn't look that way now – but the jobs are a big deal. Normally, in order to get talented people to work in state government, they're typically younger. So, it was a real blessing to have someone of her experience and wisdom that comes through life's experiences to be by my side because she helped mentor a lot of other people inside the state government.
>
> Governor John Ellis "Jeb" Bush Sr., November 16, 2017

While serving as secretary of state I did have one experience that was unsettling. After I was there for two or three months, Jeb was taking a trip to Nassau for some educational projects that the state was doing with the Bahamas. He asked me to accompany him. There were three or four of us on the state plane. During the flight in both directions the governor read clemency appeals. He indicated that he didn't like to do that, but he had hundreds of them and felt compelled to read each one personally and carefully. We did not talk on the plane, but when we got back to Tallahassee and Jeb and I were walking to the terminal together he asked, "Have you heard from

Washington?" I said, "No, on what?" And he responded, "You'll get a call." He wouldn't say anymore.

I did get a call the next day from the White House Office of Presidential Personnel. They were asking if I would take a second ambassadorial position for George W. Bush. A large country was named. They needed me to call a certain person to discuss taking the job. My first thought was, "Yes, I'd love to do that," and my second thought was, "Gosh, this one I better ask Chuck what he would think." The third thought was, "I can't do that to Jeb. I just took the job as secretary of state and Jeb has another year."

My fourth thought turned out to be the definitive controlling factor: my grandchildren were at ages three to eleven, they were happy to have me home, and came to our house often to play. I played with them, skied with them, put on the summer camps for them, and did things with them all the time in that short period when I was home between Jamaica and Tallahassee. If I left for another two or three years, as fast as children change, I wouldn't know them, and they wouldn't know me. And I knew that by the time they were in the eighth or ninth grade, somehow they would learn that it wouldn't be so much fun anymore to go play with grandmother.

The combination of circumstances, primarily leaving Chuck, sort of double-crossing Jeb by accepting a new ambassadorial post, leaving Tallahassee, and leaving my grandchildren again for at least two or three years was too hard to swallow. On the other hand, I genuinely and deeply wanted to do it. I just hemmed and hawed and told Presidential Personnel I would call them back. We had a series of calls. During this week of calls, Chuck and I were visiting with friends in Hawaii. I couldn't say anything about my dilemma because it was totally confidential. I told only Chuck. We were at the beautiful Maui home of our friends Ron and Joyce Allred with several guests including Carol and Neil Armstrong and Judi and John Temple. Periodically my phone would ring and I would have to excuse myself. The White House called at least five times in the four days we stayed in Maui. I would have to say, "Pardon me, I have to take this call." Then everybody, of course, was curious. I just said, "It's a legal matter." I was back in Tallahassee two weeks before the Office of Presidential Personnel finally said to me, "We have to know, and we have to know by Monday."

I lost sleep over the decision. I really wanted to do it. In my experience, being a US ambassador is one of the most challenging and meaningful jobs in the world. My previous long departures from normal family life were Jamaica and Mt. Everest. Each in some ways were kind of selfish endeavors because most family members really don't want you to undertake them. Despite that, there were reasons both sojourns made sense to me, but to engage in a third could actually be damaging. Chuck did not want me to go. Jeb would not have been happy about it. My grandchildren would continue to grow. The day that I got the "final" message that I really had to say yes or no, I met with Jeb and asked him for his thoughts. He basically said, "Go for it," and walked out of the room. Obviously, the governor had talked to the president and I knew they had talked to the president of the country in which they wanted me to serve. I had been told that Secretary of State Condoleezza Rice was on board with my appointment and the president was on board, the host country was on board, and even Jeb could manage a change. I knew Chuck was not on board. Apparently, as far as Washington was concerned, it was all set up. I was down to the last minute, but I decided to ask for one more extension. They said, "No." So I just thanked them for considering me. An exciting new job was off the table. I can say after the fact that the career Foreign Service officer the State Department sent to the country in question did an outstanding job and I am sure managed the difficult situations much better than I could have.

It was a blessing to have had two important, challenging, and educational jobs in state government with Governor Jeb Bush. It was a bonus in my life that I had never expected and I am grateful for those opportunities. On the second ambassadorship, I did the right thing, although I wish I had been in a position to accept. I still have pangs of regret. But the circumstances weren't right. I had in essence made a promise to Jeb in saying "Yes" to the job of secretary of state. I had made a much more important promise to Chuck many years earlier when were married in the Stanford Memorial Church. It was time to say no. Chuck and I created a partnership for life, and we have been able to share that partnership professionally, athletically, and through raising two terrific sons, seeing them with wonderful marriages of their own, and then being able to share seven very precious grandchildren. No matter how busy we've been, this family we share has been and will always be our highest priority in life. When asked about his mother and his family our son Toby observed:

My brother and I are so incredibly fortunate to have these two just amazing role models, and beyond their obvious and visible success professionally and athletically they are an amazing set of parents who love each other and reflect the true success of sixty years of incredible marriage. I am awed by them. I really am.

Tobin Templeton Cobb, November 7, 2017

"The Ambassadors," the only living and married non-career
US Ambassadors in US history, 2015. Photograph by Michael Hopkins,
Gerlinde Photography, Davie, FL.

Dedication of Cobb Stadium for Soccer, Track and Field at the University of Miami, honoring former Olympian and University of Miami Trustee, Chuck Cobb, 1999.

Jon Huntsman, former US Ambassador to Russia receiving the State Department's Sue M. Cobb Award for Exemplary Diplomatic Service at the annual awards ceremony, 2017.

With the remarkable former first lady Barbara Bush at Walker's Point, Kennebunkport, Maine, August 2015.

Supporting the work of Ambassador Brenda Johnson and Michele Rollins in the Kingston community of Rose Town with His Royal Highness Prince Charles at Rose Hall Great House, Montego Bay, Jamaica, March 2008.

With long time Stanford friend former US Supreme Court Associate Justice Anthony (Tony) Kennedy, Coral Gables, Florida, 2019.

At dear friend (First Man to Walk on the Moon) Neil Armstrong's eightieth birthday party, Cincinnati, Ohio, August 2010.

Bungee Jumping at Kawarau Bridge, Queensland, New Zealand on my sixtieth birthday, 1997, with my first senior citizen discounted ticket!

Ambassadors Glade dedication in honor of diplomats and avid skiers,
Ambassador Charles E. Cobb and Ambassador Sue M. Cobb,
owners of Durango Mountain Resort, December 2010.

Summer Camp tennis program created for Casi, Ben, Fred, and Nick with Ami Sue and Coach Andrew Stevens, 2005.

On Telluride bike ride, Sebastian, age six, celebrates grandmother, Ami Sue, 2005.

Eightieth birthday at Good Hope, Jamaica 2017, with family.
Back left to right: *Casi, Sebi, Kolleen, Charlie, Fred, Chris, Sue, Chuck, and Toby.* Front left to right: *Luis, Nick, Luisa, Ben*

Aboard liveaboard dive boat, Wave Dancer, *getting ready to dive Belize's Blue Hole, October 2000. One year later October 2001, the* Wave Dancer *flipped over in a storm killing twenty divers aboard.*

Jumping with the US Army parachute demonstration team, The Golden Knights, Homestead, Florida, February 2020.

And on we go...

Chapter Fifteen

I am what survives me.
Erik Homburger Erikson

AND ON WE GO...

Life unfolds in chapters. My government employment came to an end in 2007. The following decade opened up many new opportunities. I returned to Cobb Partners and our Miami based multi-faceted business interests, which frequently took us from sea to shining sea. There were several very positive things about this new job: I could live in my own home with my husband; I could re-engage in the practice of law as much as I wished (which was not much); I could choose most any travel destination in the world to visit and know at least a little about the country and its geopolitical position and linkages; and frequently we would visit friends serving in such destinations. But the best part of all was that I could now see and frequently be with my seven grandchildren, the oldest of whom was then twelve.

I readily confess that Chuck and I made every effort to leverage our proximity to our grandchildren to the hilt. Other than my reclusive grandfather Ed Griffin and a few days with my dad's father John McCourt who died when I was young, my brother Peter and I had no grandparental presence in our lives. My parents spoke little of them. Records were sparse. I wondered what my grandparents were like, how they lived, what influences did they have on my parents? That absence in my own life is one of the reasons I felt compelled to write down my own remembrances of growing up on a farm, my education, my varied careers in teaching, law, finance, and diplomacy, my fortunate marriage and partnership for life, as well as a few of my maybe less than rational adventures. Someday our grandchildren will wonder more deeply, as I did, about their heritage and those who influenced their own parents.

Simultaneously with having our grandchildren in our sights at malleable ages, we readjusted to a somewhat more normal existence. It was important to both Chuck and me to remain active in business, in philanthropy, and in international affairs. As Theodore Roosevelt said, "the best prize that life offers is the chance to work hard at work worth doing" which was like the Holy Grail to us. The more challenges we could find the better, whether they were income-producing or in service to others. We each still sit on numerous boards: public, private, and charitable. We remain fascinated with our own nation's foreign policy and how to address the difficult global issues of our days. I am deeply interested in long-term thinking on shaping the future resolution of current global problems. Serving on the board of trustees of the Center for Strategic and International Studies (CSIS) provides a virtual open window to a world of both intricate and grand problems. Chuck is involved with the boards of the Academy of Diplomacy, Eisenhower Fellows, and the Woodrow Wilson Center. We are both on the board of the Council of American Ambassadors. We greatly value the educational input we receive as members of the Council on Foreign Relations. You get the picture, we are kind of nerds on the international affairs front.

Our years of being associated with the institutions of our government have brought many friends, many challenges, a number of rewards, and some surprises as was our recent and unexpected opportunity to sit, at the invitation of Chief Justice John Roberts, in the Supreme Court gallery to observe the final day of the impeachment hearings of the current United States president. The night before we were included in a small private dinner at the Supreme Court where I was seated with the amazing Ruth Bader Ginsburg, an experience I treasure.

I must digress for a moment to mention the family's foreign travels that have helped to educate our grandchildren, Chuck, and me on international affairs, while significantly enhancing the bonds of our family's three generations. Every annual trip the thirteen of us have taken together has produced dozens of new "remember whens." "Remember when we saw the iguanas swimming with us in the Galápagos? Remember when we went to that huge market in Istanbul and found all those daggers? Remember when we walked on the beaches of Normandy? Remember when we dove and jumped from the cliffs of Croatia's shores? Remember when we crawled through the tunnels in Vietnam?"

One of our most recent excursions was one of the most ambitious and probably one of the most impactful. In 2015 we planned a trip we called "Asia 101." All seven of the grandchildren were old enough to appreciate historical precedents and understand the uniqueness of each of the six major cities we visited. We moved fast (no checked luggage allowed) and engaged experienced guides in each venue. In about two and a half weeks we visited the most well-known sites in Tokyo, Beijing, Hong Kong, Ho Chi Minh City, Kuala Lumpur, and Singapore (topped off by a relaxing couple of days in Waikiki). It took exquisite planning and provided for the grandchildren just a "taste" of the Orient, but we know they have many very strong memories.

In the immediate last couple of years (capturing our grandchildren before they all were absorbed by colleges), we have had the exquisite pleasure of revisiting our old stomping grounds in Iceland and Jamaica. I will leave the Iceland tales to my husband, but the Jamaica excursion was exceptionally meaningful to me. It was my family's celebration of my eightieth birthday. Though my actual birthday is in mid-August and my pronounced desire was to spend my birthday skiing in Bariloche, Argentina (which Chuck and I did), we found a date in June 2017 when all thirteen family members would be able to attend a five-day birthday party. I have always been particularly fond of GoldenEye, where Ian Fleming wrote his famous James Bond novels, so that lovely resort near Ocho Rios became our base camp.

Our enjoyment was not at all diminished by the fact that it rained every single day we were in Jamaica. We very much appreciated the indispensable help of Michele Rollins and of Major Haughton who met us at the airport, especially because on arrival at the airport and at GoldenEye, it was pouring rain. Nonetheless, we immediately bounded into the beautiful and soothing Caribbean Sea where we snorkeled, kayaked, paddle-boarded, and enjoyed a glass bottom boat tour of the coast.

With the help of our wonderful friends, Tony and Sheila Hart and their progeny, Blaise and Wendy, we found a magical rainforest full of adventures at Good Hope, in the mountains above Falmouth. We slipped and slid, climbed and rafted, then zipped about in the trees. I tell everyone that Chuck and I now hold the Jamaican National Age Group (eighty and over) Record for ziplining. (Of course, to my knowledge no such records are kept, but I'm not inquiring, because if they are, I'm sure we'd immediately lose this prestigious title.) Good Hope, a former sugar plantation, is an active family's dream.

Undertaking the obligatory climb through the waters of Dunn's River Falls near Ocho Rios was also very enjoyable and we didn't even have to change clothes to start the climb because we were already soaked from the rain when we got to the river.

Even being wet all day we were never cold due to Jamaica's delicious, stable warm climate and trade winds.

Driving around with Tony and Sheila Hart one day in historic Falmouth, where the plantation history and Georgian architecture capture hearts and minds, we encountered a very large traffic jam at the main intersection in the middle of town. We sat in the Hart's car for what seemed interminable minutes while one car inched across the intersection, alternating with a cross street vehicle crossing. The sidewalks were packed with pedestrians also trying to cross this intersection. Finally, Chuck, not known for his patience, went into action, barking: "I'm going to get out and help the flow of traffic." Sheila Hart exclaimed, "Chuck don't do that. This is so embarrassing. This corner needs a traffic cop. Don't do it." But he did.

Attired in the normal white man's khaki Bermuda shorts, old tennis shoes, a disheveled T-shirt and a big floppy white hat for the sun, Chuck got out of the car. While Sheila ducked her head below window level, he positioned himself squarely in the middle of the intersection and with hand signals motioned cars and pedestrians forward or stopped them. At that point both Harts were hiding, absolutely mortified, but as the traffic began to flow smoothly, Tony, Sheila, I and a very large number of pedestrians who had gathered around the intersection laughed and clapped enthusiastically. We got through quickly and made our way back to GoldenEye.

Our adventure in Jamaica ended on our last evening when dear friend Chris Blackwell and the GoldenEye team surprised me with an elegant and exquisite private dinner for our family of thirteen at Fleming House. James Bond and Bob Marley were in the air as reggae played in the background and Cassidy and my grandsons did their best to sing "Three Little Birds" ('don't worry about a thing...every little thing is going to be alright'). It surely was! Toby and Luisa, Luis, Charlie, and Sebi gave me a small tree which we planted at GoldenEye among the trees of an eclectic (and mostly famous) group of former visitors.

Despite the five days of rain it seems our grandchildren had as much fun as I did. After that trip, speaking on behalf of all seven grandchildren, Charlie Cobb wrote the following: (Oh, I know its gushing, but put yourself in my shoes as a grandmother, I just love it.)

Dear Ami Sue and Fam,

To all the Cobb Family members: Attached is the video footage from the GoPro I had during the entire Jamaica trip.

We are all so grateful to have such an incredible grandmother, one who can do adventurous activities like the ones we did in Jamaica. Jamaica was an unforgettable trip! Although it rained the majority of the time, it made the experience all the more memorable. It added this rainforest theme which personally, I enjoyed very much. Ami Sue, your physical and mental strength is unmatched by any other human on this planet. Luckily, I can see your genes in each and every one of the Cobb grandchildren. Thank you so much for all of the opportunities you have placed before us. From maturing us into responsible young adults, to providing us with opportunities like traveling and seeing the world with you and Afi Chuck, you have given us so much. Our time spent with you is irreplaceable and we enjoy every second of it. You light up our world.

We love you so much and thank you for being the way you are.

Love,
Charlie

What could possibly be more gratifying than a letter like that from your grandson?

Approaching the end of the decade, we generated another wonderful family celebration on February 28, 2019, the occasion of Chuck's and my sixtieth wedding anniversary. Two hundred longtime friends came to dinner at our home at Tahiti Beach. Of course, the grandchildren all gathered once again. Toby and Luisa's boys flew in from their college locations, Luis from

Georgetown in Washington, DC, Charlie from the University of Vermont in Burlington, and Sebi from University of Denver, Colorado. Chris and Kolleen have two sons remaining in Miami, Fred working for an insurance company and Ben soon to be a high school graduate and student at Southern Methodist University (SMU) in Dallas, Texas. Nicholas flew in from Tulane and Cassidy came all the way from Stanford. We were excited to see special friends from our years at Stanford, including Tony and Mary Kennedy, Nancy Page Ostrom, Deanna Amos Pollock Tarr, Carol and Paul Wiggin, and more who honored us by attending. Tony and Sheila Hart made it up from Jamaica. My dear friends Ambassador Brenda and Howard Johnson made every effort to attend, but vacationing in Jamaica, were thwarted by an airline snafu.

Because Chuck has been a leader on the University of Miami Board of Trustees for over forty years, Dean Shelly Berg and The Frost School of Music created a Broadway-style musical, covering the last sixty years of American history in song. Talented UM singers, doing the most popular songs of each decade, sang a narrated video of news highlights as the years rolled across the big screen. Chris and Toby introduced the show and our gifted friend, Broadway tenor Dennis McNeil participated as a singing commentator. Sue and Chuck photos were interspersed in the hour-long history presentation. UM's School of Communications recorded the action, creating a memorable video. Because many of our guests were somewhere close to our age range and knew the popular songs, it became something of a sing along. Following the show, our guests moved to dinner where our grandchildren got the spotlight, doing a second version of Bob Marley's "Three Little Birds." What an entirely joyful evening! The show, written by John Softness and conducted by Shelly Berg, was magnificent. And yes, we were honored with the presence of former US senators,

Supreme Court justices, Florida governors, and other high-profile friends such as Coach Don Shula, Mary Anne Shula and Dick Anderson of the famed 1972 Miami Dolphins football team with its 17–0 record still standing.

Well, sixty years is a very long time and Chuck and I are very lucky people. We were absolutely thrilled that so many good friends could come from around the country, as well as from international locations, including Jamaica and Iceland. The evening was more heart-warming than I could ever put into words.

In case a reader might think by now at my advanced age I've outgrown my taste for new adventures, in February of this year, 2020, a member of the US Army parachute demonstration team, The Golden Knights, called to ask if I'd like to do a parachute jump with the team. The answer was of course, yes.

It is a good place to stop reminiscing, which I shall do while I'm still young enough to eagerly await what may be coming around the next corner.

Epilogue

Be kind, for everyone you meet is fighting a great battle.
Origin Disputed

I have tried to tell the story of my life, about growing up in what was for all practical purposes the Old West, with little money but abundant resources; about a little girl who went to Stanford; about my over sixty year marriage to a remarkable man; about family and friends; about my sons, grandsons, and a granddaughter who followed me to Stanford; about Telluride and Cat Cay, skiing, scuba diving, mountaineering; adventures in faraway places (South America, Africa, Asia, Tibet, Mt. Everest, Nepal) and more; working in places closer to home (Tallahassee and Washington, DC); about warm places (Jamaica) and cold places (Iceland) and worldwide travel; about lawyers and diplomats and world affairs.

I offer in my reflections only thoughts on a life of work, a life of daring to act, of taking advantage of opportunities that arose, which I would hope also reflects a humble life of caring for others.

I was not necessarily on top of each of the ladders I climbed. I completely understand how transient and self-indulgent most achievements are. I realize that no achievement is accomplished alone, and that any success can quickly be reversed to a failure.

I do not have an inflated sense of my personal worth or accomplishments. But when a challenge came along, I always said "yes" to the opportunity to try. I worked hard at each juncture. I worked very hard at one point very far from home and as a result almost touched infinity.

I worked hard when I had the honor of representing my country. Over the years I learned a great deal about the work of my Foreign Service colleagues, both career and non-career. I have the highest respect for those who serve, particularly our Senior Foreign Service officers. They are extraordinarily skilled men and women rendering outstanding service to our country in frequently very difficult circumstances.

My time in Kingston was challenging, rewarding and educational. I'd like to think that I helped to influence and expand the very positive bilateral relationship between the United States and Jamaica. When the prime minister of Jamaica labeled me "The Lady of Silk and Steel," I actually sort of liked it and have used the steel part over the years to keep Chuck, my boys, and my grandsons in line.

It is true that the biggest lesson I learned on the biggest mountain in the world is that it is not, after all, about the peak; it is about the journey and the people with whom we are traveling. And probably the second biggest lesson I have learned along the way is, as my friend Courtney Skinner said: "Everyone has an Everest inside." Our challenges may be different but human capacity is expandable. You may have noticed the quote of this Epilogue: "Be kind, for everyone you meet is fighting a great battle." I believe this to be true and I've learned over these many years that we can help those with whom we are traveling by simply being kind.

So, the culmination of an incredibly interesting and exciting eighty plus years, though perhaps undeserved, is this: I have been blessed beyond words. I am deeply grateful for those blessings and to those who have supported me and guided me along the way. I have concluded that all my immediate family love me deeply and always will. I love all twelve of them equally deeply and always will. And I know love never ends.

Acknowledgments

THE ASSOCIATION FOR DIPLOMATIC STUDIES AND TRAINING (ADST): My book project started when Charles Stuart Kennedy, "Stu," called me to see if I would engage in an oral interview to be placed along with those of other diplomats on the websites of the Library of Congress and ADST. Stu would do the interviews on behalf of ADST, headquartered on the grounds of the National Foreign Affairs Training Center in Arlington, Virginia. I agreed and met several times in 2011–13 with Stu, a very astute interviewer, and responded to his queries. At the conclusion of our talks ADST transcribed Stu's recordings and provided the original transcript to me for review and editing. That transcript provided the skeleton of this book. I am grateful to Stu for his fine work.

Critical to progress in writing and reviewing was the acute judgment of the brilliant ADST book series editor, Margery Boichel Thompson. I also greatly appreciated the critique and editing provided by career Foreign Service member Lisa Terry, who was detailed to ADST. Moreover, I thank the indomitable Susan Johnson, president of ADST, and the entire team at this unique, historically-minded nonprofit for their initiative and efforts to preserve the experiences of US diplomats through diplomatic oral histories and book series programs.

DR. LAURA TANNA, OD: I consider myself very fortunate that my friend and colleague Laura Tanna agreed to help keep me on track as I filled in the blanks of my outline, trying to unravel and record an energetic, intense, and unconventional life. Author of two books and hundreds of newspaper and magazine articles and interviews, Laura holds a BA in Comparative Literature, an MA and PhD in African Languages and Literature, has lived in the USA, England, Uganda, France, and Jamaica, has served on numerous Jamaican boards, and is a fellow director of New York-based American Friends of Jamaica. In 2014 the Government of Jamaica awarded her one of its national honors, the Order of Distinction, for her "invaluable contribution in the fields of Literature and Culture." Laura and her urbane Ugandan-born husband, Dhiru, have traveled worldwide and had amazing experiences of their own. She has given advice and directions that could only come from a skilled observer and author. I am deeply grateful for her guidance, her patience, and her constant effort to enhance my work.

I am grateful to family, friends, and colleagues in the United States and Jamaica, especially those listed in the INTERVIEWS section, who took time to help round out my remembrances in their interviews with Dr. Tanna. Their individual comments are deeply meaningful to me.

The Cobb Family Foundation, Inc. staff members Lissette Vazquez-Andujar, Mary Jo Stasi, and Mercy Perdomo all added value to my project. I particularly thank Lissette, my administrative assistant, for many hours of her time typing this manuscript and retyping my changes, errors, and inserts and for her amazing ability to read my handwriting.

I am impressed with and grateful to Ian Randle Publishers for the quality of the company's work over its thirty-year history, for its sage editing, for its encouragement when due, and for the dispatch with which it executes productions. I extend my special personal thanks to the gracious Christine Randle, managing director of Ian Randle Publishers.

This is not a scholarly biography so notes and bibliographies are not included. Content is based on the author's personal sources, including books, documents, letters, articles, photos, newspaper and magazine articles, and on Dr. Tanna's extensive interviews with family, friends, and colleagues. I accept full responsibility for any misstatements or errors, none of which are attributable to Ian Randle Publishers, Dr. Tanna, ADST, or those interviewed or recognized in this memoir.

And, of course, to Chuck I express my eternal gratitude for far more than support in writing a book.

Interviews

Personal Interviews by Charles Stuart Kennedy

Ambassador Sue McCourt Cobb, September 8, 2011
Ambassador Sue McCourt Cobb, December 1, 2011
Ambassador Sue McCourt Cobb, April 12, 2012
Ambassador Sue McCourt Cobb, May 16, 2012
Ambassador Sue McCourt Cobb, March 15, 2013

Personal Interviews by Laura Tanna

Governor John Ellis "Jeb" Bush Sr., November 16, 2017
Ambassador Charles E. Cobb Jr., June 8, 2018
Christian McCourt Cobb, September 23, 2017
Christian McCourt Cobb, February 5, 2019
Ambassador Sue McCourt Cobb, August 5, 2017
Ambassador Sue McCourt Cobb, August 24, 2017
Ambassador Sue McCourt Cobb, October 15, 2017
Ambassador Sue McCourt Cobb, November 14, 2017
Ambassador Sue McCourt Cobb, November 15, 2017
Ambassador Sue McCourt Cobb, January 4, 2018
Ambassador Sue McCourt Cobb, February 12, 2018
Ambassador Sue McCourt Cobb, February 13, 2018
Ambassador Sue McCourt Cobb, April 15, 2018
Tobin Templeton Cobb, November 7, 2017
The Hon. Orette Bruce Golding, May 13, 2018
Rear Admiral Hardley Lewin, October 18, 2017
Peter Edmond McCourt, October 9, 2017
The Most Hon. P. J. Patterson, March 10, 2018
Dr. Peter Phillips, February 24, 2018
General Colin Powell, November 17, 2017
Ambassador Thomas Shannon Jr., January 18, 2018
Courtney Skinner, January 2, 2018

About the Author

SUE M. COBB, OJ: Sue M. Cobb served as the United States Ambassador to Jamaica (2001–2005) and is currently a principal of Cobb Partners, LLC, and president of the Cobb Family Foundation. She is a trustee of the Center for Strategic and International Studies and the Council of American Ambassadors and a member of the Council on Foreign Relations and the Association for Diplomatic Studies and Training.

Ambassador Cobb has also served as secretary of state of Florida, CEO of the Florida Lottery, partner at the Greenberg Traurig Law Firm, and multiyear member and three-time chair of the Miami Federal Reserve Bank. She has been an officer and director of several public, private, and charitable boards and has received numerous awards, including national honors from Iceland and the Order of Jamaica, that nation's highest honor for a non-citizen. The United States Department of State annually names the *Sue M. Cobb Award for Exemplary Diplomatic Service* to the individual selected in worldwide competition as the most outstanding non-career United States ambassador.

A graduate of Stanford University and the University of Miami School of Law, Sue Cobb is a skilled alpine skier and high altitude climber who has scaled mountains worldwide and published *The Edge of Everest: A Woman Challenges the Mountain* (1989), a chronicle of her travels across China and Tibet and her climb of Mt. Everest. She is married to Charles E. Cobb Jr., former undersecretary of the US Department of Commerce and US ambassador to Iceland.

Related ADST Memoirs
Series Titles

Joys and Perils of Living Abroad:
Memoirs of a Foreign Service Family
Diego and Nancy Asencio

Terrorism, Betrayal, and Resilience:
My Story of the 1998 US Embassy Bombings
Prudence Bushnell

Diversifying Diplomacy:
My Journey from Roxbury to Dakar
Harriet Elam-Thomas

Behind Embassy Walls:
The Life and Times of an American Diplomat
Brandon Grove

Paying Calls in Shangri-La:
Scenes from a Woman's Life in American Diplomacy
Judith M. Heimann

The Unofficial Diplomat
Joanne Huskey

American Ambassadors:
The Past, Present, and Future of America's Diplomats
Dennis Jett

Distinguished Service:
Lydia Chapin Kirk, Partner in Diplomacy, 1896–1984
Edited by Roger Kirk

American Diplomats: The Foreign Service at Work
Edited by William Morgan and Charles Stuart Kennedy

Plunging into Haiti: Clinton, Aristide, and the Defeat of Diplomacy
Ralph Pezzullo

Forever on the Road:
A Franco-American Family's Thirty Years in the Foreign Service
Nicole Prévost Logan

Not to the Manner Born
Helen Lyman

Witness to a Changing World
David D. Newsom

A Long Way from Runnemede:
One Woman's Foreign Service Journey
Theresa Tull

Abroad for Her Country:
Tales of a Pioneer Woman Ambassador in the U.S. Foreign Service
Jean Wilkowski

Arabian Nights and Daze: Living in Yemen with the Foreign Service
Susan Wyatt

Peregrina: Unexpected Adventures of an American Consul
Ginny Carson Young

For a complete list of series titles,
visit <adst.org/publications>

Index